IMAGES
of America

OAKLAND AVIATION

ON THE COVER: The first Naval Reserve air station to receive a jet plane after World War II was Naval Air Station (NAS) Oakland. The new North American FJ-1 Fury, predecessor to the famous USAF F-86 fighter, was first delivered to Oakland in August 1949. It was such a special occasion that this very special lettering was painted on the nose of the planes—the only such decoration ever used on any of the navy FJs. This NAS Oakland photograph shows three in a right echelon formation over San Francisco Bay with Treasure Island in the upper right background.

IMAGES
of America

OAKLAND AVIATION

Ronald T. Reuther and William T. Larkins

ARCADIA
PUBLISHING

ISBN 978-0-7385-5600-0

Published by Arcadia Publishing
Charleston SC, Chicago IL, Portsmouth NH, San Francisco CA

Printed in the United States of America

Library of Congress Catalog Card Number: 2007934167

For all general information contact Arcadia Publishing at:
Telephone 843-853-2070
Fax 843-853-0044
E-mail sales@arcadiapublishing.com
For customer service and orders:
Toll-Free 1-888-313-2665

Visit us on the Internet at www.arcadiapublishing.com

Contents

ACKNOWLEDGMENTS

We wish to thank all of the people who have been generous in their contributions of information and photographs for this project, in particular Lindy Boyes, John Corpening, Melvin Grassi, Dick Lindsay, Fred McElwain, Woodruff Minor, Tom Northrop, and Jay Wright. We owe a special thanks to Gerald "Sarge" Stein for his contributions, knowledge, and enthusiasm. Additional photographs are from the Reuther and Larkins collections.

In addition, we appreciate the help and assistance of the staffs of the Oakland Aviation Museum (formerly the Western Aerospace Museum), Oakland Museum of California, Oakland Public Library, *Oakland Tribune*, Pacific Aerial Surveys, and the Port of Oakland.

Author's note: The completion of this book was delayed by the unexpected death of Ronald Reuther in late 2007. For additional photographs and information about Oakland aviation, see the Arcadia Publishing book *San Francisco Bay Area Aviation*.

—William T. Larkins

INTRODUCTION

Just when the first manned flight took place in California is not known definitely, but most likely it was the flight of the balloon *California* on August 28, 1853. This was also recorded as the first manned flight west of the Rocky Mountains. The *California*'s owner, a man known only as Mr. Kelly, was probably one of the many aerial impresarios of the 1850s who went from city to city across America taking balloon flights. Kelly advertised in the San Francisco papers that on August 28 at 1:00 p.m. in Contra Costa County (actually now Oakland in Alameda County) he would ascend in the largest balloon ever made in America. The *California* consisted of a yellow silk envelope 40 feet in diameter with a basket suspended below. Three ferryboats were kept busy steaming across San Francisco Bay that day, their decks crowded with passengers destined to watch the flight. The balloon was inflated on a small lot on Third Street, near Broadway, in Oakland. A volunteer, 16-year-old Joseph "Ready" Gates, was the passenger. Using a small hoop with a 4-inch-wide board as a seat, Gates drifted at an altitude of about 1,000 feet over Martinez, Benicia, and into Solano County. Gradually the gas began to escape, and at about 8 feet above the Suisun Plain, Gates jumped, spraining both ankles as he landed.

This initial venture in Oakland aviation was followed by a torrent of activities and evolution of flight. Many prominent pioneers were connected with Oakland aviation, including John J. Montgomery, who with his brother James lived in Oakland and pursued some of his early aviation research on their ranch. He launched man's first controlled flight (a glider) on August 28, 1883, from the Otay Mesa near San Diego. Also included was Thomas Scott Baldwin, who flew his Curtiss motorcycle-engine-powered dirigible *California Arrow* from Idora Park on its initial flight on July 29, 1904, and on August 3 piloted it out over San Francisco Bay and back—the first successful controlled dirigible flight in America. He built and flew dirigibles, balloons, and airplanes and made over 3,000 ascensions without an accident.

Some of the early builders and pilots in Oakland, beginning in 1908, were Fong Yue (the first Chinese aircraft builder in the United States), the Christofferson brothers, Stanley Hiller Sr., Weldon Cooke, the Jacuzzi brothers, and others. Later names were Bessie Coleman (the first licensed black pilot in the United States, who worked in Oakland for a time as an aerial demonstrator), Allan Lockheed, Henry J. Kaiser, Stanley Hiller Jr., and others. The Hall-Scott Motor Company was one of the first, if not the first, to design and build engines for airplanes. Durant Field in east Oakland was the first Oakland airport and was named after pilot Clifford Durant, vice president of the General Motors/Chevrolet plant in east Oakland. He was also president of the Durant Aircraft Company that built the Durant Standard J-1.

The current Oakland Airport is one of the most historic in the world and certainly in the United States. The original field, now called North Field, dedicated by Charles Lindbergh on September 17, 1927, was officially designated as a historic landmark by the Oakland City Council in February 1980. It served as the departure point for all of the land plane trans-Pacific flights to Hawaii and beyond. Army lieutenants Maitland and Hegenberger flew the Fokker *Bird of Paradise* from Oakland to Oahu, Hawaii, on June 28, 1927. This was followed shortly by Ernie

Smith and William Davis in the Travel Air 5000 *City of Oakland* and Art Goebel and Emory Bronte in the Dole Race–winning Travel Air *Woolaroc*. On May 31, 1928, Australian Charles Kingsford Smith and crew flew the first "transpac" across the breadth of the Pacific in the Fokker *Southern Cross*.

Oakland was one of the most modern airports in the country in the early years, and many aviation systems and technologies were initially developed here. Some of these were the "Model Airline"; the first airport hotel; early air navigation and radio aids and techniques; Department of Commerce Aeronautics activities, which have evolved into major FAA facilities and operations; and the Boeing School of Aeronautics. In addition to early airline service, Oakland was the western headquarters for early U.S. Airmail service and air ferry service across the bay. After World War II, it was a center for nonscheduled and irregular passenger service and the home of the largest of these—Transocean Air Lines and World Airways.

It had one of the earliest Naval Reserve bases, starting in 1928, and the largest in the United States in the postwar period. It was taken over by the Army Air Forces in World War II in conjunction with the navy operating its Naval Air Transport Service. Business executive aircraft and a large increase in air cargo flights have led to increased facilities and operation since the 1950s.

One

Early Oakland Aviation

Oakland's first manned flight was probably the flight of the balloon *California*, owned by aerial impresario Mr. Kelly, on August 28, 1853. John J. Montgomery experimented with flight on his ranch near Fortieth Street and Telegraph Avenue before making man's first controlled flight in a glider near San Diego. Thomas Scott Baldwin, an associate of Montgomery, flew his powered dirigible *California Arrow* on its initial flight from Idora Park in Oakland on July 29, 1904. Roy Knabenshue and Lincoln Beachy were two of his young helpers.

Many prominent pioneers were connected with Oakland aviation. There were a number of early aircraft and engine builders and pilots in Oakland beginning about 1908, such as Chinese Fung Joe Guey (also known as Fung Yue), who built an airplane and engine and flew at Oakland in 1909; others were the Christofferson brothers, the Jacuzzi brothers, Bessie Coleman (the first licensed black pilot in the United States who worked at Oakland as an aerial demonstrator for a brief time), Allan Lockheed, and others.

Stanley Hiller Sr. built an original design Paterson-Hiller mono-hydroplane powered by a 60-horsepower original rotary engine that made its first successful public flight in the spring of 1913 at Lake Merritt with "Flying Dutchman" Stevens at the controls. Hiller contributed to the advancement of aviation and incorporated original ideas and designs. He became a successful designer and builder of helicopters, starting in Oakland. In 1909, the Hall-Scott Motor Car Company built engines at Snyder Avenue and Fifth Street in Oakland. The company built 1,255 engines during World War I with Elbert J. Hall as manager and chief engineer.

The Maupin-Lanteri *Diamond* was built at the Lanteri Shipyards in Pittsburg, California, in 1911 and is often called the "Black Diamond." A young Oaklander, Weldon B. Cooke, became the pilot and was in Oakland as part of the 1911 Columbus Day celebrations at Lake Merritt. Cooke was licensed by the Aero Club of America with a flight in 1912 and given License No. 95. Oakland mayor Frank K. Mott presented Cooke with a silver loving cup and a purse of $300. The flight marked the first time a Californian flying a California-built plane had tried for this honor and the first time for anyone west of St. Louis. While Cooke's new plane was in the course of construction at Elmhurst, a suburb of Oakland, he went to Santa Rosa, where he met Ben Noonan and obtained the Wiseman biplane. Cooke assembled the plane and made several flights before bringing it to Oakland and entering the Third International Aviation Meet in 1912.

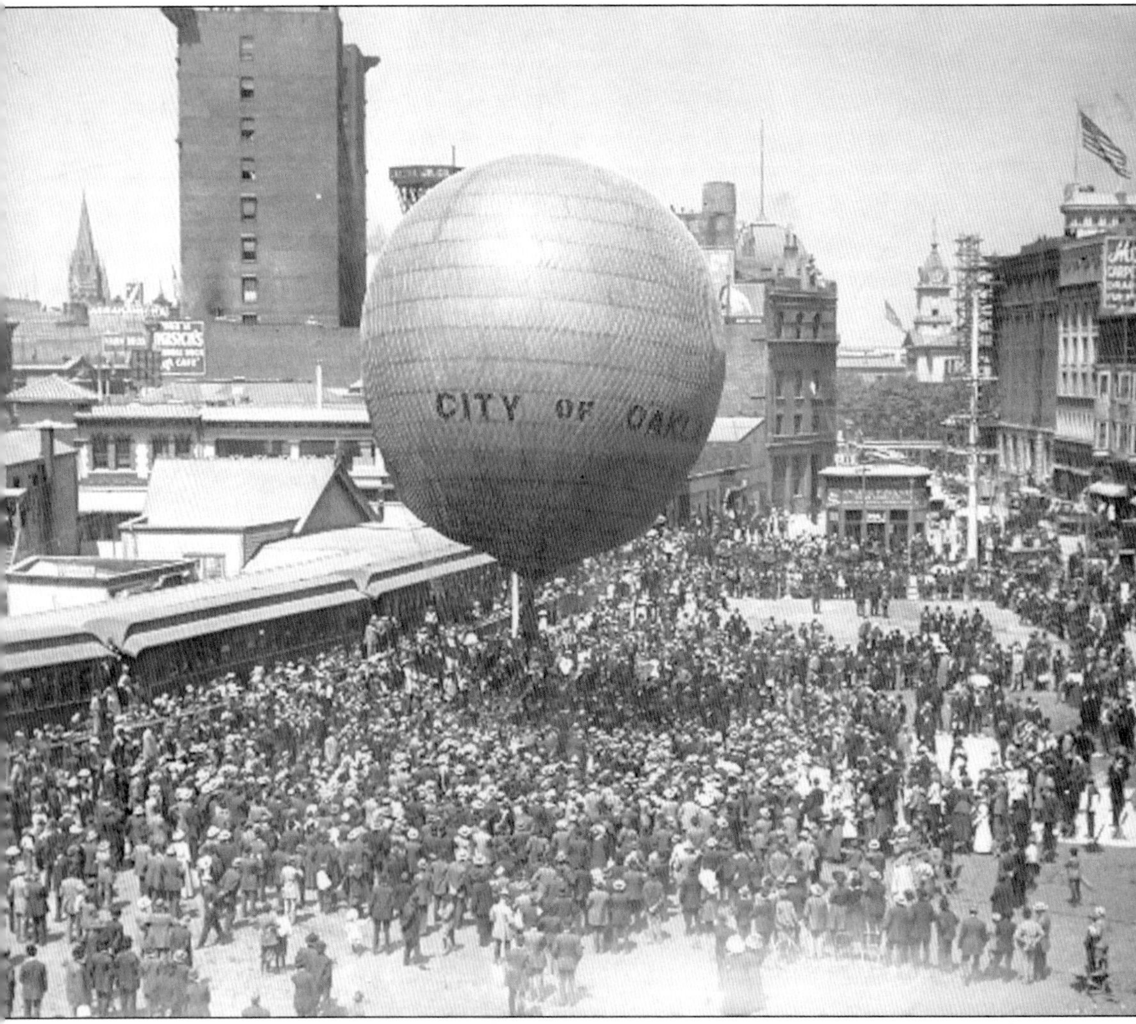

Balloon ascensions were popular before the advent of the "aeroplane," and Oakland was no exception. This photograph shows the balloon *City of Oakland* ready for flight at Fourteenth and Franklin Streets in downtown Oakland on August 14, 1905.

The first controlled flight of a dirigible in the western hemisphere was accomplished by the *California Arrow*, shown here at Idora Park in July 1904 with its designer, builder, and pilot Capt. Thomas Baldwin in the undercarriage below the dirigible.

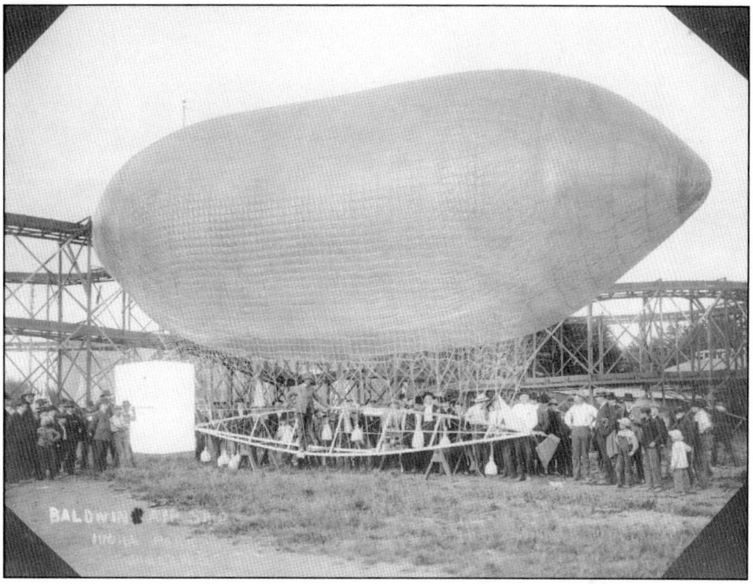

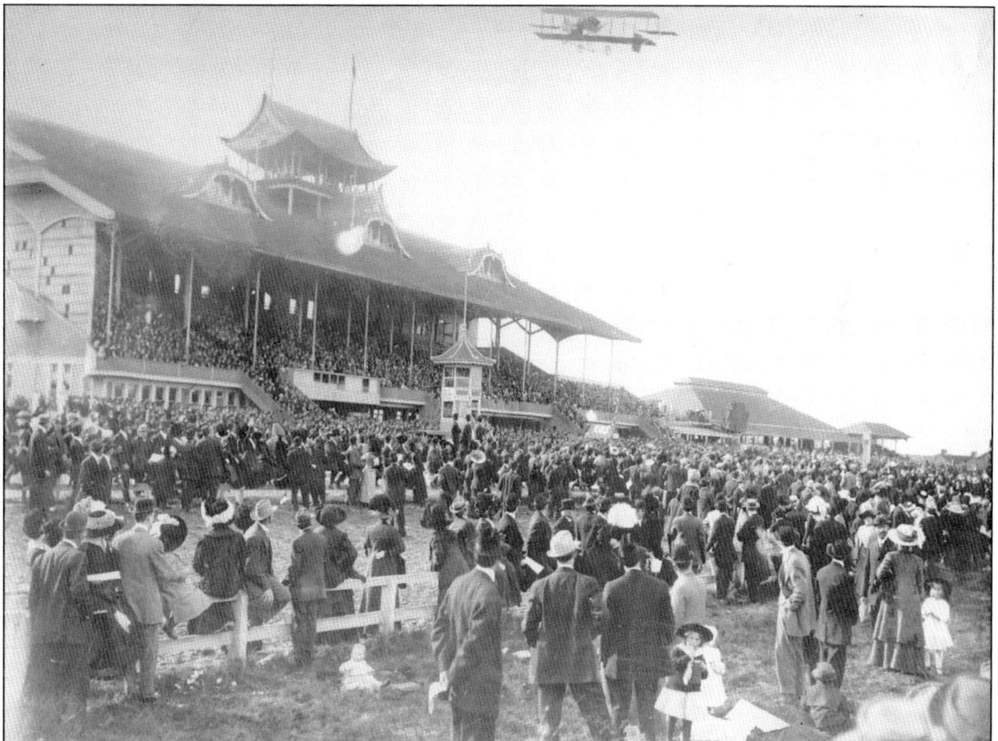

Fred Wiseman, M. W. Peters, and Ben Noonan pooled their resources to build an aircraft. Construction was started on the Wiseman-Noonan plane in San Francisco in October 1909. Wiseman made the first airmail flight from Petaluma to Santa Rosa on February 11, 1911. The plane passed to Weldon Cooke in 1912, then to the Oakland Port Commission as a gift from Dr. Robert Cooke in 1933, and finally to the Smithsonian Institution in Washington, D.C., in 1948 after being in the exhibit building at Oakland Airport for about 10 years.

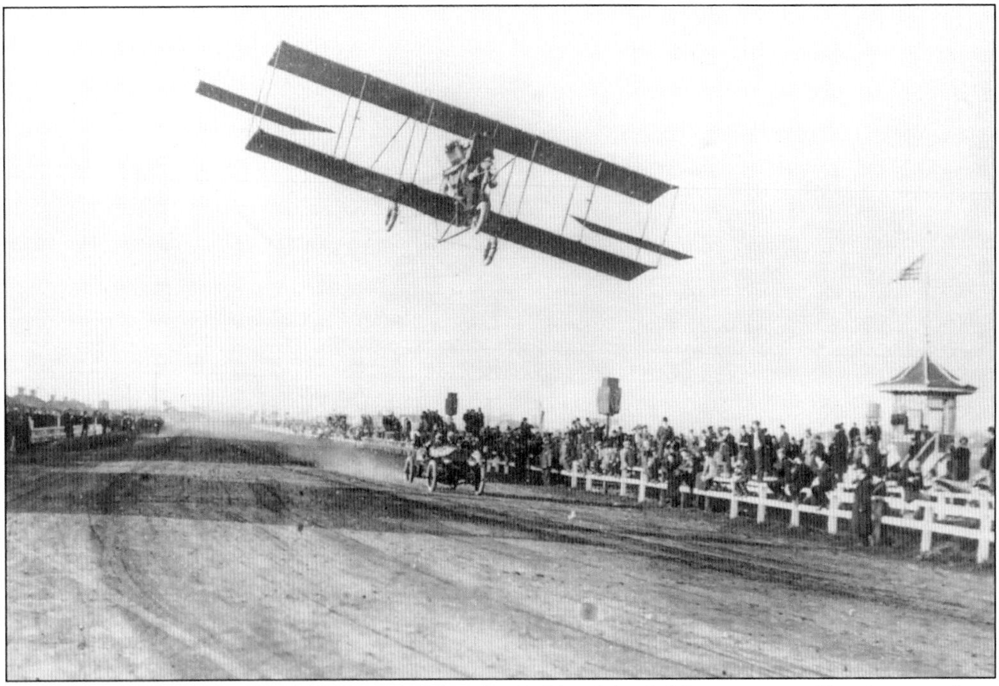

The Third International Air Meet was held at the Oakland Airfield, a name used by the city when they rented the racetrack in Emeryville for this event in 1912. The photograph shows Barney Oldfield racing his car against Lincoln Beachy in the airplane.

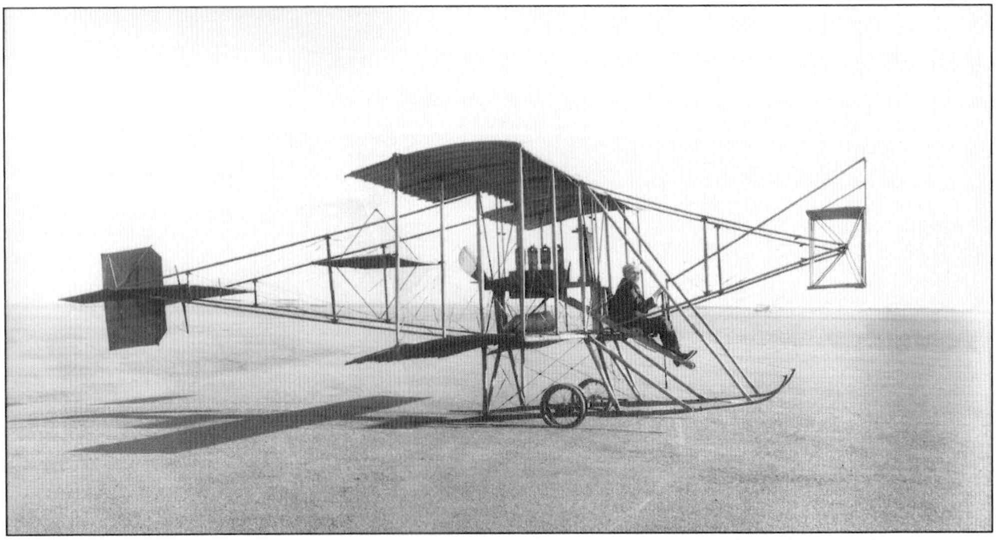

The *Diamond* aircraft was built in Pittsburg, California, in the spring of 1911 by Land B. Maupin (captain of one of the large dredgers working on the Sacramento River) and Bernard P. Lanteri (owner and operator of the Lanteri Shipyards at Pittsburg). It is sometimes called the "Black Diamond," as that was the former name of the town that became Pittsburg. The plane flew on its first trial flight with Lanteri at the controls at a field by the shipyard. Weldon B. Cooke flew this plane over Lake Merritt in 1911 and at Los Angeles in 1912. It was given to the Port of Oakland in 1933 and displayed in the exhibit building between Hangars 2 and 3. In 1948, it was given to the Smithsonian Institution.

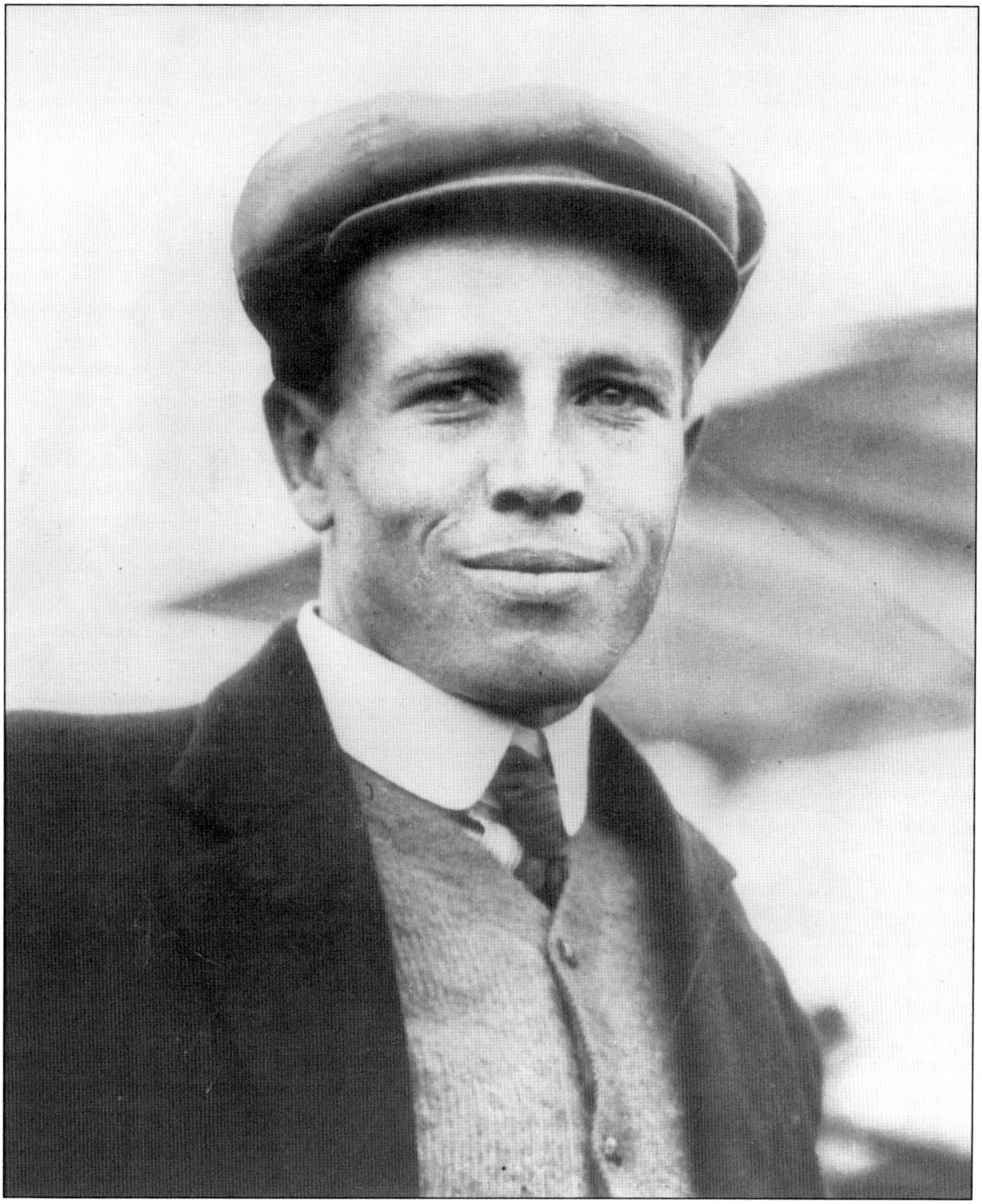

Weldon B. Cooke flew several of the historic Oakland aircraft, including the Wiseman-Noonan, the *Diamond*, and the Christofferson brothers' *Aermaid*. His flying the *Diamond* in January 1912 at Lakeside Park was the first Californian flying a California-built plane west of St. Louis to obtain a license from the Aero Club of America.

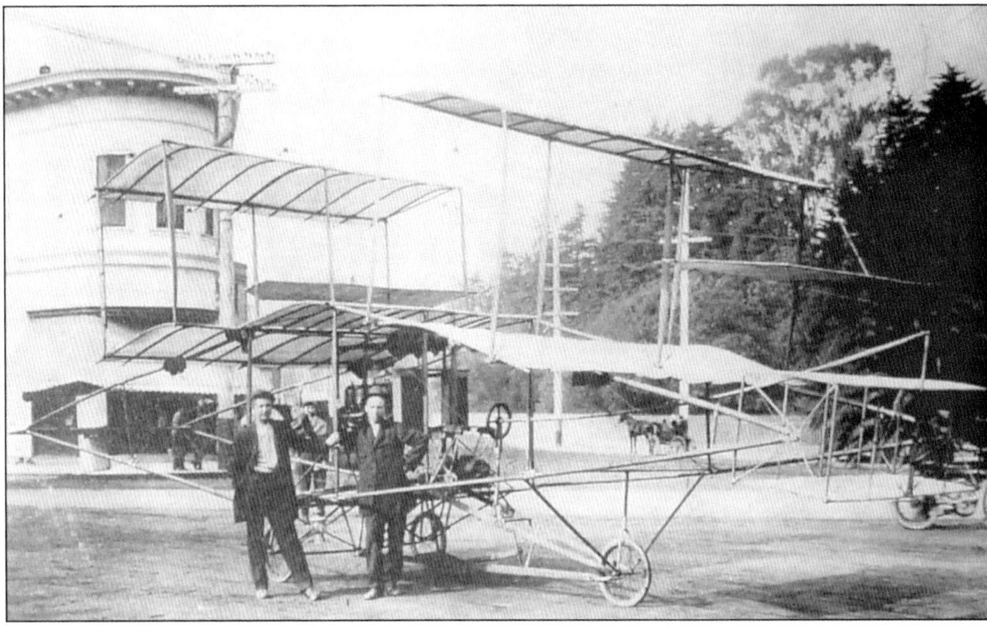

Peter and W. P. English, father and son, lived in Fruitvale, now a part of Oakland. They became interested in flying in 1902–1903 and in 1906 built a full-scale aeroplane. This photograph shows it being towed through Twenty-fourth and Harrison Streets in Oakland. It was unsatisfactory and was damaged in attempting to fly.

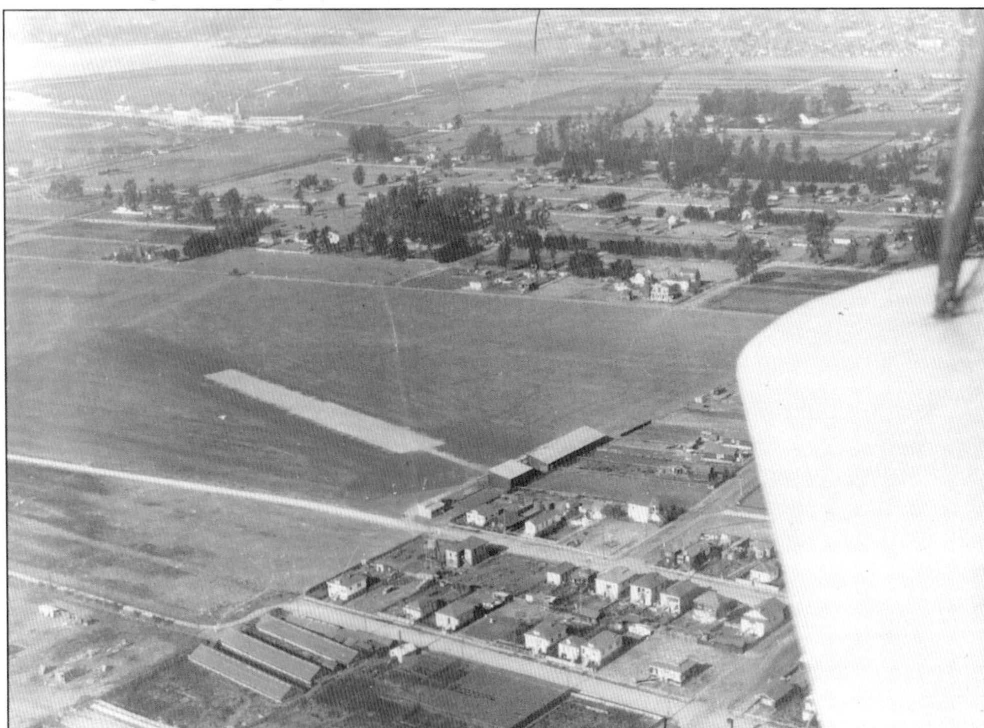

An aerial view of Durant Field in East Oakland, located near the site of the present-day Oakland Coliseum, shows the first official "Oakland Airport," which existed from about 1910 to 1926.

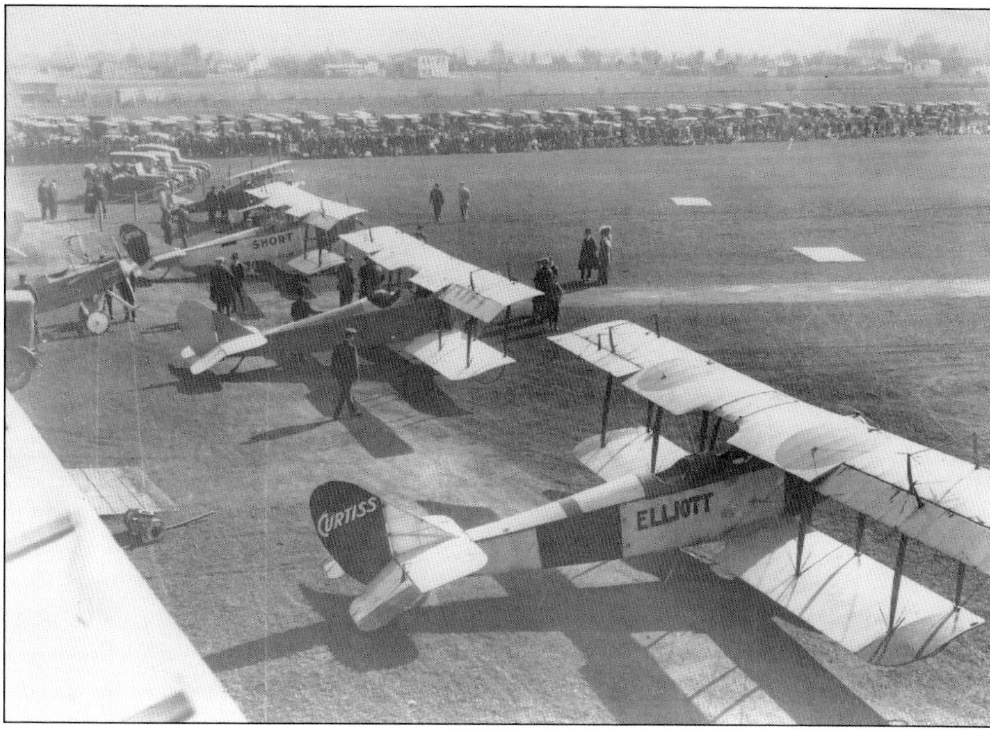

Curtiss JN-4 Jenny planes line up at Durant Field in May 1920 during an air derby.

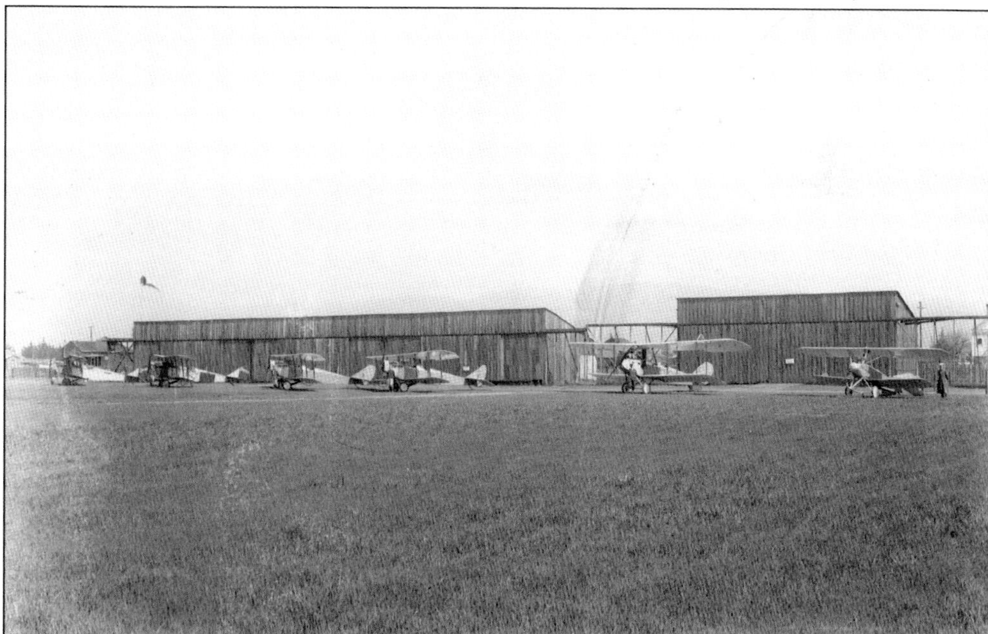

Six aircraft, including four Curtiss JN-4 Jennies on the left, are shown parked in front of the wooden hangars at Durant Field in east Oakland. The field was named for Clifford Durant, vice president of the General Motors–Chevrolet plant in east Oakland and president of the Durant Aircraft Company.

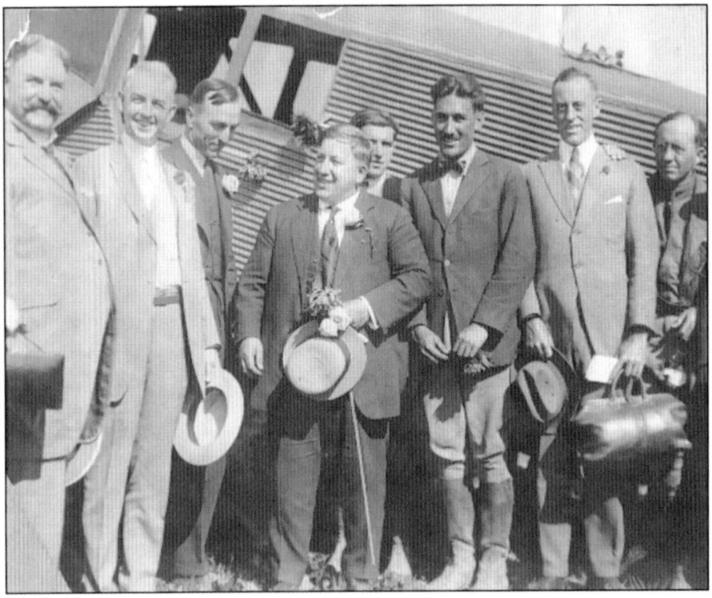

This August 1920 photograph shows one of three Junkers-Larsen metal aircraft flown from New York with the first U.S. airmail to Oakland. From left to right are unidentified, Oakland mayor Davis, Eddie Rickenbacker, John M. Larsen, unidentified, Bert Acosta, Oakland postmaster J. J. Rosborough, and unidentified.

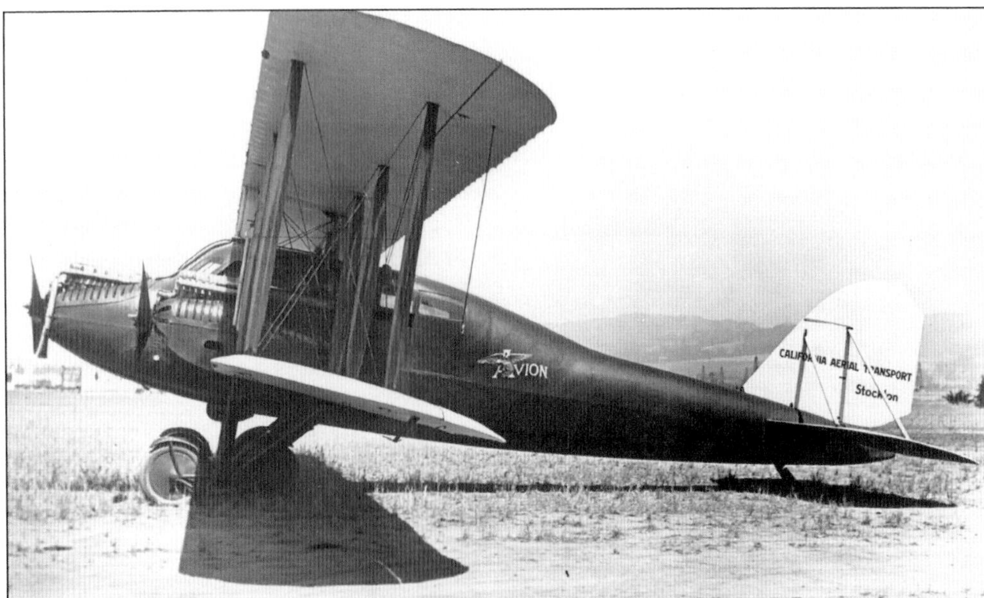

In April 1920, George Pond inaugurated the second scheduled airline in the West with the California Aerial Transport Company. With offices in Stockton, a route was laid out from Concord to Los Angeles via Oakland (Durant Field), Stockton, Fresno, and Bakersfield. A new Curtiss Eagle named *Avion* was purchased with the first flight on June 7, 1920. On June 26, the plane crashed in Los Angeles, causing the company to disband.

Two

Early Days of Current Oakland Airport

In 1925, Oakland city leaders appropriated over a half million dollars to purchase 600 acres for an airport near the border with San Leandro and adjoining farming area known as Bay Farm Island. Thus the new field was unofficially known as "Bay Farm Field" or "Bay Farm Airport." In February 1927, the Oakland City Council adopted an ordinance placing the airport under the jurisdiction of the newly formed Oakland Port Commission. In addition to a purchase of 225 more acres of land, the commission added 20 acres for use as a deepwater channel direct to the hangars.

On June 28, 1927, army lieutenants Lester Maitland and Albert Hegenberger left Oakland for Hickam Field, Hawaii, in the Fokker *Bird of Paradise*. Hegenberger Road at Oakland Airport is a tribute to him and the flight. In 1962, Generals Hegenberger and Maitland were reunited at the dedication of the new Oakland International Airport. On July 14, 1927, "Ernie" Smith and Emory Bronte took off in the *City of Oakland* and landed at Molokai, thus becoming the first civilians to make this flight.

James Dole of Hawaii funded a race by offering $35,000 in prize money, promoting the greatest aviation contest up to that time. Following the announcement, 30 fliers from throughout the world gave notice of their intention to enter, but only 16 of these actually did. Officially named the North American–Honolulu, Hawaii, Trans-Pacific Flight, it was soon shortened to Pacific Air Race, but the press changed that to the Dole Race.

On August 16, 1927, the first plane, *Aloha*, a modified Bresse monoplane made in San Francisco, got under way with Martin Jensen as pilot and Paul Shluter as navigator. Twenty-eight hours and 15 minutes later, they arrived at Wheeler Field, Honolulu. They won second prize after Dole Race winners Art Goebel and Emory Bronte in the *Woolaroc*. On May 31, 1928, Australian Charles Kingsford Smith and crew flew the first Trans-Pacific flight from Oakland in the Fokker *Southern Cross*.

Oakland was one of the most modern airports in the country in its early years, and many aviation systems and technologies were initially developed here, such as the "Model Airline," the first airport hotel, and early navigation and radio aids. Early transcontinental and north-south routes and commercial airlines served Oakland, it was the western headquarters for early U.S. mail operations, and an air ferry service operated across the bay from Oakland to San Francisco.

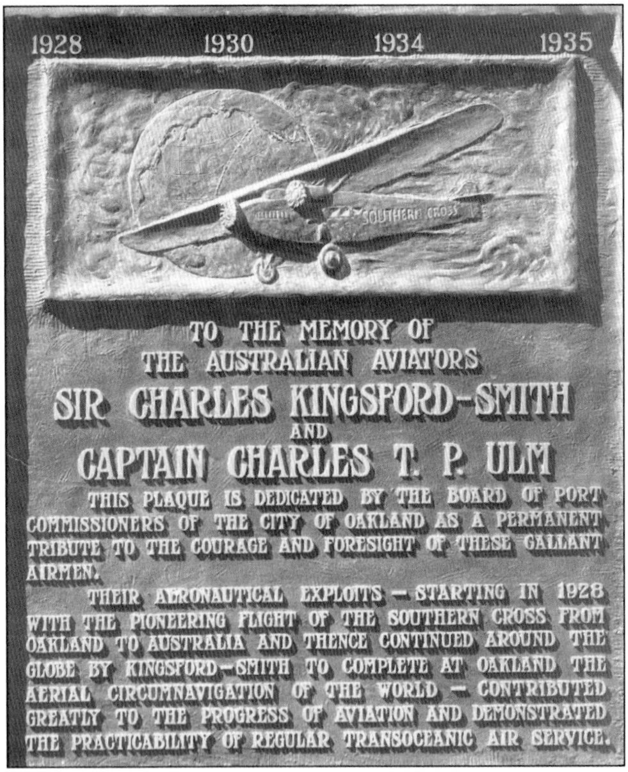
1928 1930 1934 1935

TO THE MEMORY OF
THE AUSTRALIAN AVIATORS
SIR CHARLES KINGSFORD-SMITH
AND
CAPTAIN CHARLES T. P. ULM

THIS PLAQUE IS DEDICATED BY THE BOARD OF PORT COMMISSIONERS OF THE CITY OF OAKLAND AS A PERMANENT TRIBUTE TO THE COURAGE AND FORESIGHT OF THESE GALLANT AIRMEN.

THEIR AERONAUTICAL EXPLOITS — STARTING IN 1928 WITH THE PIONEERING FLIGHT OF THE SOUTHERN CROSS FROM OAKLAND TO AUSTRALIA AND THENCE CONTINUED AROUND THE GLOBE BY KINGSFORD-SMITH TO COMPLETE AT OAKLAND THE AERIAL CIRCUMNAVIGATION OF THE WORLD — CONTRIBUTED GREATLY TO THE PROGRESS OF AVIATION AND DEMONSTRATED THE PRACTICABILITY OF REGULAR TRANSOCEANIC AIR SERVICE.

On May 31, 1936, this large bronze plaque was mounted on a permanent base directly in front of the old Administration Building at what is now North Field. It is a tribute to both the Fokker *Southern Cross* and its crew—pilot Sir Charles Kingsford Smith, copilot Charles T. P. Ulm, navigator Harry W. Lyons, and radioman James W. Warner. In addition, it commemorates Kingsford Smith as an individual who made additional flights from Oakland shown by the dates at the top of the plaque. The flight was made possible by philanthropic donations from Capt. Allan Hancock of Santa Maria.

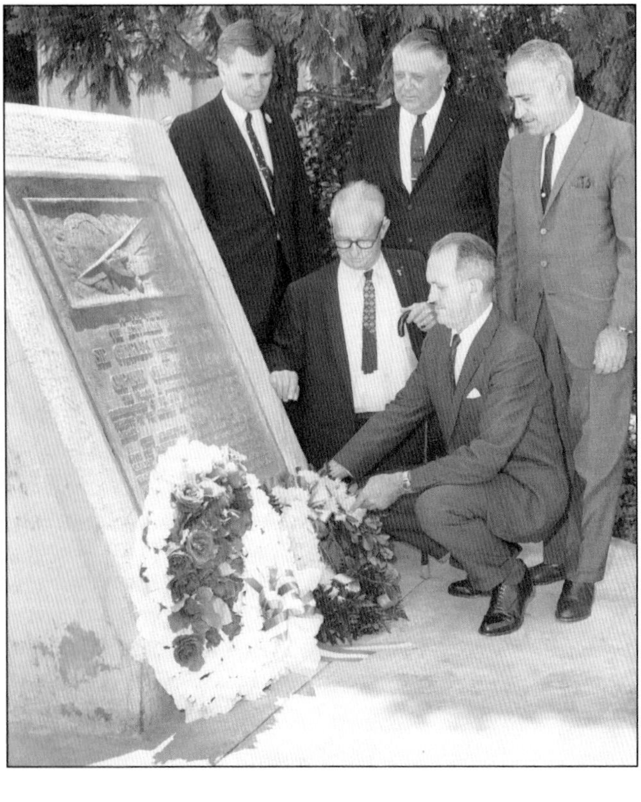

This photograph shows a group in the 1950s laying wreaths at the foot of the monument. James Warner, the radioman, is kneeling with the cane in the center of the photograph. This memorial monument is still there today in 2008, and the old Administration Building is now an upgraded executive terminal for pilots and passengers.

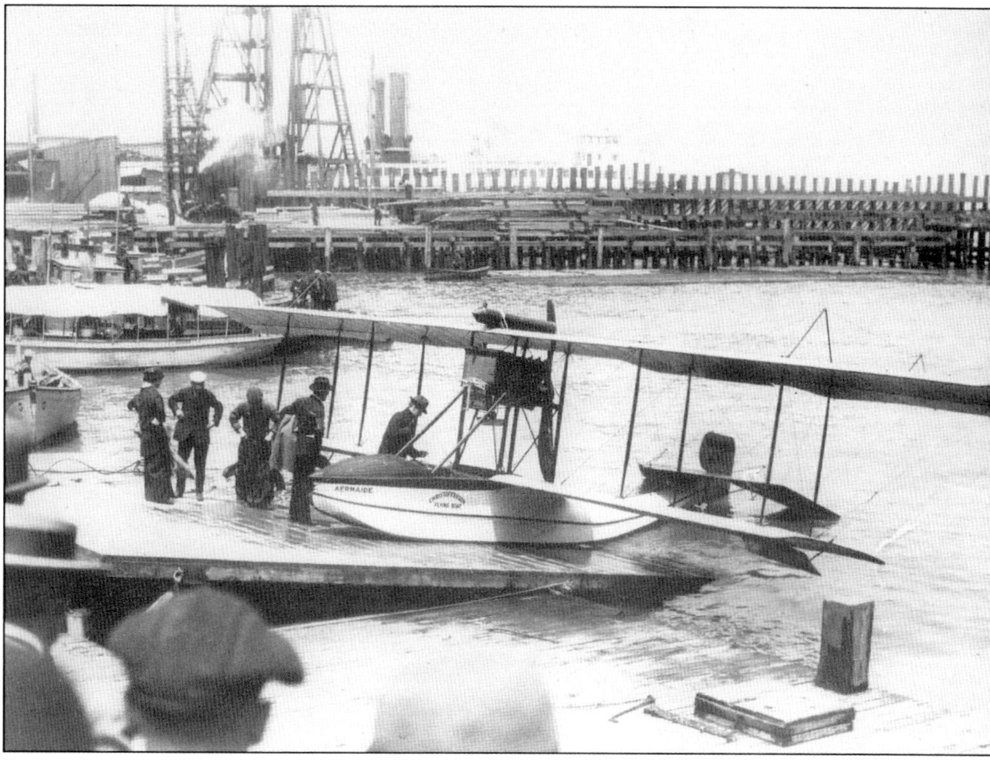

Pictured is the Christofferson Flying Boat *Aermaid* at the Oakland Estuary dock at the foot of Webster Street. This first air ferry service to the foot of Mission Street in San Francisco started in May 1914 but made only a few flights before service was terminated. Their first pilot was Weldon Cooke.

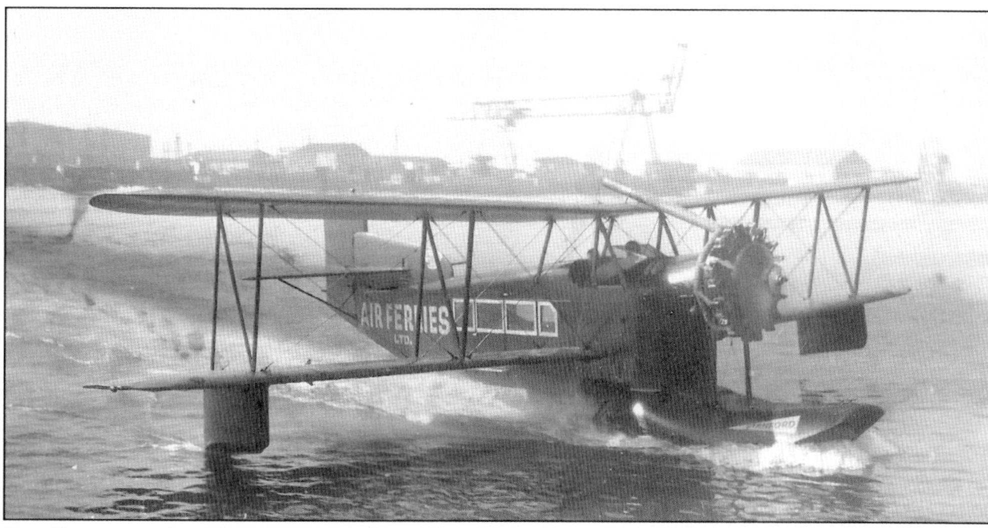

San Francisco Air Ferries provided a unique commuter service between the foot of Franklin Street in Oakland and Pier 5 in San Francisco in 1930. With a fleet of Keystone-Loening "Air Yachts," the airline set a record of flying 60,000 passengers across the bay in one year. At the peak of its operation, with four planes, a flight was made every 20 minutes. Maintenance was done at Oakland Airport.

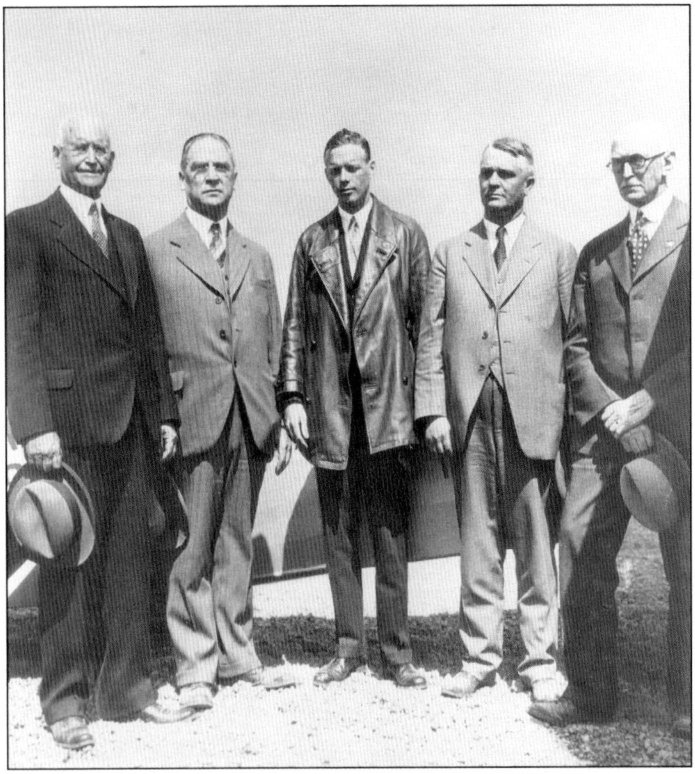

Pictured are Charles Lindbergh (center) and Port of Oakland officials at the dedication of Oakland Airport by Lindbergh on September 17, 1927.

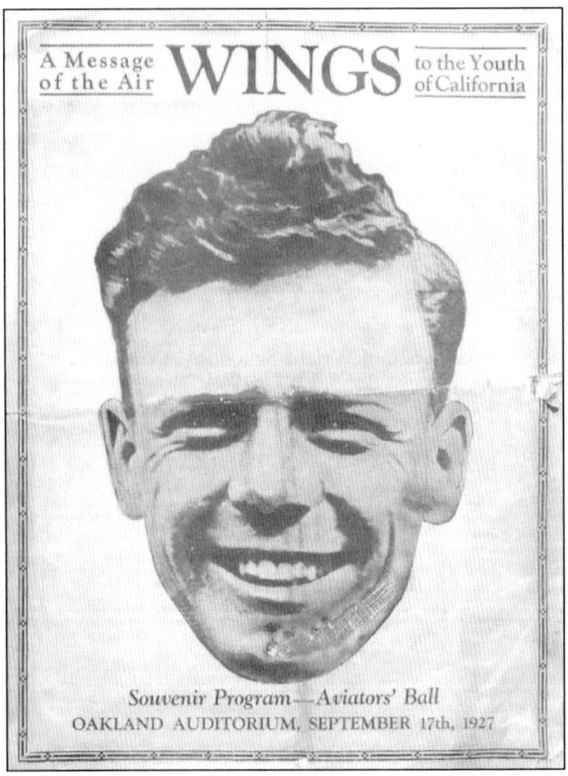

This is the cover for the souvenir program of the Aviators Ball at Oakland on September 17, 1927. Unfortunately, Lindbergh could not attend, as he was at Oakland for only four hours before flying to Sacramento for the evening.

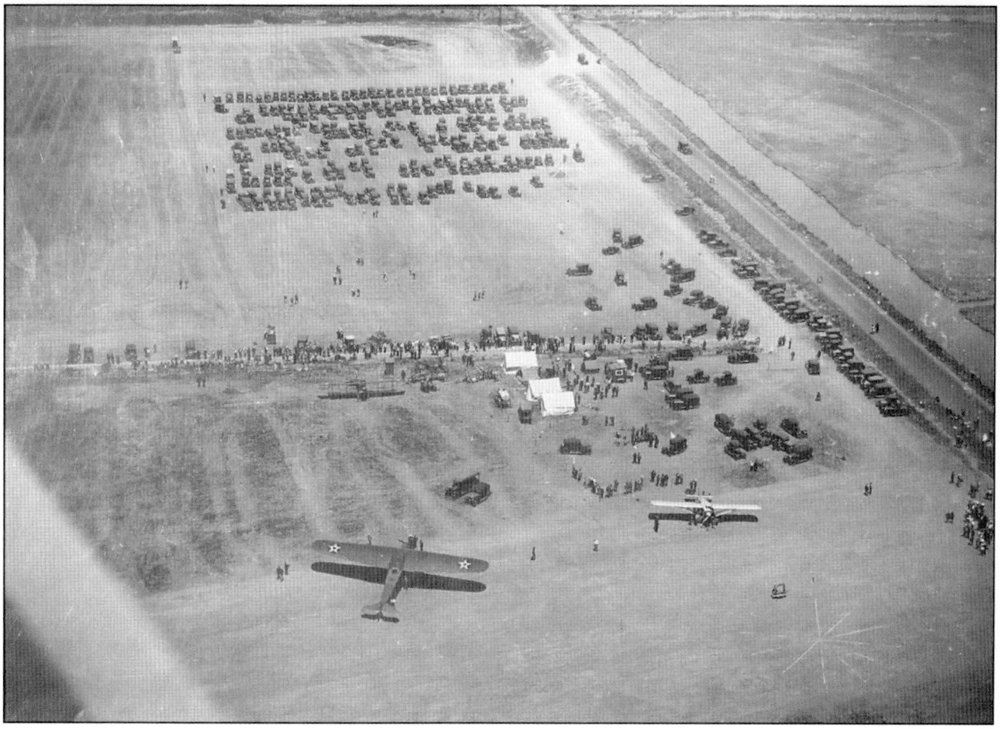

The army *Bird of Paradise* (lower left of center with the large wing and stars) and the civilian *City of Oakland* (on the right) are pictured at the end of the field that was to become Oakland Airport. The crowd is awaiting the departure of the *Bird of Paradise* for Hawaii on June 28, 1927.

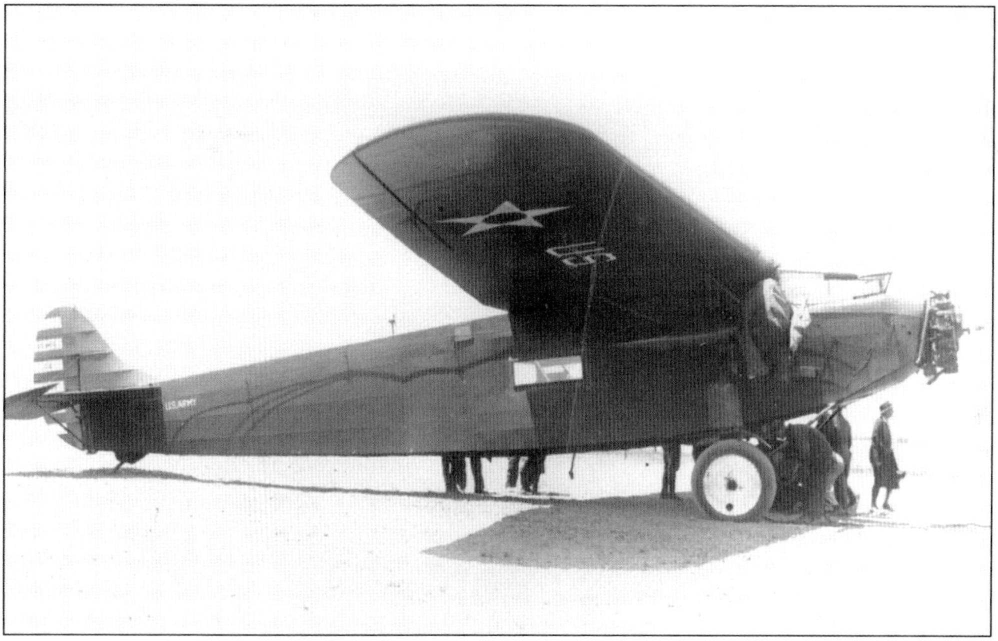

This is a close-up view of the U.S. Army Air Service Fokker C-2 *Bird of Paradise* that made the first flight of an airplane from California to Hawaii. The 2,407-mile nonstop flight took 25 hours and 50 minutes.

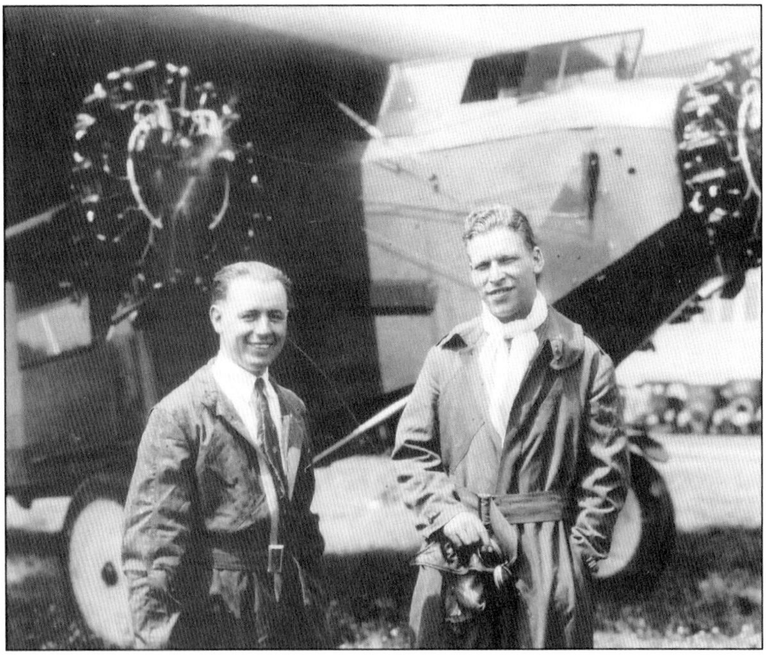

Shown here are Lt. Lester Maitland (left), pilot, and Lt. Albert Hegenberger, copilot/navigator, standing by the nose of their Fokker before the flight to Hawaii. Lindbergh said of the Maitland-Hegenberger flight, "It was the most perfectly organized and most completely planned flight ever attempted."

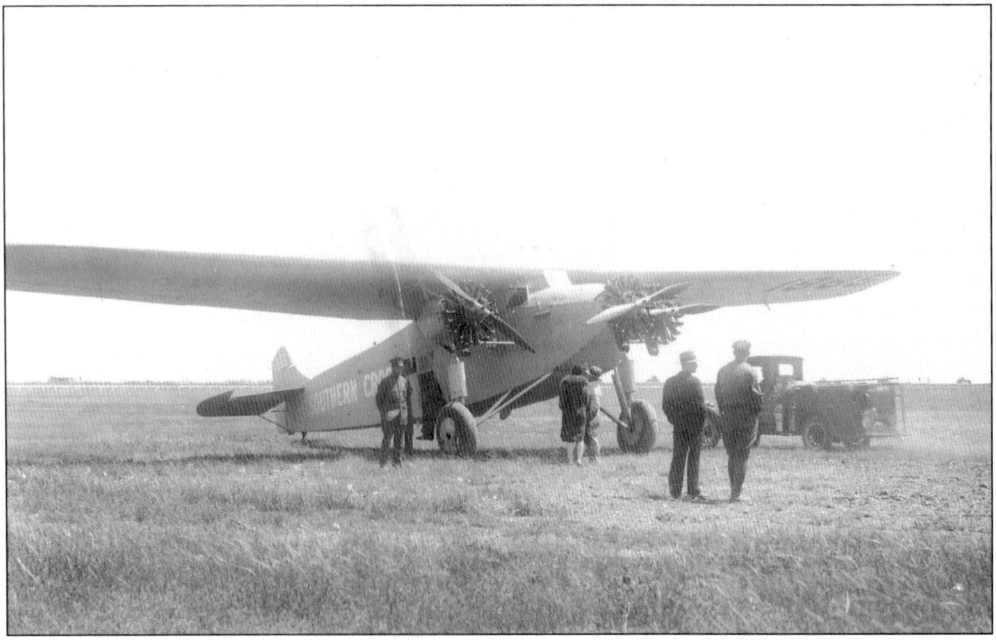

The Fokker F.VIIb/3m trimotor *Southern Cross*, with Charles Kingsford Smith as pilot, took off from Oakland on May 31, 1928, to make the astounding 7,800-mile flight to Brisbane, Australia. With Australian Charles Ulm as copilot and Americans Harry Lyons and James Warner as crew, the plane accumulated 88.5 flying hours in this first record-making transpacific flight.

On July 14, 1927, pilot "Ernie" Smith and navigator Emory Bronte took off from Oakland Airport in a 225-horsepower overloaded Travel Air monoplane named *City of Oakland* and landed in a breadfruit tree on Molokai, Hawaii, after 25 hours and 35 minutes. This second crossing of the Pacific was the first achieved by a nonmilitary aircraft.

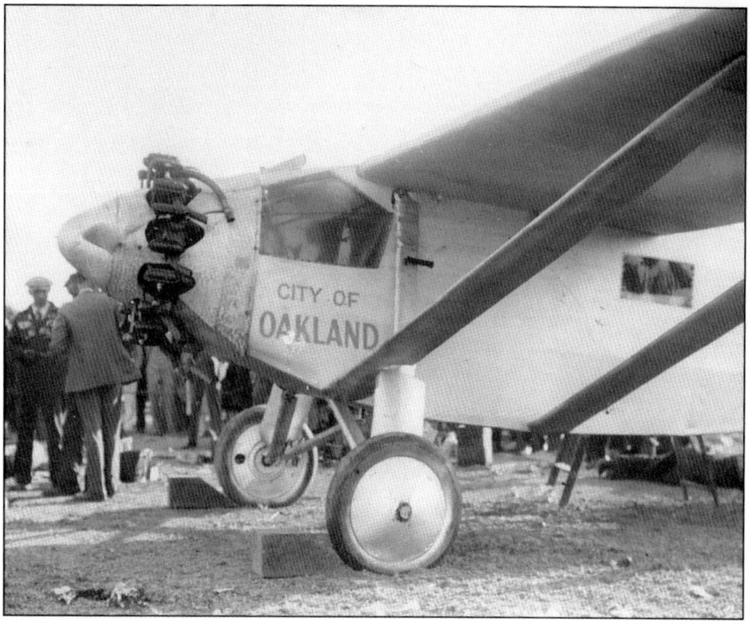

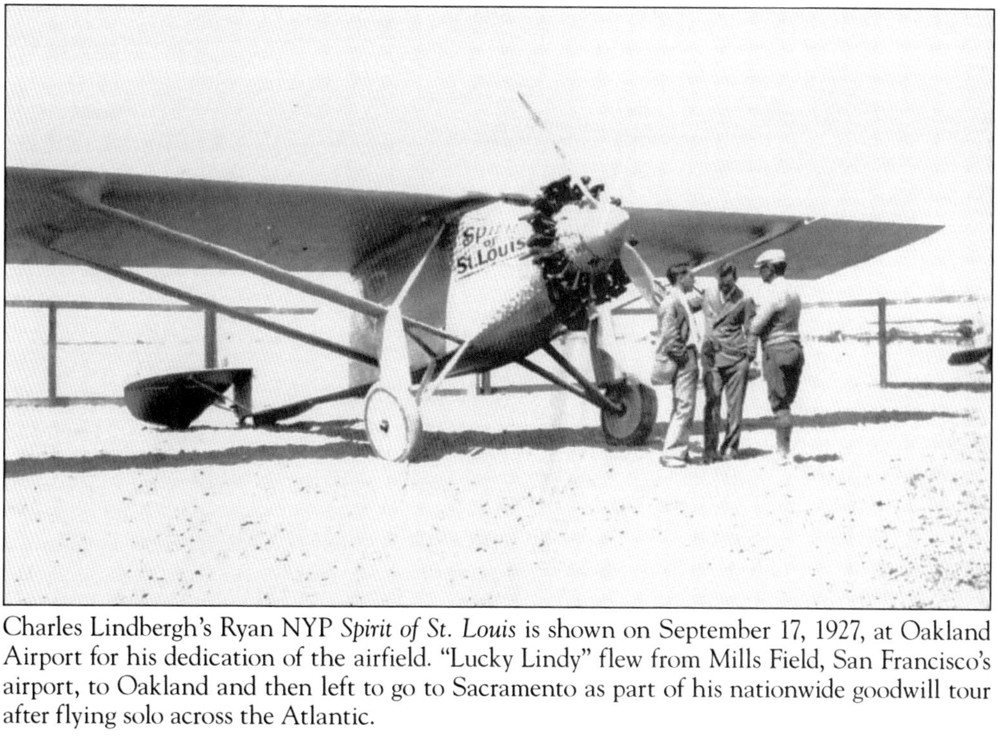

Charles Lindbergh's Ryan NYP *Spirit of St. Louis* is shown on September 17, 1927, at Oakland Airport for his dedication of the airfield. "Lucky Lindy" flew from Mills Field, San Francisco's airport, to Oakland and then left to go to Sacramento as part of his nationwide goodwill tour after flying solo across the Atlantic.

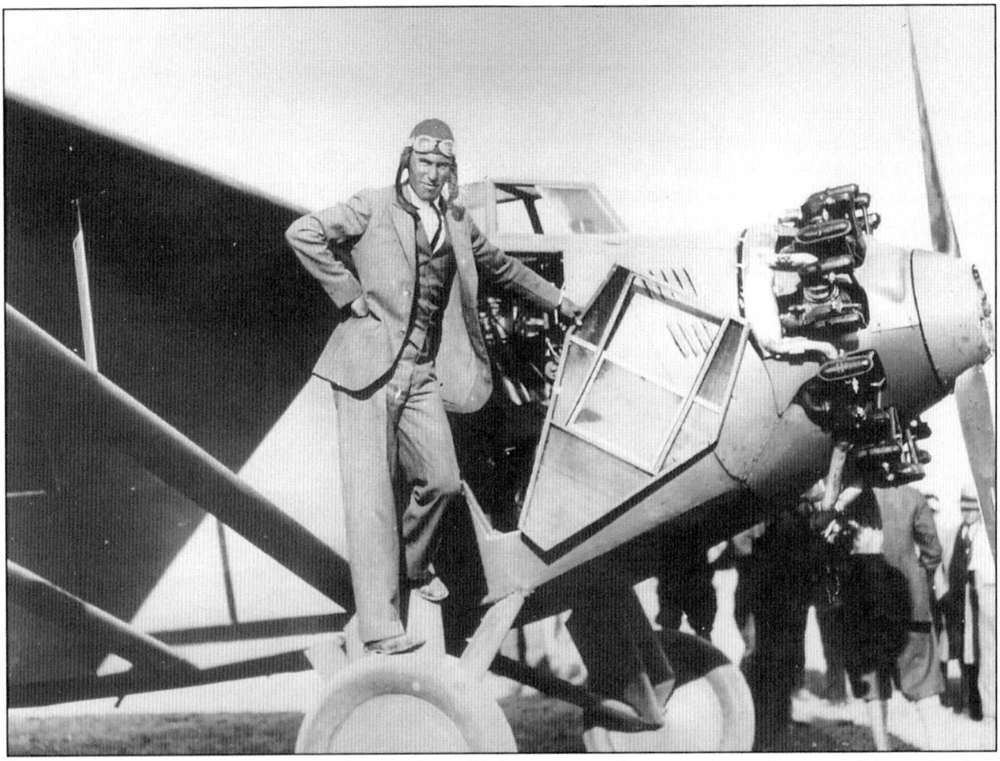

Shown here is Arthur Goebel, pilot of the *Oklahoma*, standing on the right tire of the winning plane in the Dole Race. With navigator navy lieutenant William V. Davis, they took off as one of the last participants in the race but arrived in Oahu ahead of Martin Jensen and his Breese monoplane *Aloha*.

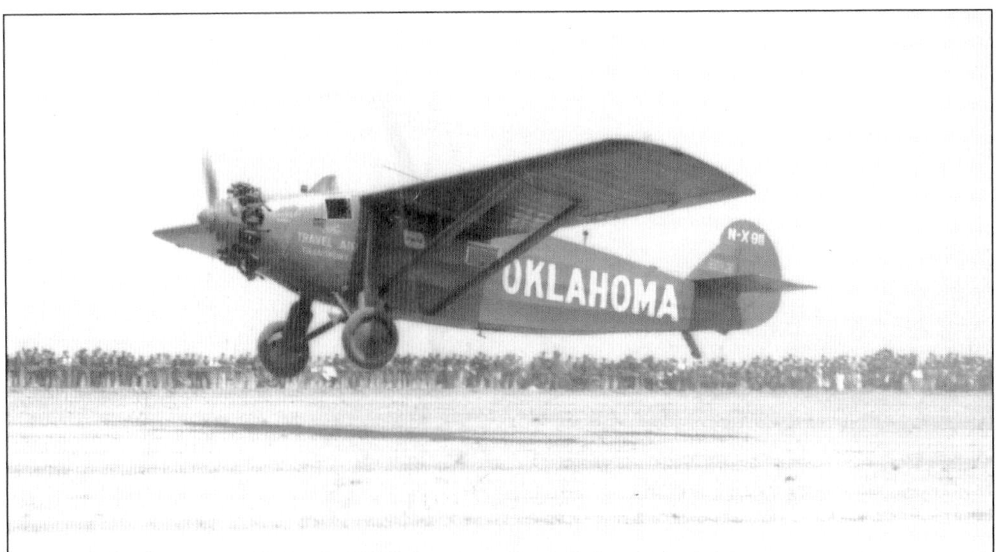

This is the modified Travel Air 5000 *Oklahoma* leaving the runway at Oakland Airport on August 16, 1927, for its record flight to Hawaii as part of the Dole Race, or Dole Derby. It landed in Oahu 26 hours and 17 minutes later to win the first prize of $25,000.

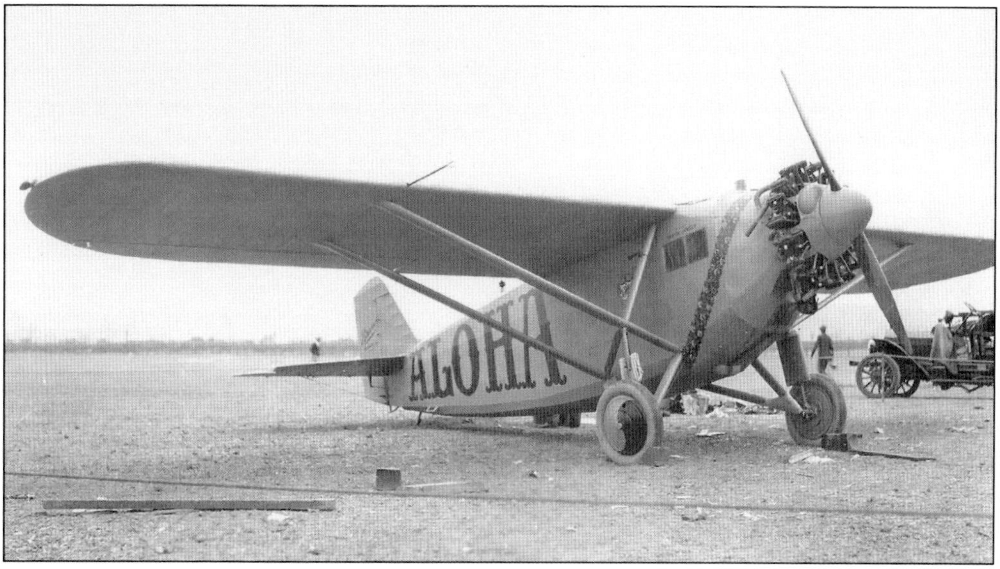

The Breese monoplane *Aloha* would have won the Dole Race had it not gotten off course and taken 28 hours and 15 minutes to finish the flight. Pilot Martin Jensen and navigator Paul Shluter were lucky to have gotten there, as at one time they hit an ocean wave while in flight.

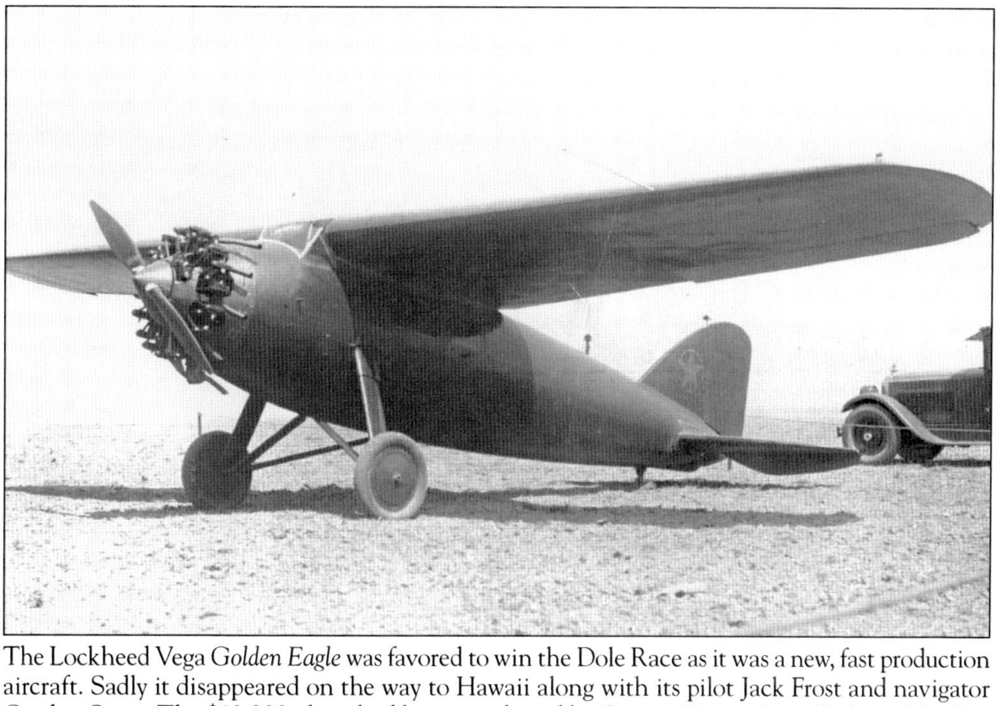

The Lockheed Vega *Golden Eagle* was favored to win the Dole Race as it was a new, fast production aircraft. Sadly it disappeared on the way to Hawaii along with its pilot Jack Frost and navigator Gordon Scott. The $12,000 plane had been purchased by George Hearst Jr., publisher of the *San Francisco Examiner*, just for the race. The plane and crew were never seen again.

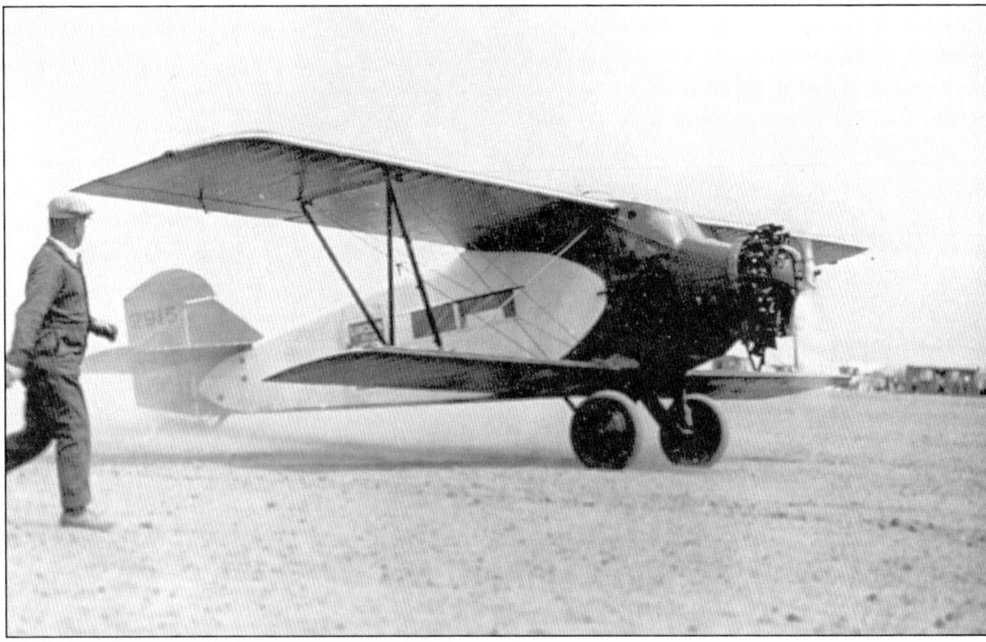

The Buhl biplane *Miss Doran*, along with the Lockheed, was a tragic loss. In addition to pilot John "Augy" Pedlar and navigator Lt. Vilas R. Knope, it carried a much publicized passenger: Mildred Doran. As the only woman to fly in the Dole Race, she received a lot of attention before the flight and more after the plane and three people were lost at sea. The last sighting of *Miss Doran* was as it flew west over the Farallon Islands.

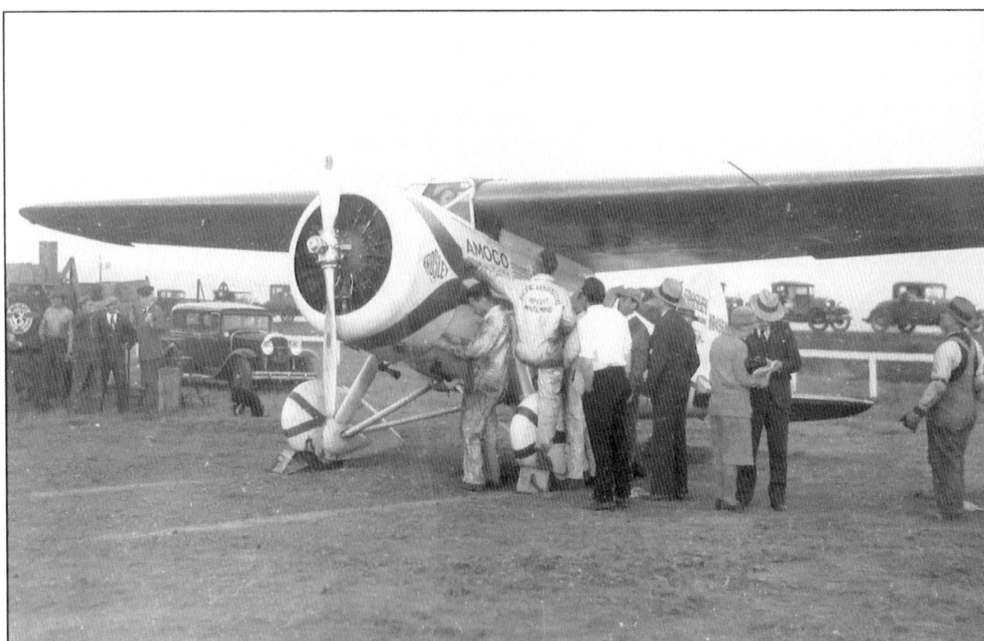

Ruth Nichols is shown preparing to take off from Oakland for a record flight in her Lockheed Vega *The New Cincinnati* on October 24, 1931. She set a woman's distance record of 1,977 miles nonstop in 14 hours, flying from Oakland to Louisville, Kentucky.

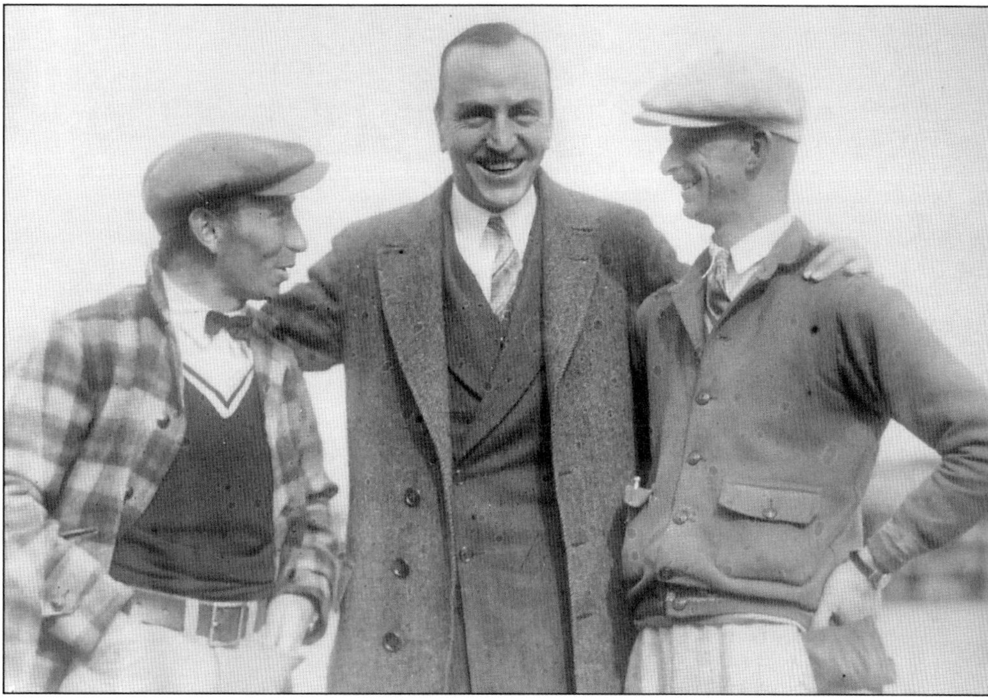

From left to right are well-known local pilot Ralph Virden, Eddie Rickenbacker, and Livingston Irving. Irving was an unsuccessful entrant in the Dole Race as pilot of the *Pabco Pacific Flyer*, which crashed on takeoff.

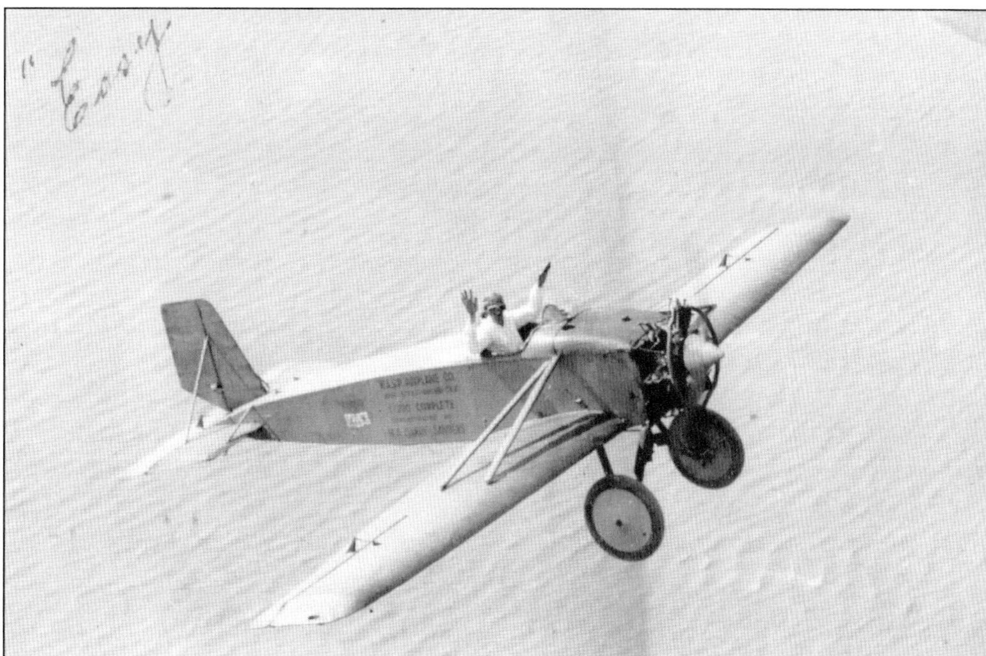

W. A. "Sandy" Sanders is demonstrating the hands-off capability of a new airplane built in the late 1920s. It was designed and built as a $1,200 single-place sport plane by the WASP Airplane Company of Oakland.

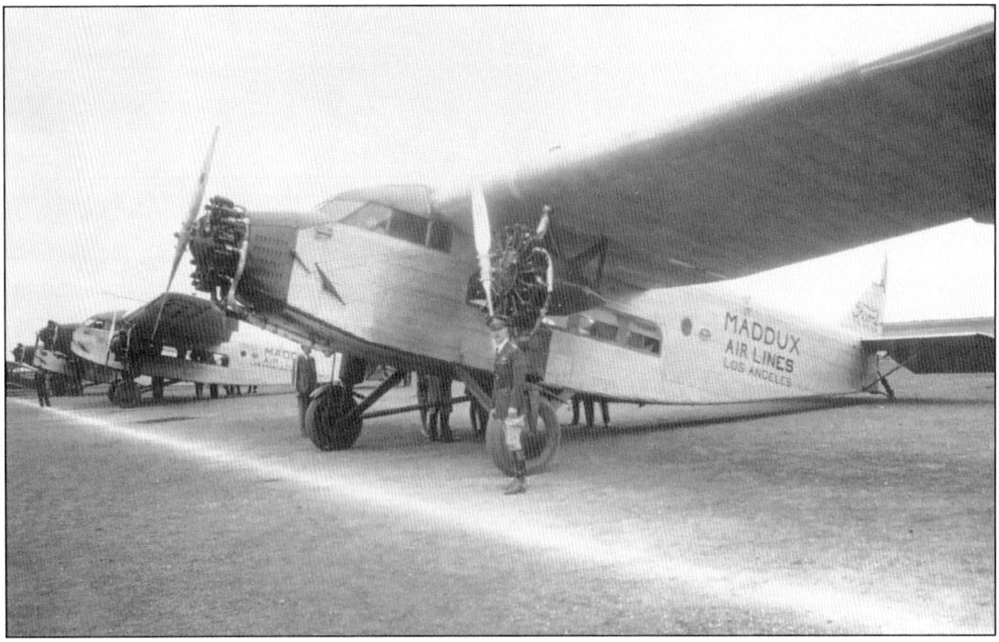

Maddux Air Lines operated the Ford 4-AT trimotor in service from Oakland to Los Angeles from February 1929 to August 1930, with later service in newer Ford 5-ATs to Alameda Airport.

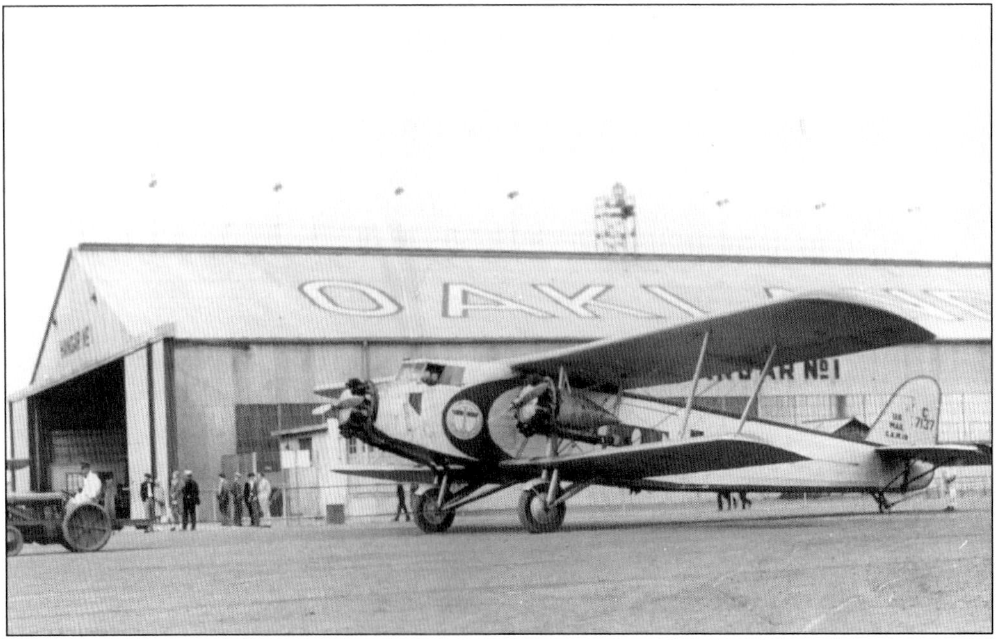

United Air Lines offered service from Oakland to Seattle in the then-luxurious Boeing 80A trimotor. This was a vast improvement over the prior service in the Boeing 40B, flown by Pacific Air Transport (PAT). Boeing Air Transport, which merged with PAT to form United Air Lines, flew Boeing 40Bs from Oakland to Chicago.

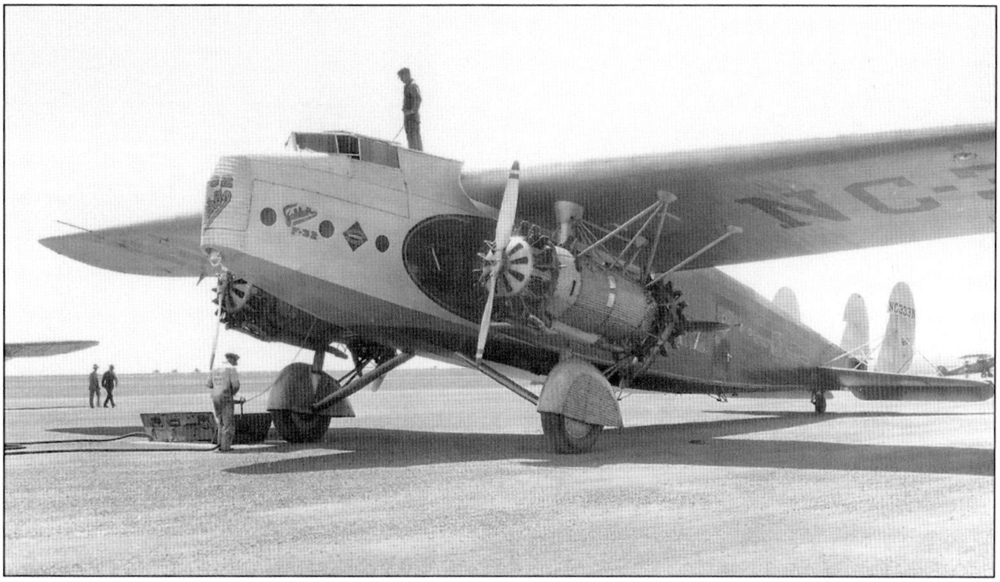

The "giant" four-engine Fokker F-32 was to be a great advancement for Western Air Express service from Oakland to Alhambra, but it was not successful. The design of the engines, one in front of the other, resulted in excess fuel used and did not produce the expected increase in performance, so the F-32s had a short period of service in 1931.

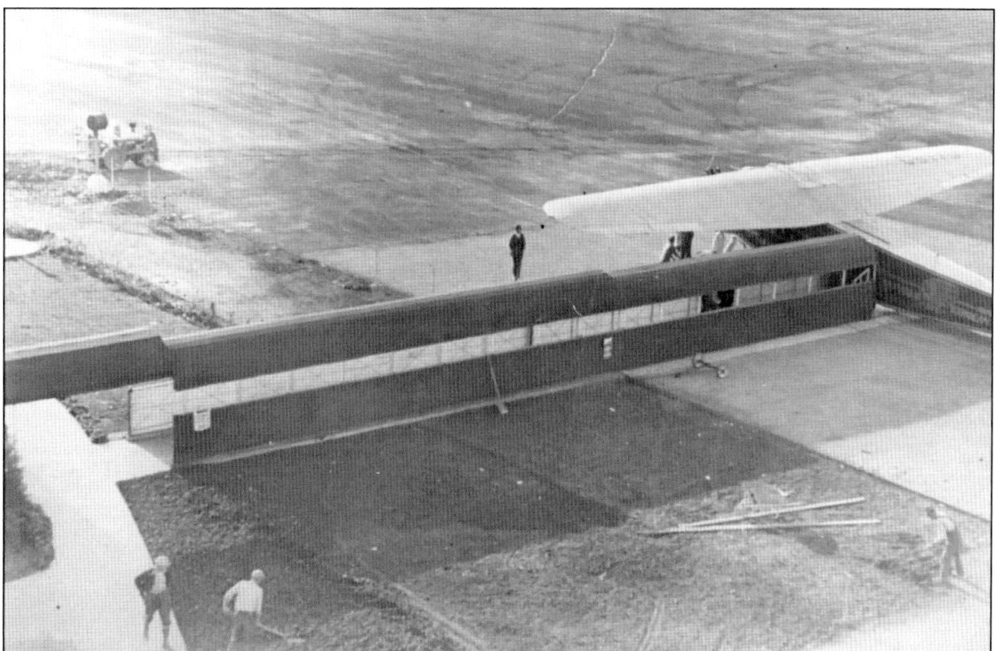

This photograph shows very early use of the covered passenger loading gate leading to the Western Air Express Fokker F-10. Prior to this, and for many years after, passengers at Oakland and other airports had to walk out in the weather from the terminal to the airliner.

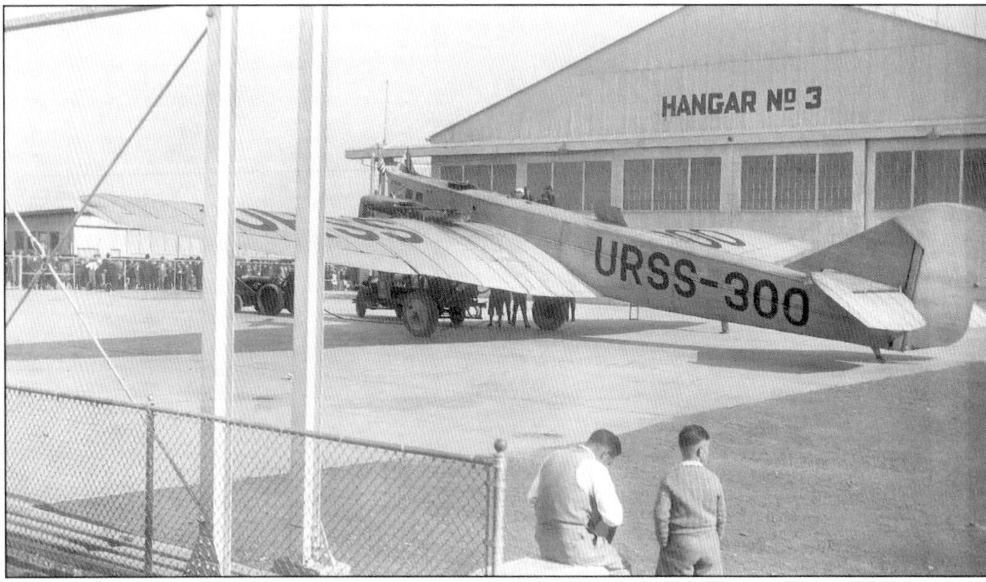

The Russian Antonov ANT-4 *Land of the Soviets* landed at Oakland Airport on October 19, 1929, during a goodwill flight from Moscow to New York City. After leaving Oakland, the four-man crew flew to Salt Lake City and on to New York. The total flight took 142 flying hours and covered 13,300 miles.

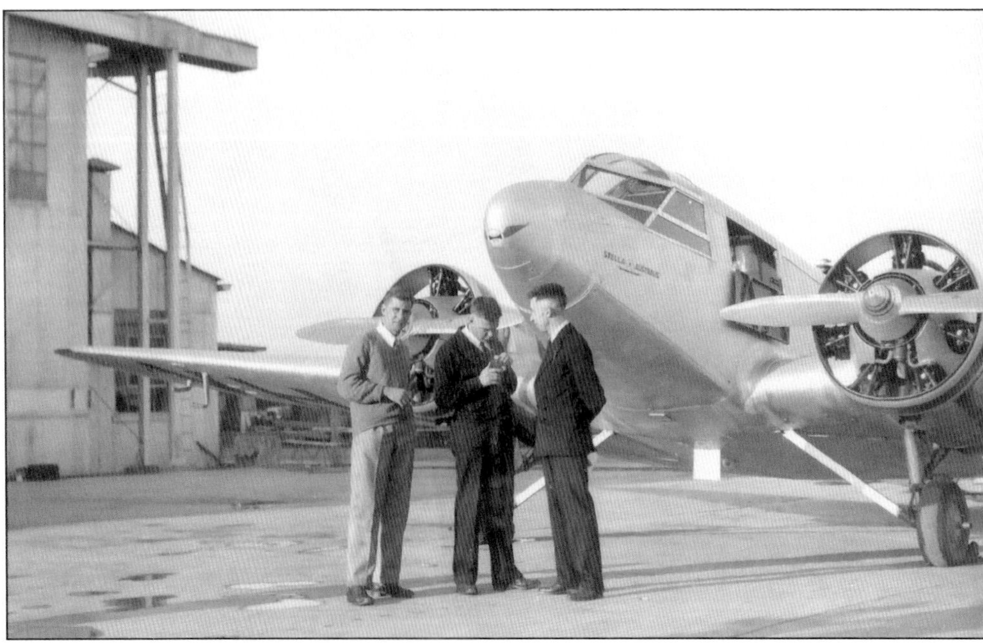

Charles Ulm, the Australian copilot with Kingsford Smith on the first flight from Oakland to Brisbane, returned with his plane, a British Airspeed Envoy named *Stella Australis*. With George Littlejohn and J. S. Leon Skilling, he left Oakland for Australia on December 3, 1934, to chart a proposed commercial route to Australia. The plane and crew disappeared at sea somewhere in the vicinity of the Hawaiian Islands.

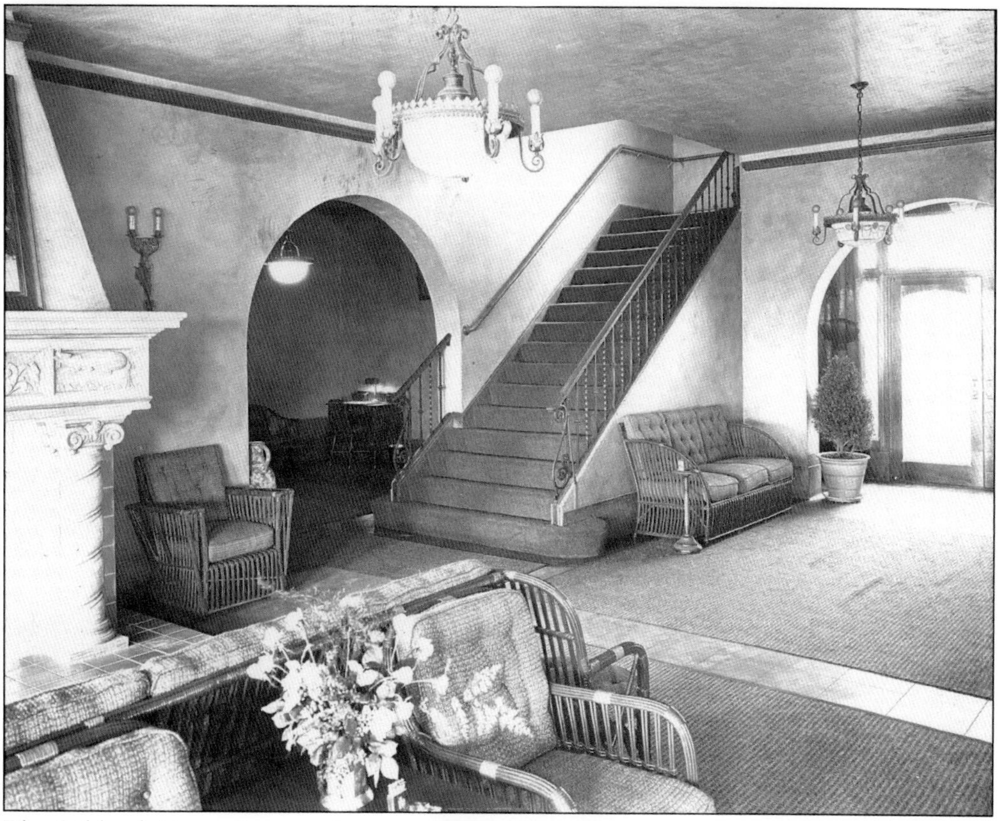

The Oakland Airport Inn was the first airport hotel to be built in the United States. The doors opened on July 15, 1929, to this 37-room two-story hotel with a restaurant to serve 200 people. It included a barbershop, which was probably also the first at an airport in the United States. It has served as office space and an aviation school in more recent years, and the building is still in operation.

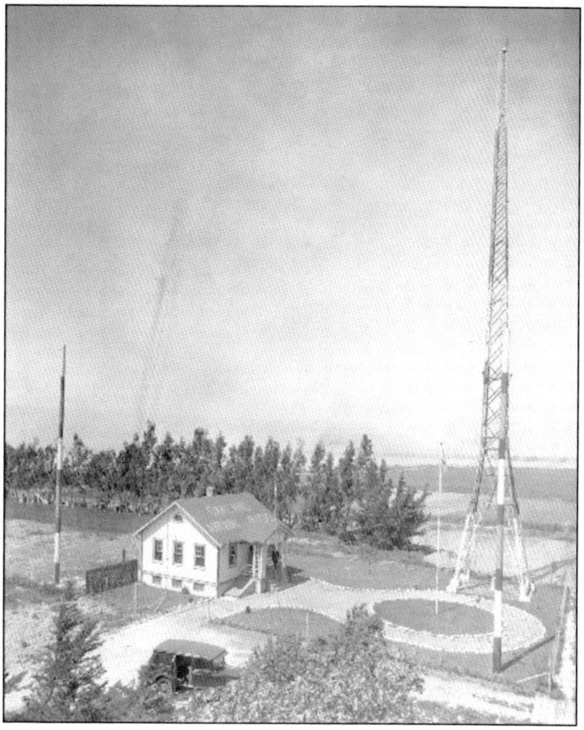

This is a rare photograph of the early radio tower serving Oakland Airport. The name on the roof of the small building reads, "OAKLAND AIRWAY RADIO." The advent of aircraft radios in the 1920s was a major change in the ability to navigate, especially at night. The previous system, built for the U.S. Airmail Service, consisted of rotating beacons. There were 616 beacons in operation from 1923 to 1927 from New York to San Francisco.

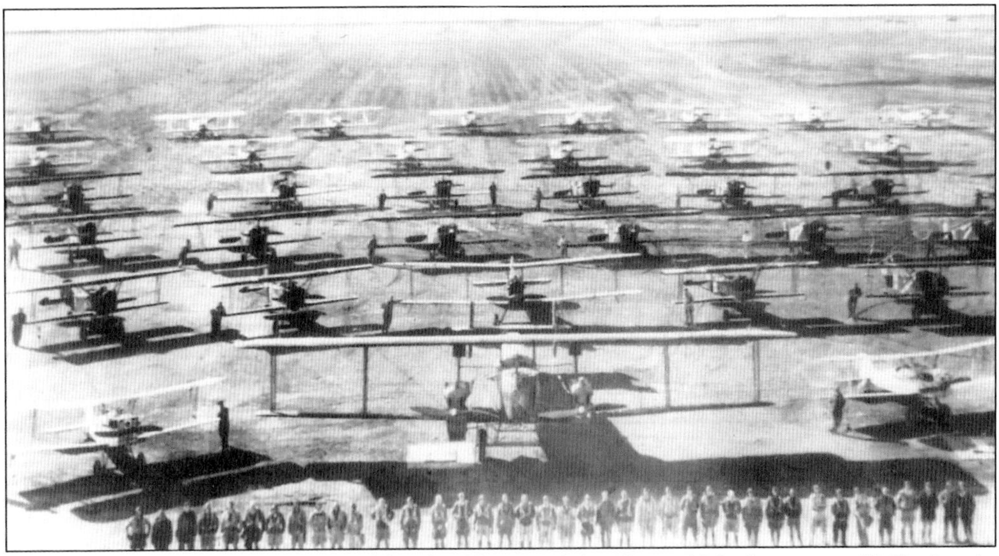

This large group of planes was used for the filming of the Howard Hughes movie *Hell's Angels*. First filmed as a silent movie with many scenes over the Oakland hills, it was redone with the advent of the "talkies." The planes consisted of some authentic World War I fighters but also used private planes modified and painted to represent them. Some of the planes in this photograph were camera planes, carrying large 35-millimeter cameras strapped to the fuselage or top wing.

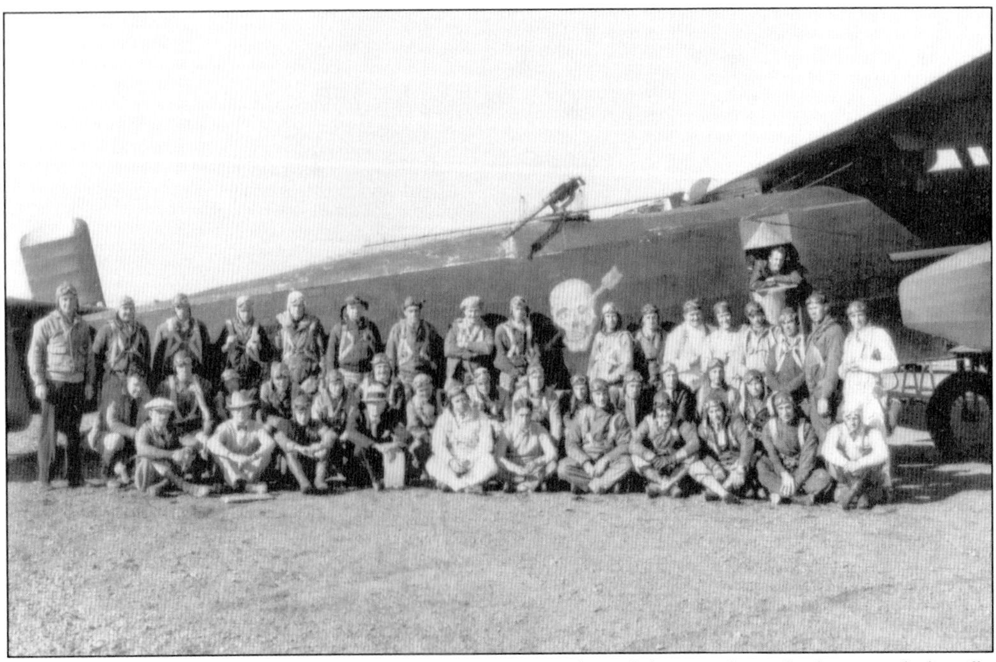

This photograph, taken at Oakland Airport, gives an idea of the number of pilots needed to fly the planes for *Hell's Angels*. The large plane was actually a civilian Sikorsky S-29 painted as a German World War I Gotha bomber. It was lost during the filming along with a cameraman in the rear when the crew had to bail out with their parachutes—some of which can be seen on the pilots standing to the right.

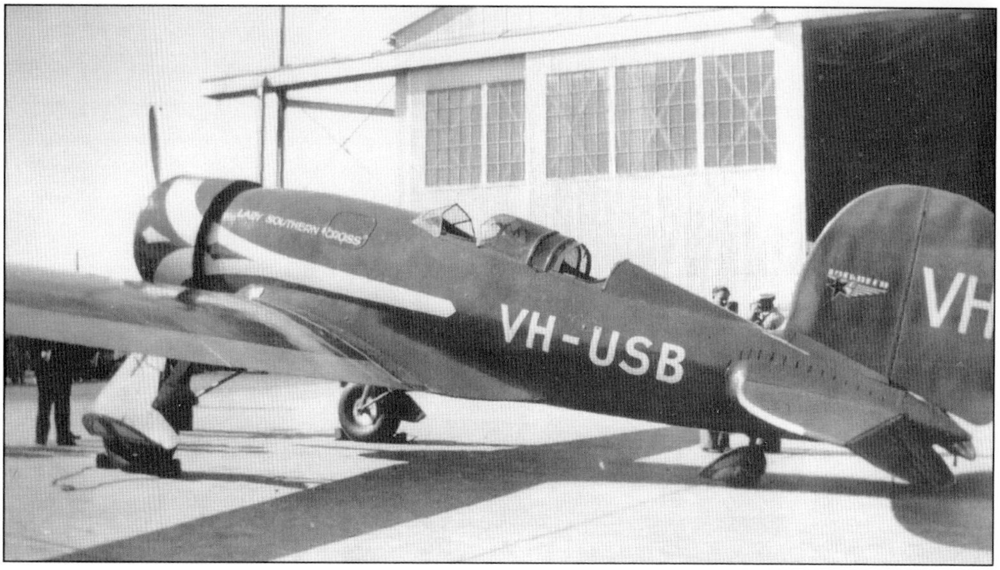

Sir Charles Kingsford Smith arrived at Oakland on November 4, 1934, in a new Lockheed Altair named *Anzac* with Capt. P. G. Taylor as navigator. The flight from Honolulu took a total flying time of 7 hours and 44 minutes. Kingsford Smith and the Lockheed were lost during a storm flying across the Bay of Bengal on the way to Singapore in November 1935.

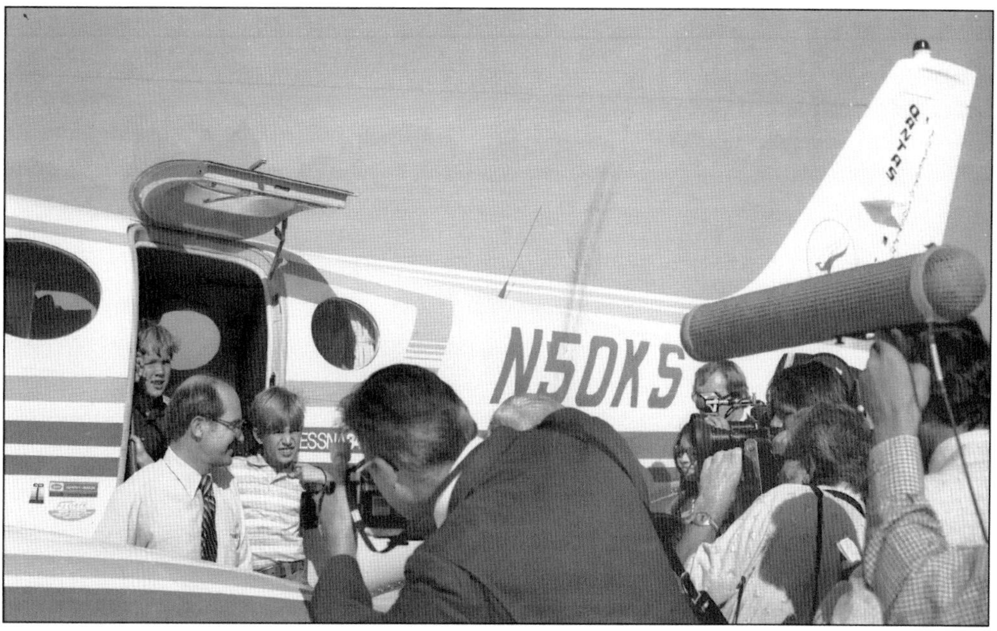

In May 1978, his son Charles A. Kingsford-Smith flew a twin-engine Cessna 340 from Oakland to Australia, following his father's route to commemorate the 1928 flight of the *Southern Cross*. This photograph shows him about to leave Oakland surrounded by his family and the press.

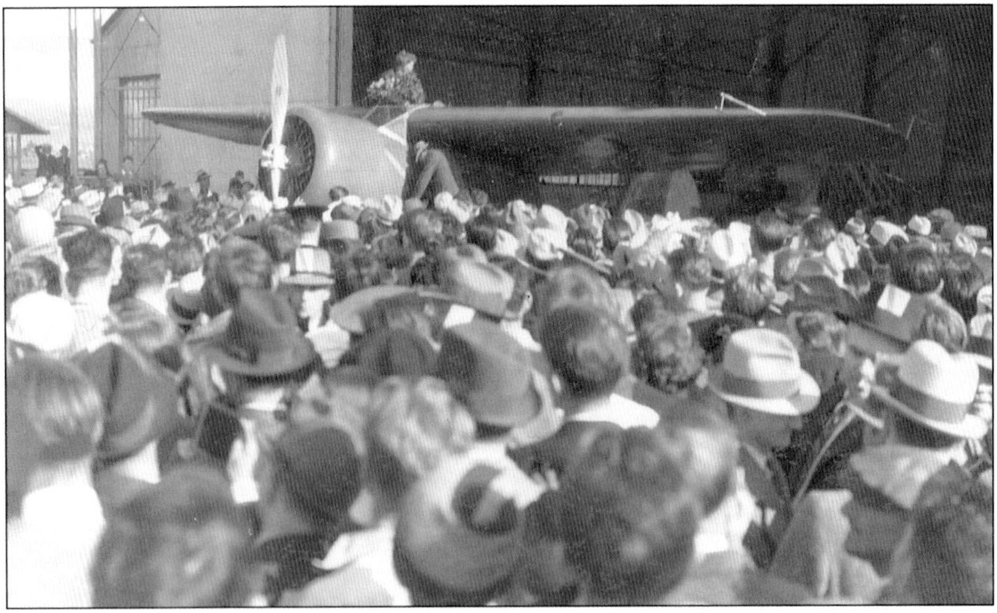

Amelia Earhart in her Lockheed Vega *Little Red Bus* is surrounded by a crowd after arriving at Oakland from Honolulu, Hawaii, on January 12, 1935. She was the first person and first woman pilot to fly solo from Hawaii to the United States. She carried 522 gallons of gas for an 18-hour flight. In April, the airport road was renamed Earhart Road in her honor, sponsored by the Ninety-Nines and the Oakland Junior Chamber of Commerce.

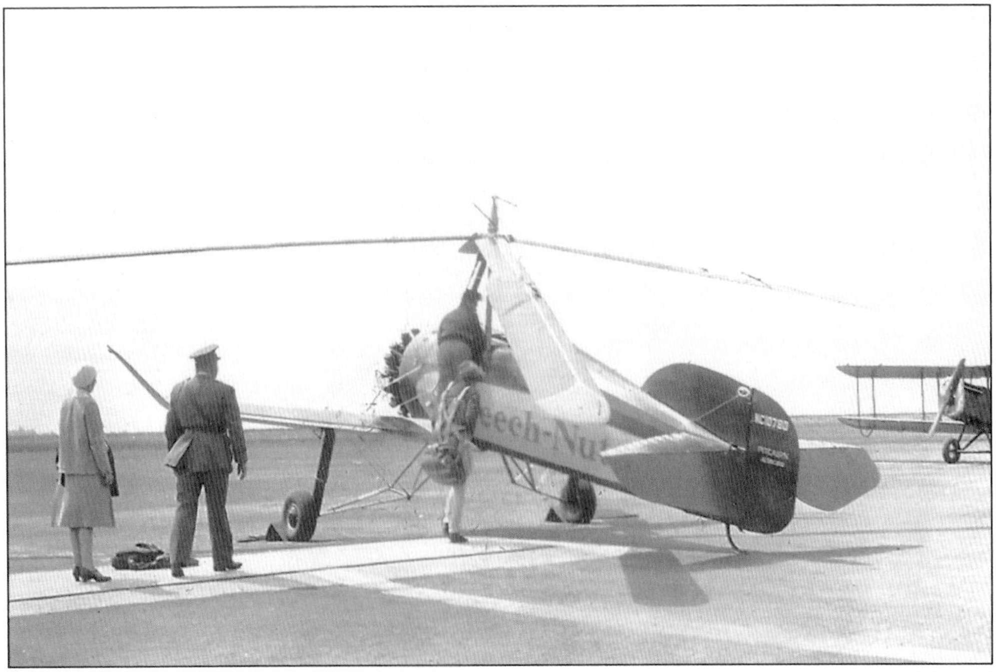

Amelia Earhart flew this Pitcairn PCA-2 autogiro across the United States, landing at Oakland on June 6, 1931. She was sponsored by Beech-Nut, who owned the autogiro and had planned for her to make the first transcontinental autogiro flight, but this did not happen. Amelia had set an autogiro altitude record of 18,415 feet in Pennsylvania the previous April.

Three

Growth of Commercial Aviation, Testing, and Training

Under political pressure, airmail routes and subsidies were cancelled in 1934, and for 80 days, the Army Air Corps carried the mail. Under Maj. Clarence L. Tinker, commander of the Oakland–Salt Lake City–Cheyenne route with headquarters in Oakland, flights were started on February 19. Other routes had multiple accidents, and the death toll forced the government to reopen civilian bids on April 20, requiring complete reorganization of the airlines. Contracts were again let for civilian airlines to operate the mail routes, and the last army mail flight left Oakland on May 7, 1934.

Robert F. Six attended St. Mary's High School in Oakland, took flying lessons from Walter Varney, bought a Travel Air, and started Valley Flying Service. With Monty Mouton, he formed the company Mouton and Six. Six later purchased an interest in Varney Air Transport in 1936 and in 1937 became its president. On July 1, 1937, he changed the name to Continental Airlines.

In March 1934, the Army Air Corps took the DC-1 on bailment from Trans World Airlines (TWA) for a series of radio and navigation flights out of Oakland. Capt. Clayton Bissell and Capt. Albert Hegenberger were assigned to evaluate the new Sperry autopilot and Kreusi radio compass. Many flights were conducted, most of them far out to sea. In May 1936, United Air Lines at Oakland was the site of a successful series of tests of the nation's first practical "blind" landing system. Engineers Thorp Hiscock and William Lawrenz, together with Herbert Hoover Jr., worked with Western Electric Company–assigned technicians, and over 7,000 test landings were conducted.

In 1938, the Duck Flying Service at Oakland provided a specially equipped Stinson Reliant to the U.S. Forest Service for fire prevention tests. All through its history, Oakland Airport has been home to significant training schools, such as the Boeing School of Aeronautics, TALOA (Transocean), Aero Tech Industries Institute, Sierra Academy of Aeronautics, Kaiser Air Center, and, more recently, Wyotech.

On January 12, 1935, Amelia Earhart arrived from Honolulu in her Lockheed Vega *Little Red Bus*. On March 17, 1937, Earhart departed Oakland destined for Honolulu on an around-the-world flight with Paul Mantz, Paul Manning, and Fred Noonan. Two days later, while taking off at Oahu, the Lockheed 10E crashed. After it was repaired, she started out a second time from Oakland on May 20, 1937, on an eastward flight around the world. On July 2, she and the plane disappeared approaching Howland Island in the middle of the Pacific.

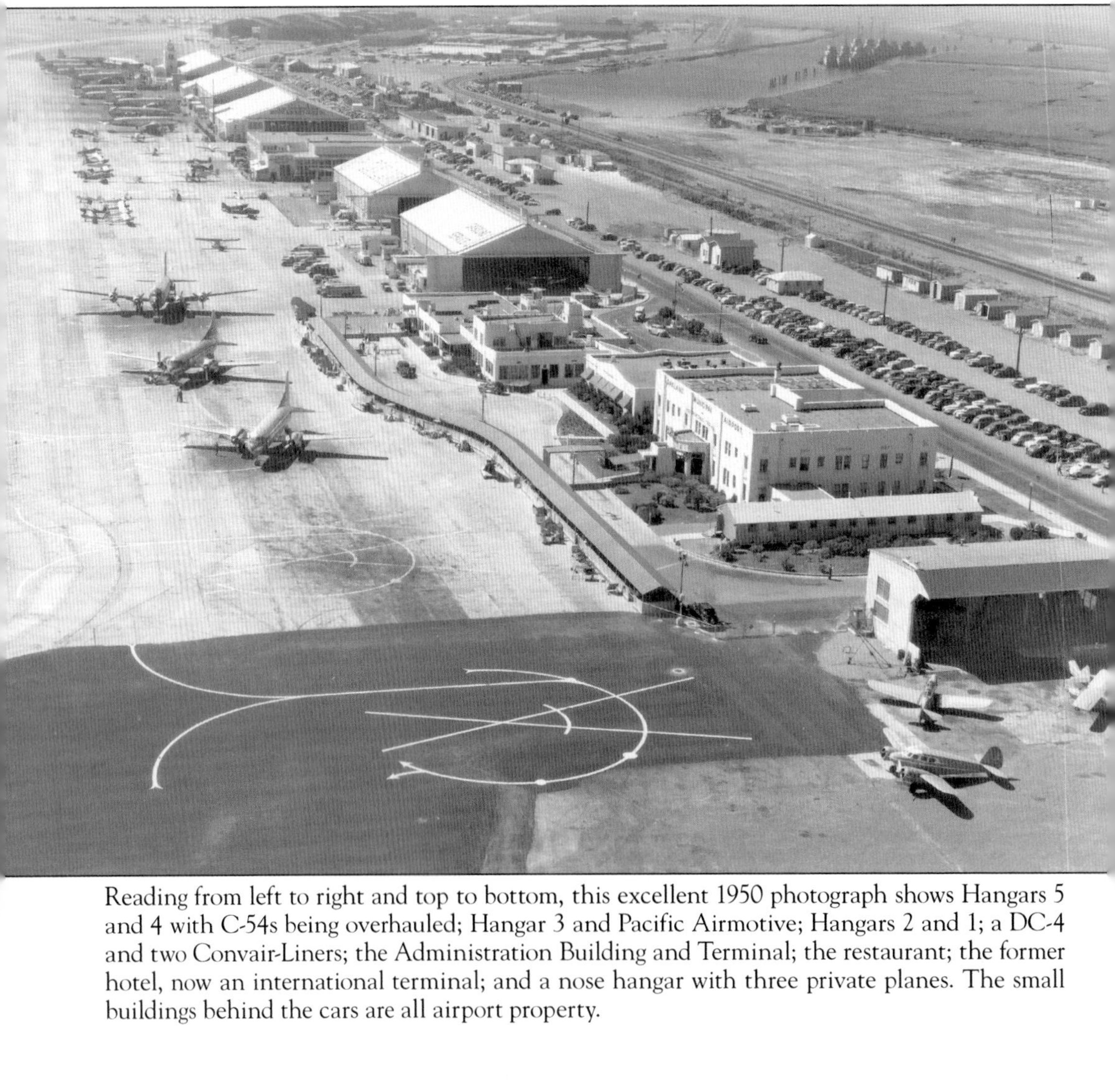

Reading from left to right and top to bottom, this excellent 1950 photograph shows Hangars 5 and 4 with C-54s being overhauled; Hangar 3 and Pacific Airmotive; Hangars 2 and 1; a DC-4 and two Convair-Liners; the Administration Building and Terminal; the restaurant; the former hotel, now an international terminal; and a nose hangar with three private planes. The small buildings behind the cars are all airport property.

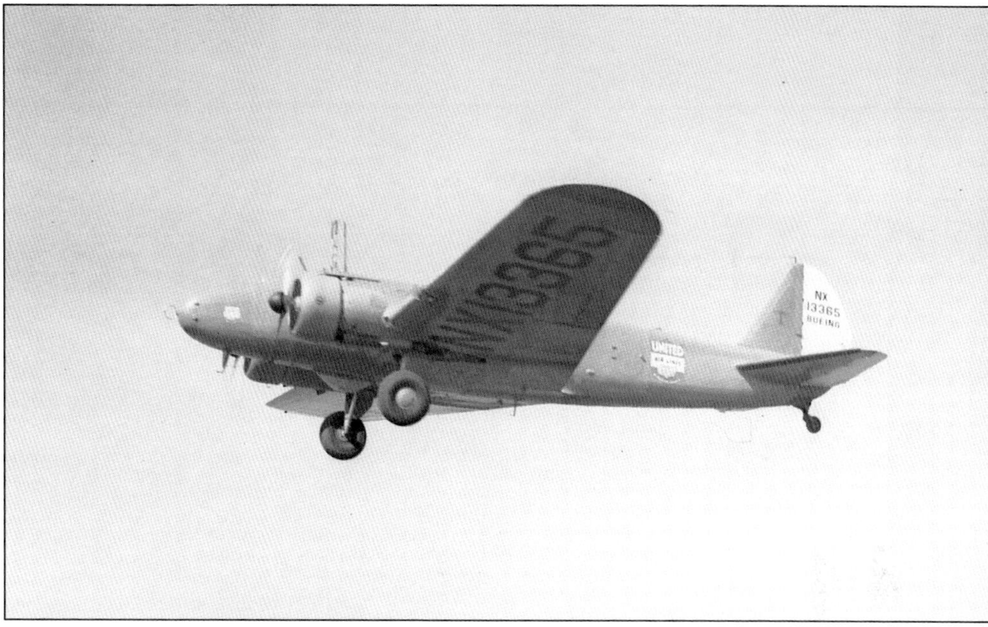

United Air Lines took one Boeing 247D (NX.13365) out of airline service and used it for radio research for several years. This photograph shows its early appearance in dark gray in 1938 before it was redone in red and white. A special radio antenna can be seen above the cockpit.

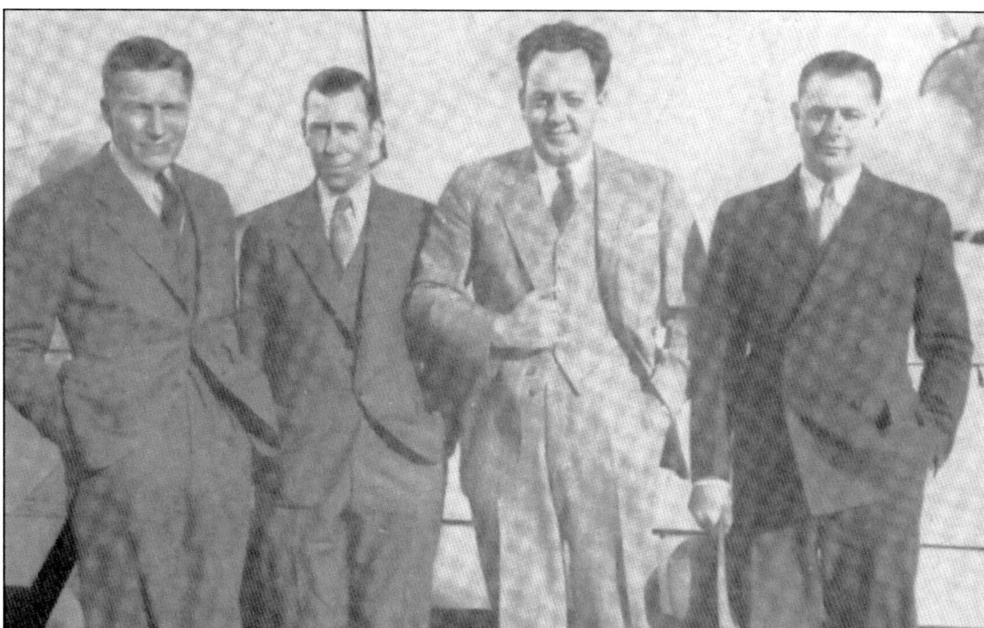

In 1934, the new Douglas DC-1 was used by the Department of Commerce to test new navigation and radio devices in anticipation of commercial ocean air travel. With considerable secrecy, flights were conducted testing the new Sperry autopilot and the Kreusi radio compass. Pictured from left to right are Eugene Vidal, director of the Bureau of Air Commerce; Clayton Bissell; Herbert Hoover Jr.; and Albert Hegenberger.

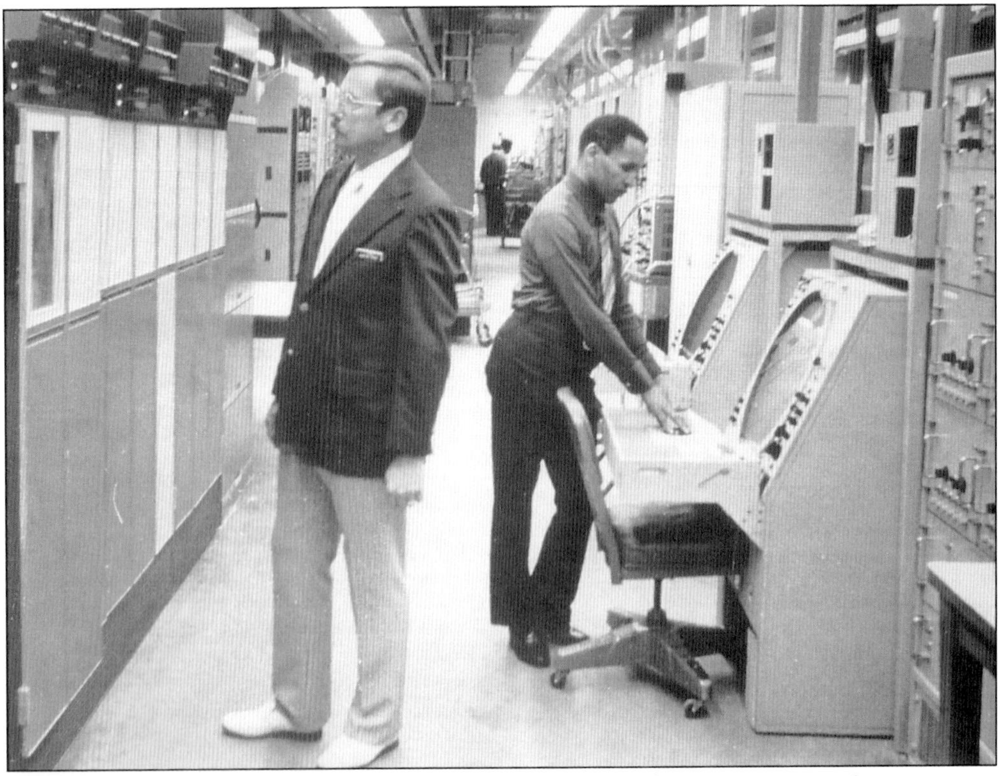

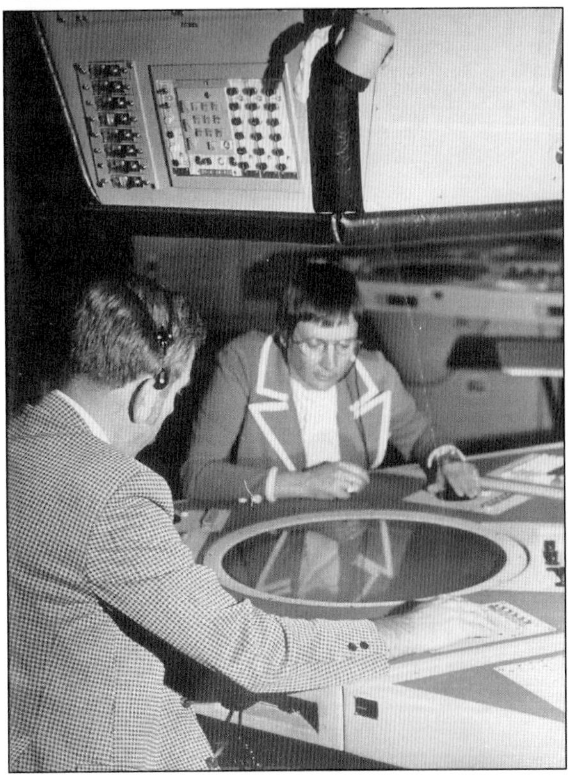

Weather reporting was always important for flight planning and management. This photograph shows a well-equipped modern weather office at Oakland Airport.

This photograph shows the early use of a radar scope for air traffic control. Today's equipment fills a large room with banks of vertical screens. Oakland Center Control was not at the airport.

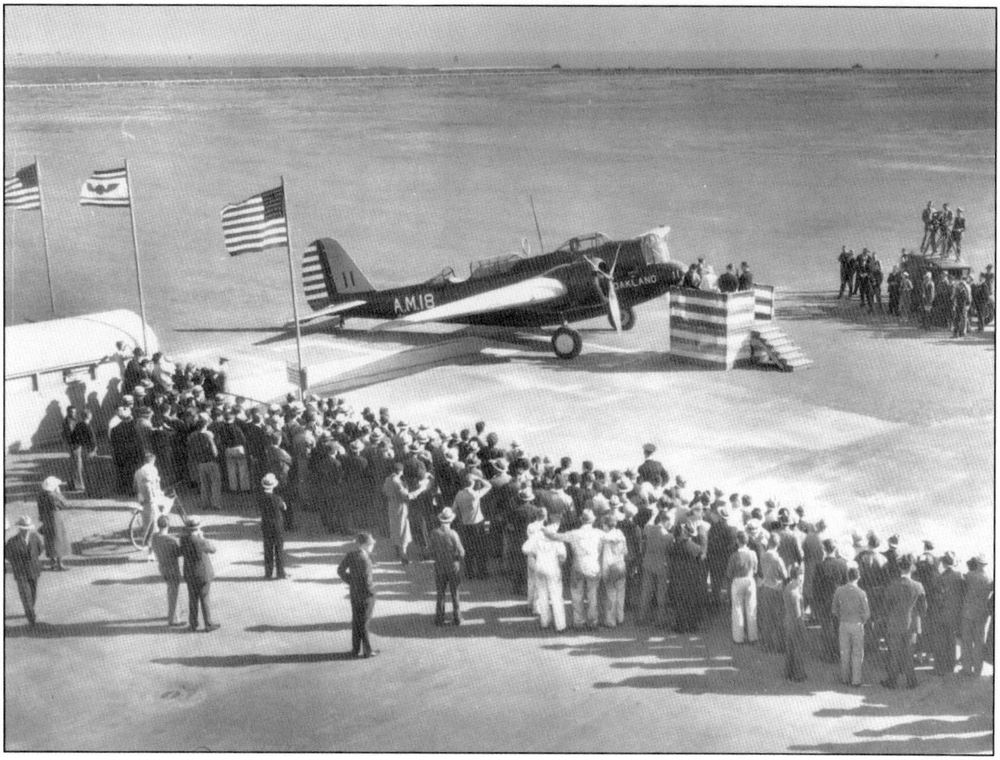

When the Army Air Corps took over the delivery of airmail in the United States in February 1934, this Martin B-10 bomber was christened the *City of Oakland* at a ceremony at Oakland Airport on April 19. After fatal crashes in bad weather in the East, the airmail service was returned to the airlines, and the last flight out of Oakland was on May 7.

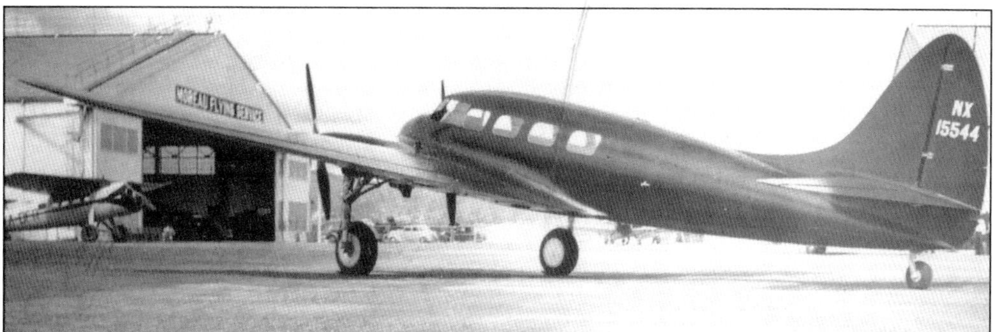

Alan Lockheed formed a company to design and build a twin-engine passenger plane at Oakland. The plane was built in one half of Hangar 4, and test flights were conducted as far as Burbank. Unfortunately it was lost during a high-speed test over the bay when flutter developed. The two-man test crew parachuted safely from the plane into the mudflats off the airport.

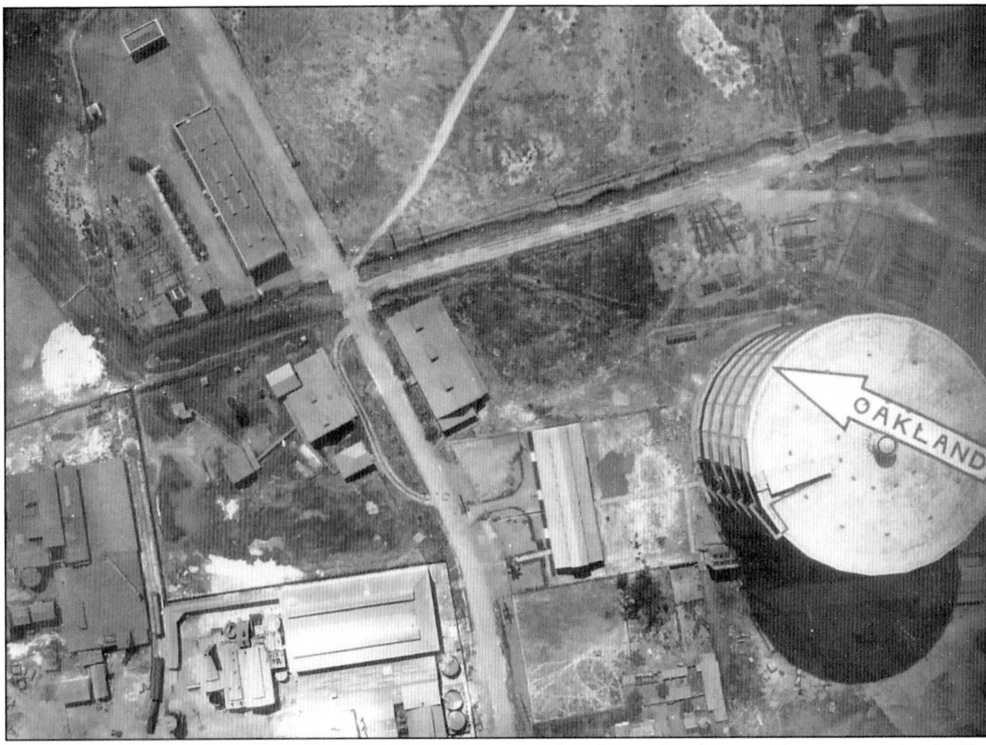

Painting compass arrows on the roofs of hangars and buildings had been done since the 1920s, as shown by this large directional arrow on the top of the PG&E Natural Gas Storage Tank in Oakland. It achieved some fame later in a scene in the movie *Thirty Seconds over Tokyo* as the B-25s were bombing that city.

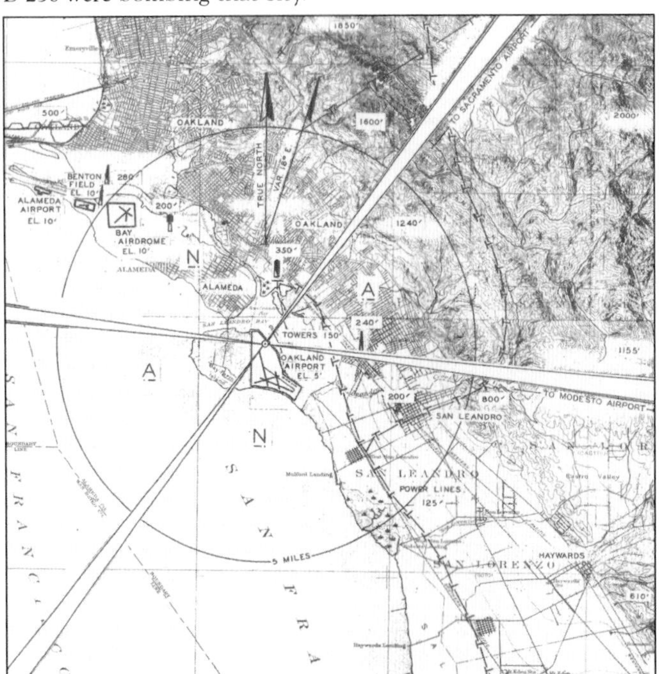

This January 1940 United Air Lines pilot map of the Oakland area shows the developing sophistication of flying aids that led up to today's multicolored aeronautical charts. It shows the short-lived Benton Field started for the Army Air Corps in Alameda and the interesting use of the word "Haywards."

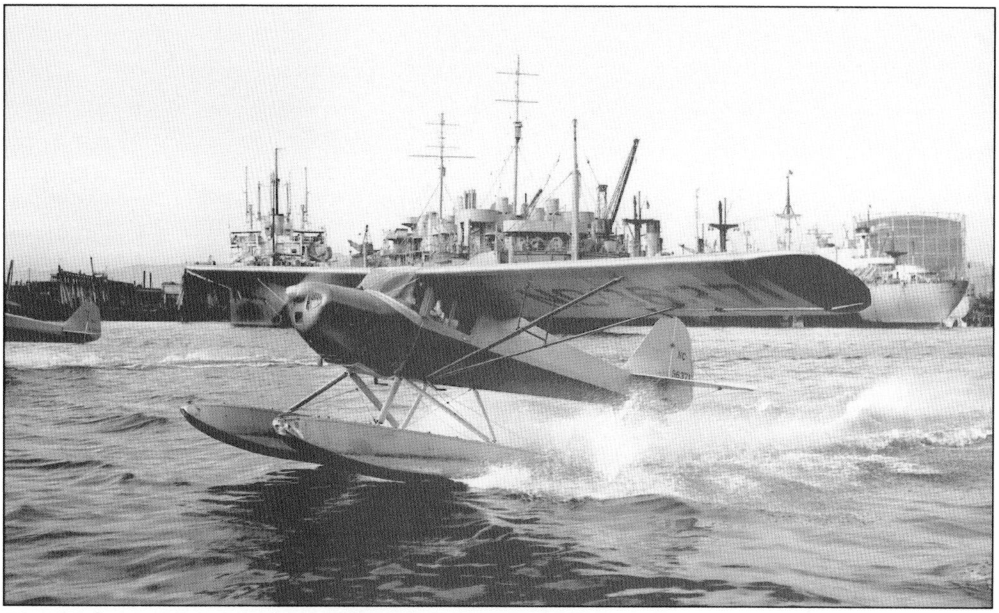

This Taylorcraft BC-12D (N96371) of the Norton Marine Air flight service is shown taking off in April 1947 from the Oakland Estuary near the foot of Broadway with the Alameda shipyards in the background.

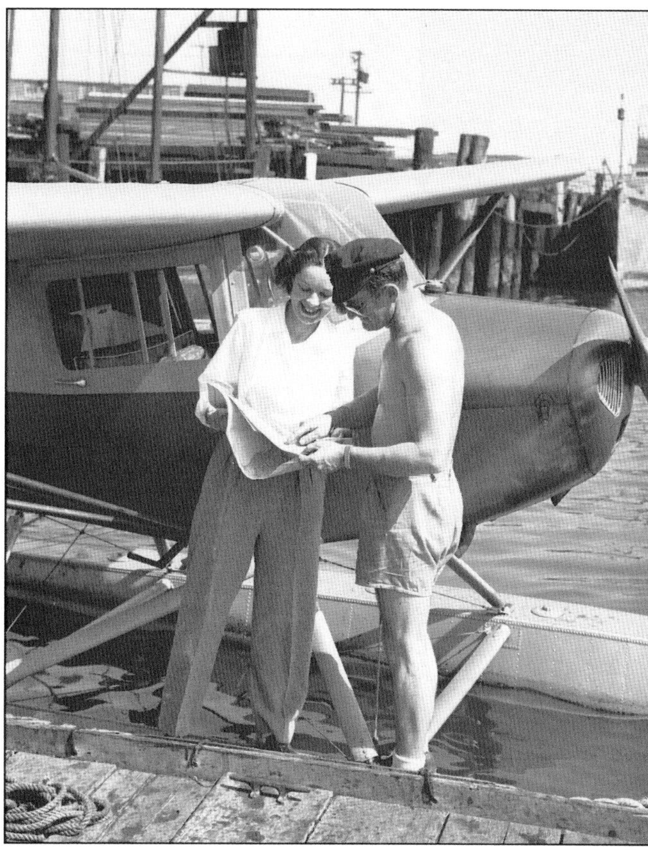

In this posed publicity photograph, Howard Norton is shown briefing a student before a flight in his Taylorcraft BC-12D floatplane. Flight instruction, aircraft rental, and charter service were part of the business at the foot of Webster Street.

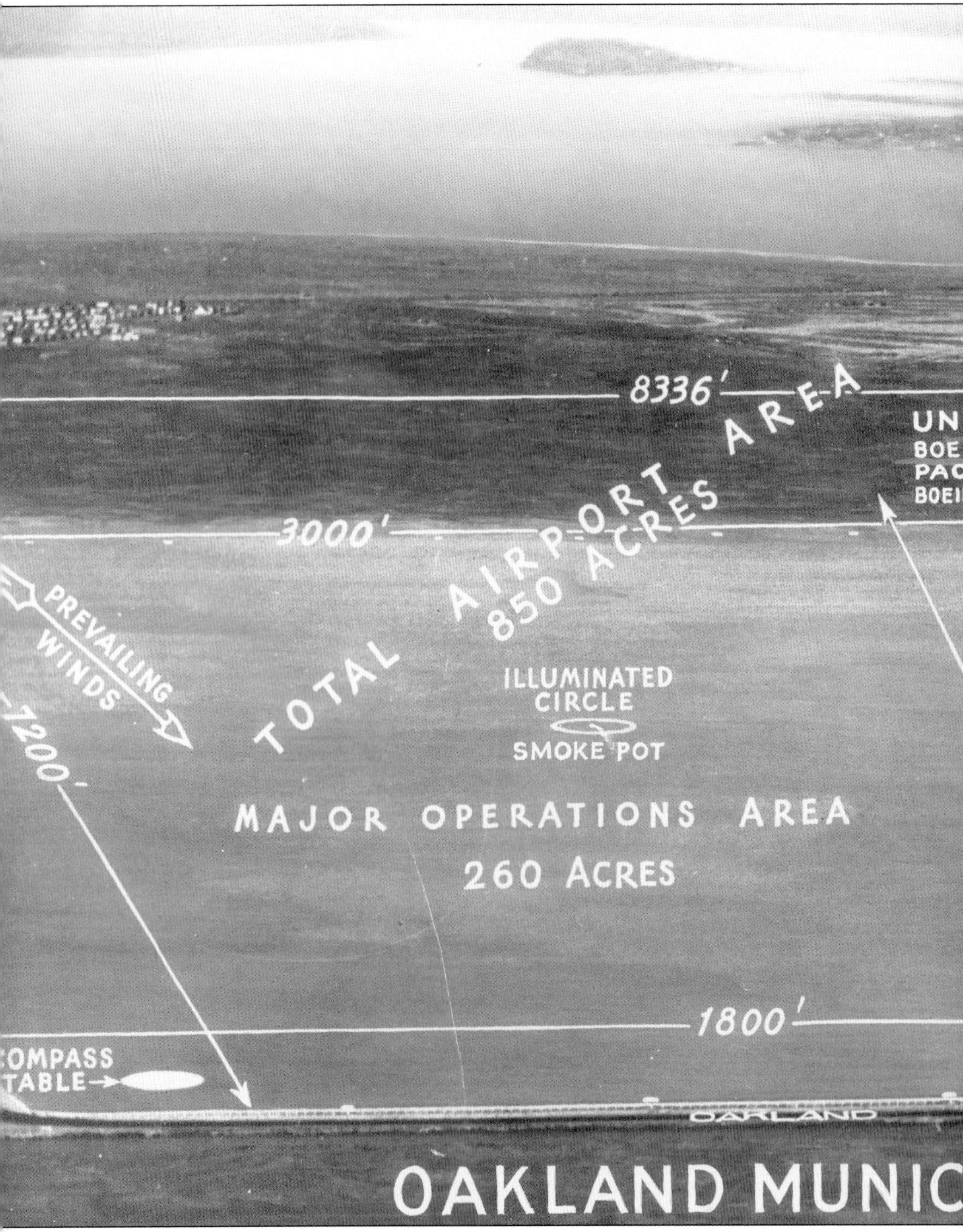

This excellent description of the airport is the result of retouching an aerial photograph taken about 1936. The field has been painted out, which eliminates the runways and planes but provides a clearer background for the lettering. A two-lane public road, labeled "Oakland" on the photograph, ran around the outside of the airport and over to Bay Farm Island. The Airport

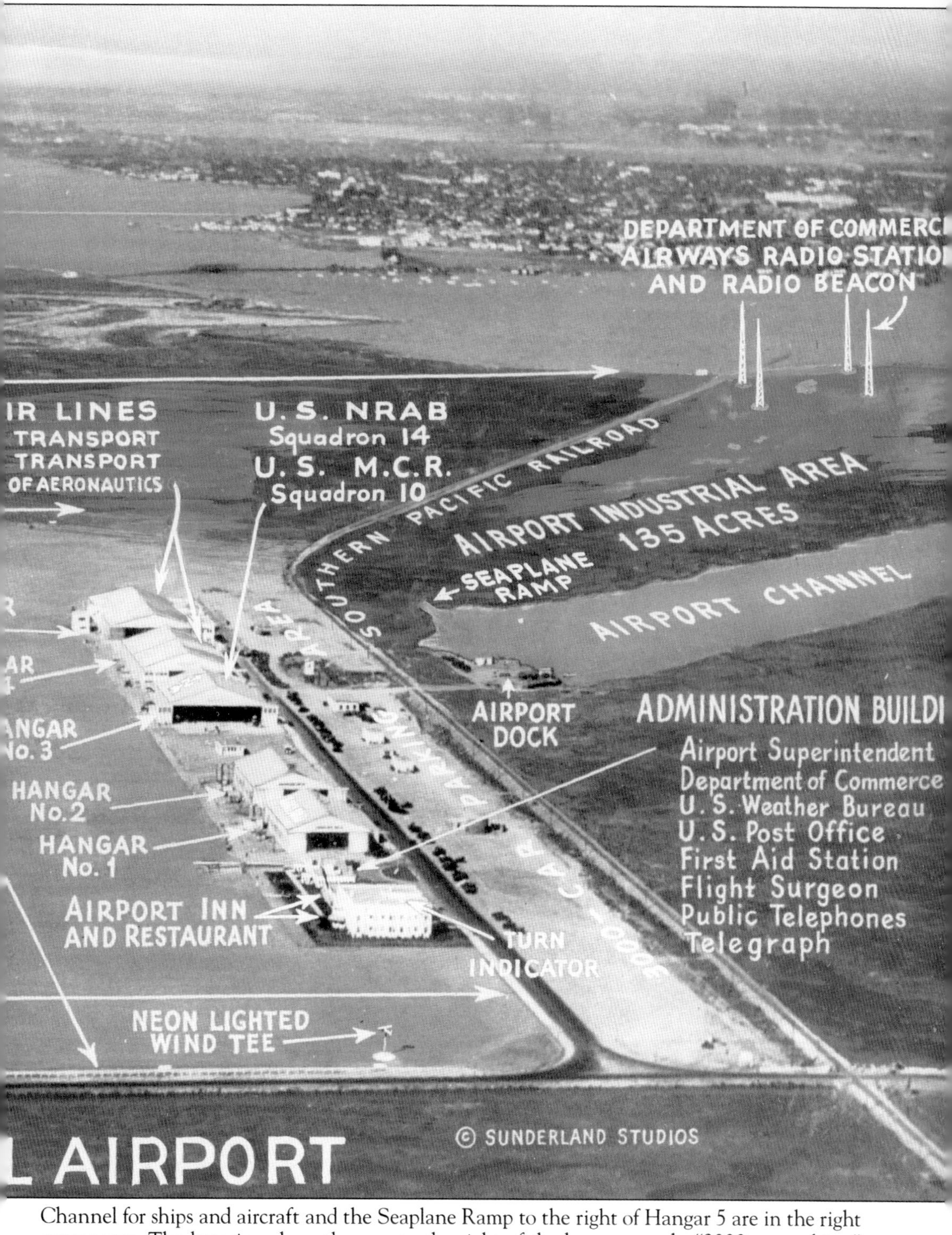

Channel for ships and aircraft and the Seaplane Ramp to the right of Hangar 5 are in the right center area. The lettering along the cars to the right of the hangars reads, "3000 car parking." Hangar 3, with the doors open, is the home of VN-14R of the 12th Naval District and VO-10MR Marine Reserve.

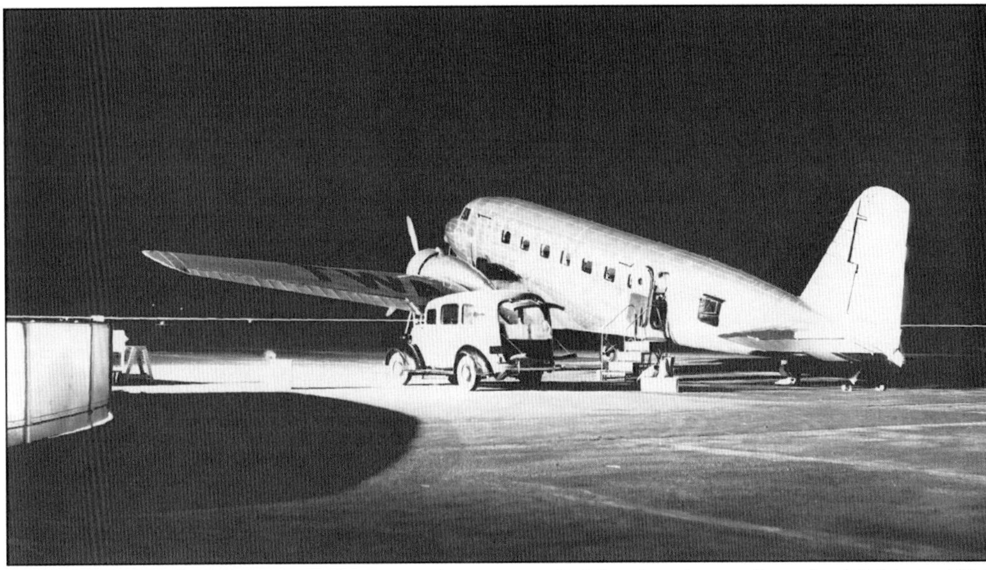

Transcontinental and Western Air started service to Oakland with new Douglas DC-2s in 1934. This was an improvement over the Ford trimotors used by the previous Transcontinental Air Transport and an interim step before introduction of the more successful DC-3.

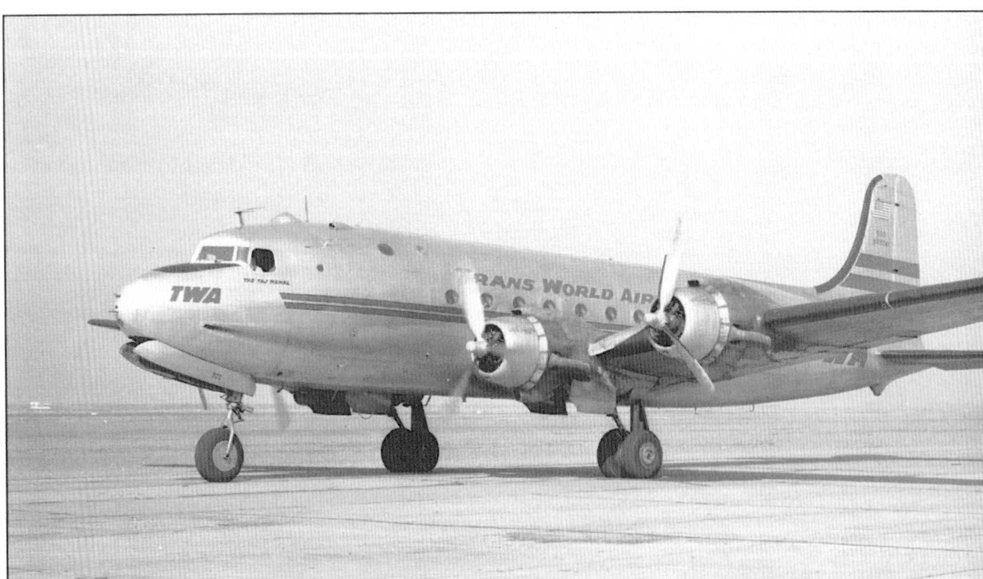

After World War II, many former AAF Douglas C-54 transports were rebuilt to DC-4 passenger configuration and put into service by all of the major airlines in the United States. TWA was quick to introduce them to service at Oakland and San Francisco.

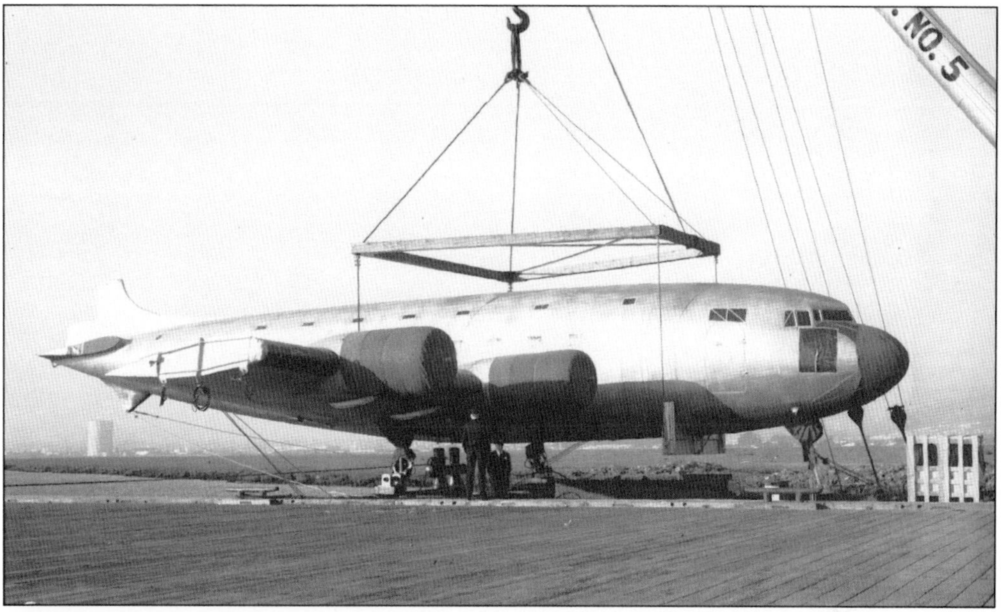

United Air Lines and Douglas teamed up to develop the original triple-tail DC-4E passenger plane in 1939. It was distinctly different than the later DC-4s that were a result of military design and production. After a nationwide tour, the DC-4E was sold to Japan, dismantled at Oakland in September, loaded on a Haviside Company barge in the airport channel, and then taken to a Japanese freighter in the bay.

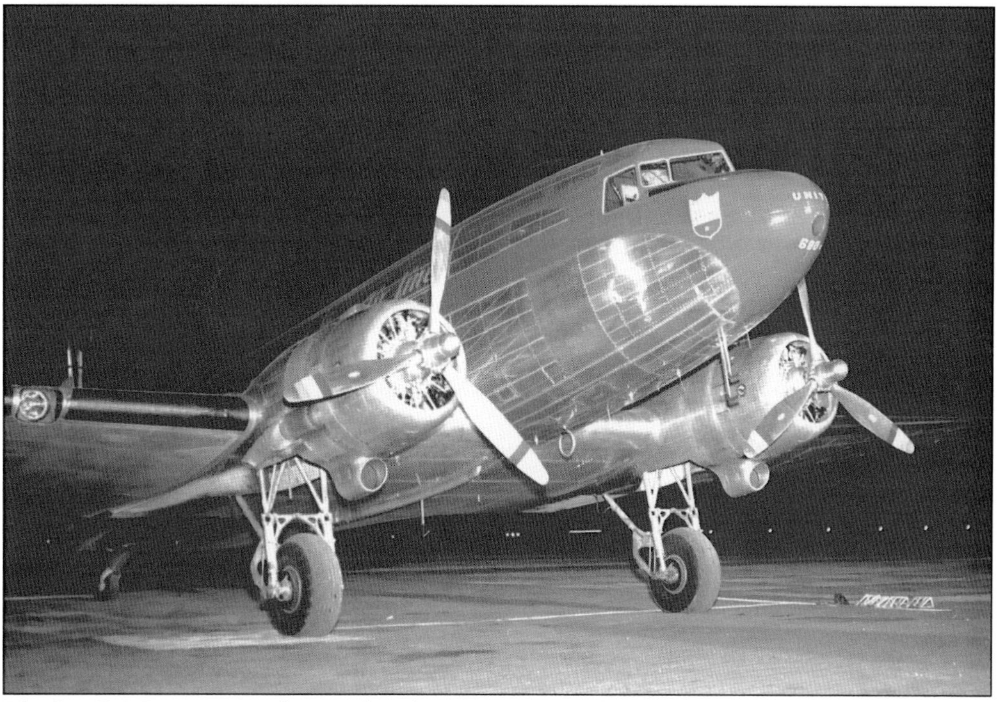
The first DC-3s were actually Douglas Sleeper Transports (DSTs) and this photograph shows one of the first for United Air Lines, NC-25680. It was delivered in February 1940; this photograph was taken at Oakland a few months later. It became *Mainliner North Platte*.

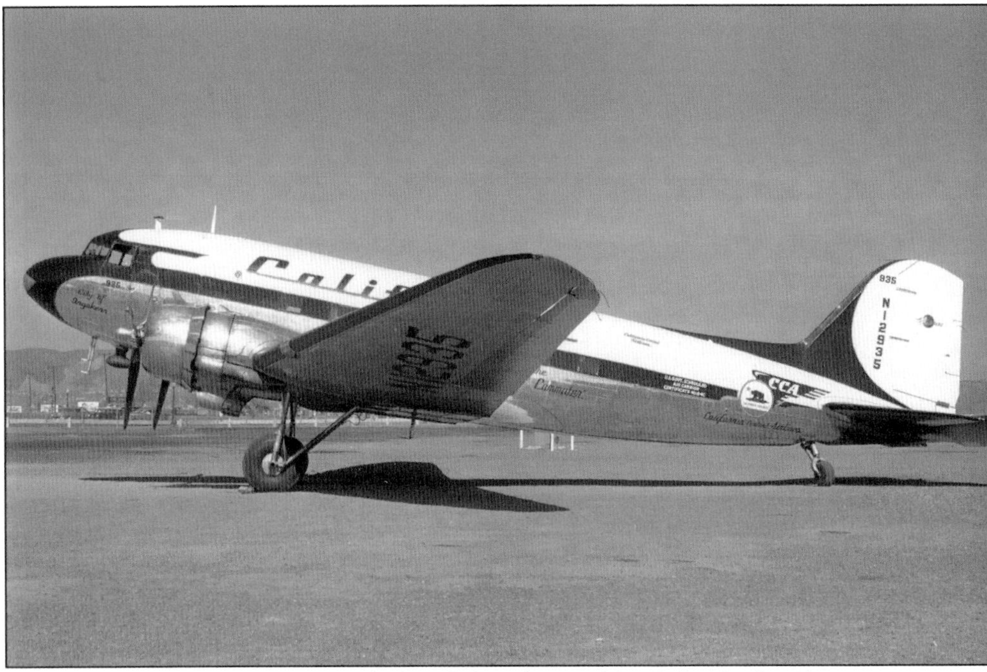

California Central Airlines (CCA), founded and owned by Col. Charles Sherman, operated a low-fare commuter airline between Oakland and Burbank from 1949 to 1954 before filing for bankruptcy. A popular route with an intrastate approval only, in competition with the regular scheduled airlines, it painted the following next to the door, "U.S. Gov't Scheduled Air Carrier, Certificate No.6-4C." N12935 was a surplus AAF C-49K transport and was named *City of Inyokern*.

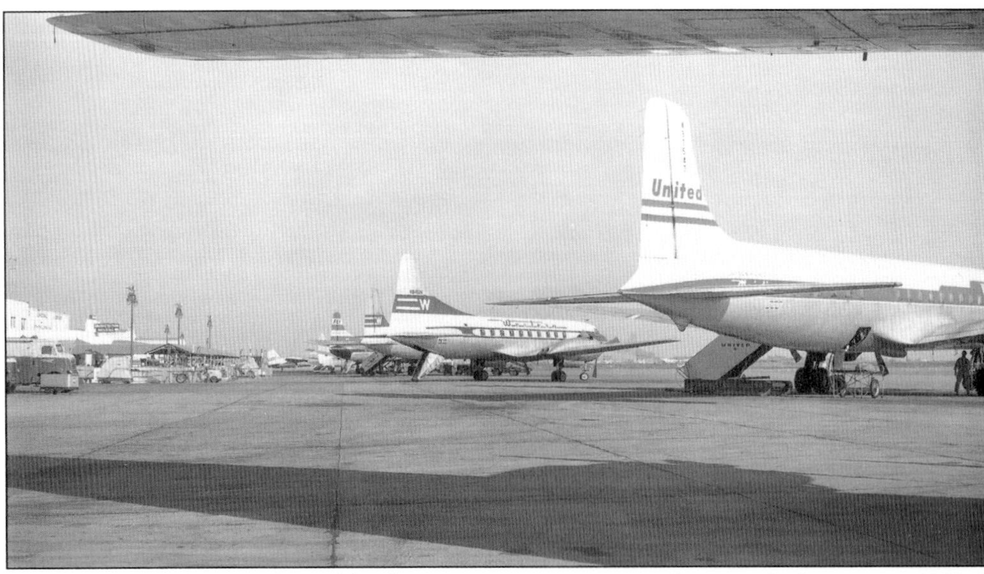

This lineup of airliners at the Oakland Airport passenger terminal is typical of activity in 1952. It was taken from under the tail of a United DC-4 and shows, from left to right, a Pacific Southwest Airways DC-3, a Transocean Curtiss C-46, a California Central Martin 2-0-2, a Western Airlines DC-4, a Western Airlines Convair-liner 240, and a United Air Lines DC-6.

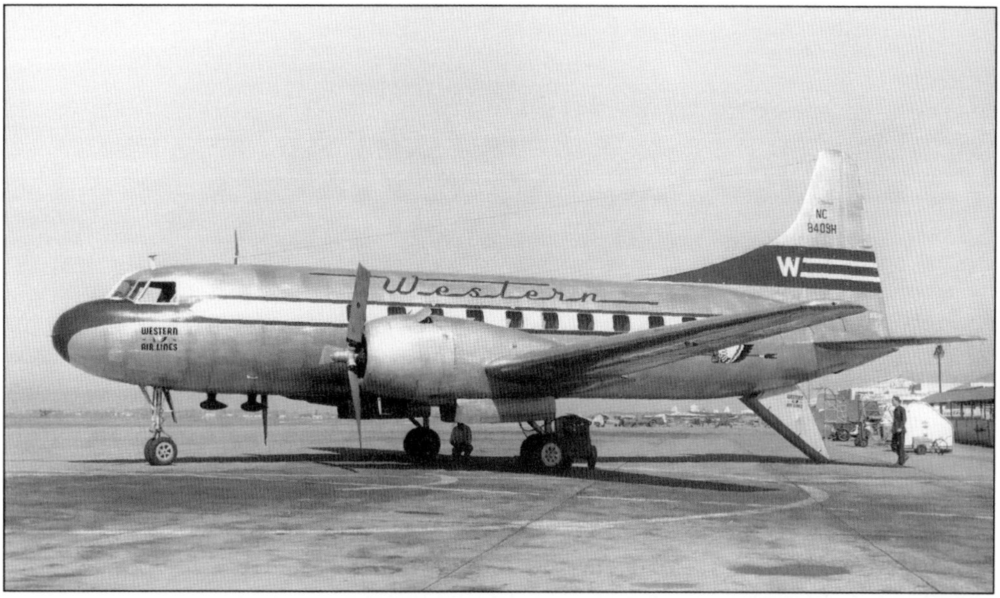

Western Airlines was the first to introduce the new Convair 240 to passenger service at Oakland. It was a new, fast competitor to the DC-3 and featured an air stair door at the rear of the fuselage. This photograph shows N8409H at Oakland on August 26, 1948, preparing for the first passenger service to Los Angeles on September 1.

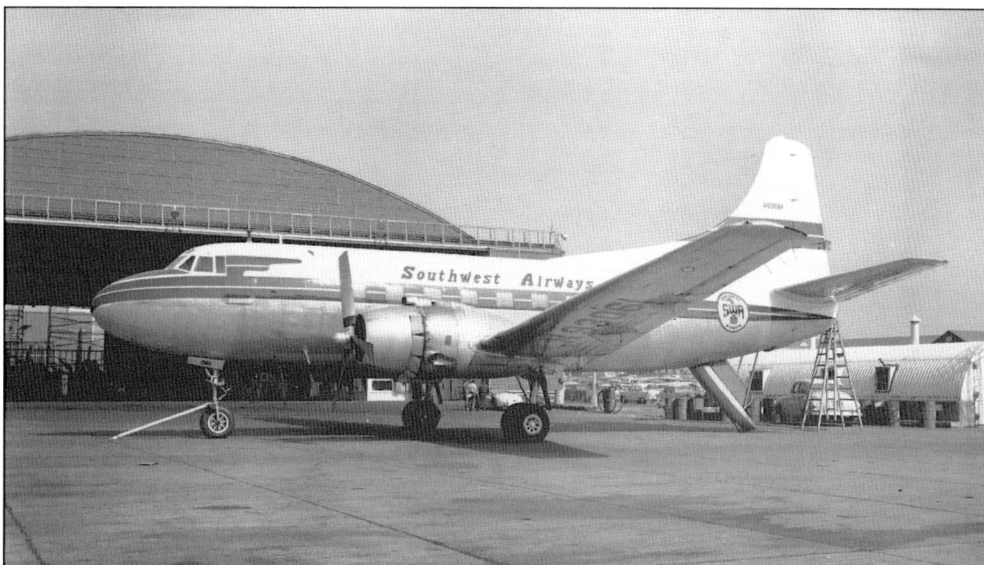

Similar in appearance, the Martin 2-0-2 airliner also flew into and out of Oakland with Southwest, Transocean, and California Central. Both carried 40 passengers and were used on airlines throughout the United States. This Southwest Airways 2-0-2 is at the north end of the field in 1952.

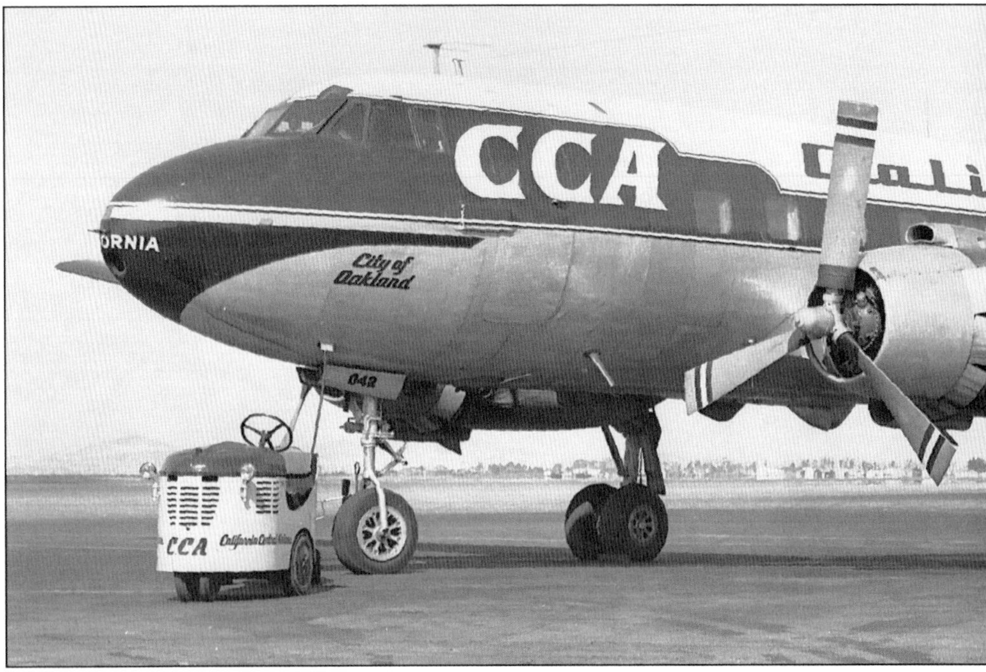

The most colorful of the twin-engine airliners in the 1950s was the Martin 2-0-2 of California Central Airlines in its bright red-white-and-blue colors. Of the five in service in 1952, this one, NC93042, was named *City of Oakland*. TWA Martin 2-0-2A (N93202) was named *Skyliner Oakland* in the 1950s.

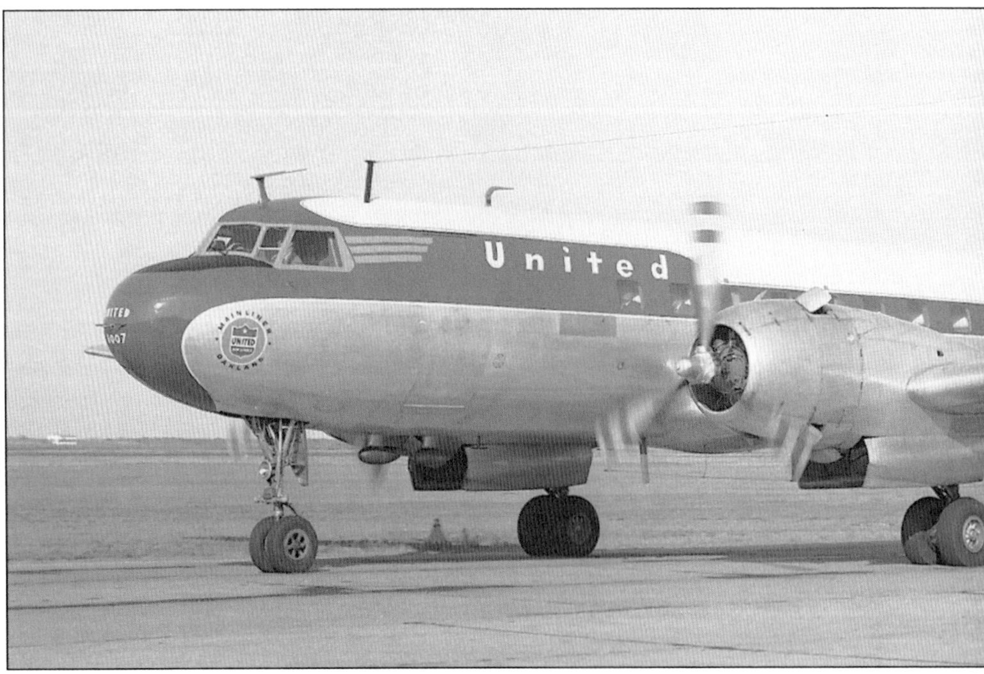

United Air Lines named all of their planes "Mainliners" with the addition of the name of a city served by them. This Convair 340 (N73107) coming in from a landing in 1954 is *Mainliner Oakland*. American Airlines (AA) had a Convair 240 (N94248) as its *Flagship Oakland*.

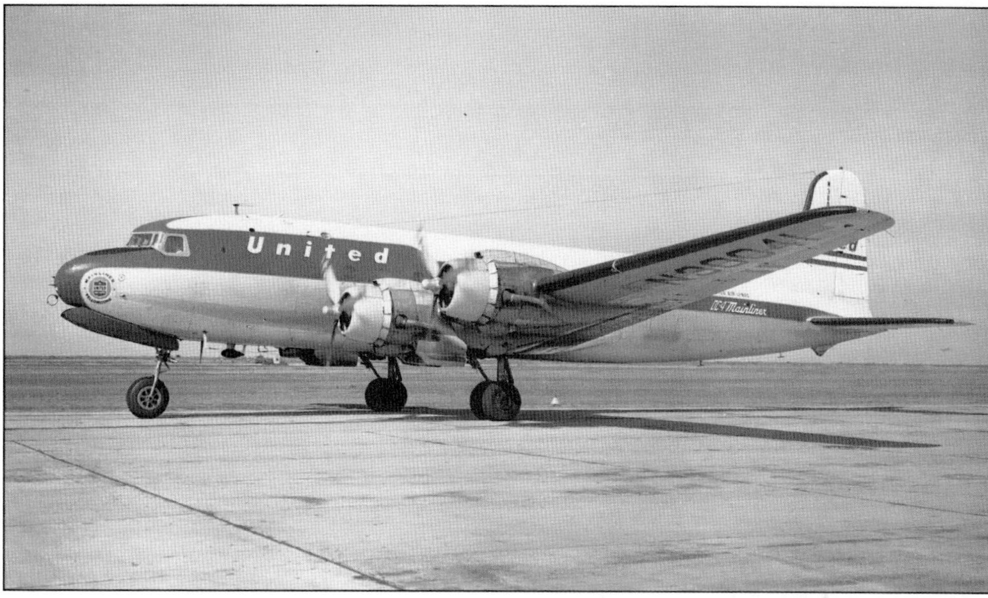

United Air Lines operated Douglas DC-4s from Oakland for several years until they were replaced by DC-6s. The first flight was from Oakland to Portland on March 18, 1946. This photograph shows *Mainliner Yellowstone* (N30041) arriving at Oakland in June 1954. Western Airlines started service with the DC-4 at Oakland on September 3, 1946, flying to Los Angeles but moved to San Francisco in November 1948.

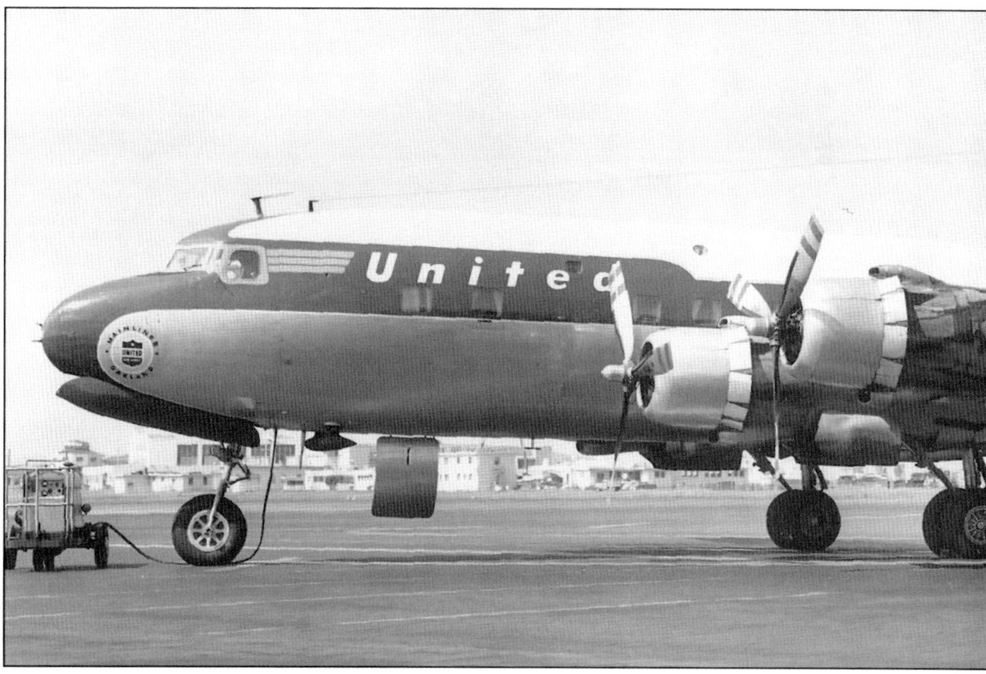

Replacements for the United Douglas DC-4s continued with the even newer Douglas DC-6Bs. The first United Air Lines service at Oakland with the DC-6 was on August 1, 1947, with a flight to Chicago. This is DC-6B (N37561) *Mainliner Oakland.*

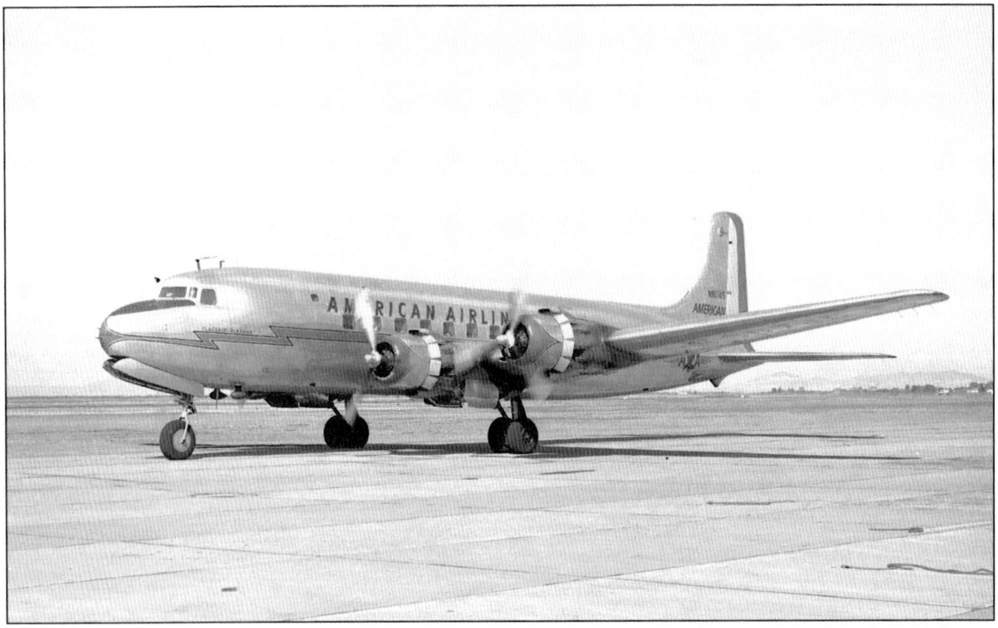

American Airlines also served Oakland with the Douglas DC-6. This is AA's *Flagship Alabama* arriving at Oakland in June 1952. American Airlines started service at Oakland with a DC-4 flight on July 7, 1947. A Douglas DC-7 of Dooley Airlines in 1966 named their plane (N6321C) *City of Oakland*.

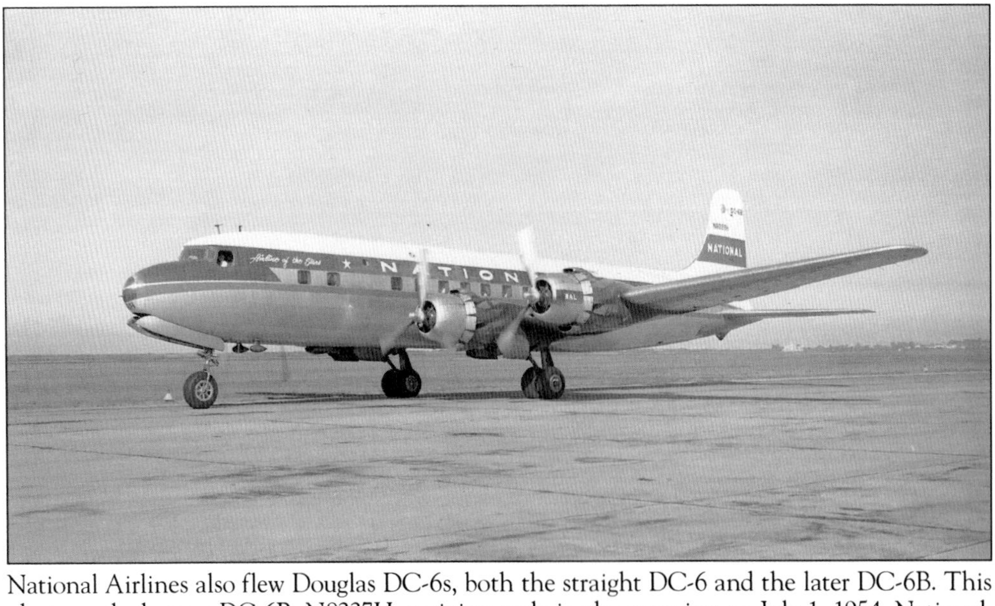

National Airlines also flew Douglas DC-6s, both the straight DC-6 and the later DC-6B. This photograph shows a DC-6B, N8227H, arriving early in the morning on July 1, 1954. National, known as "The Airline of the Stars," did not have individual plane names on the nose.

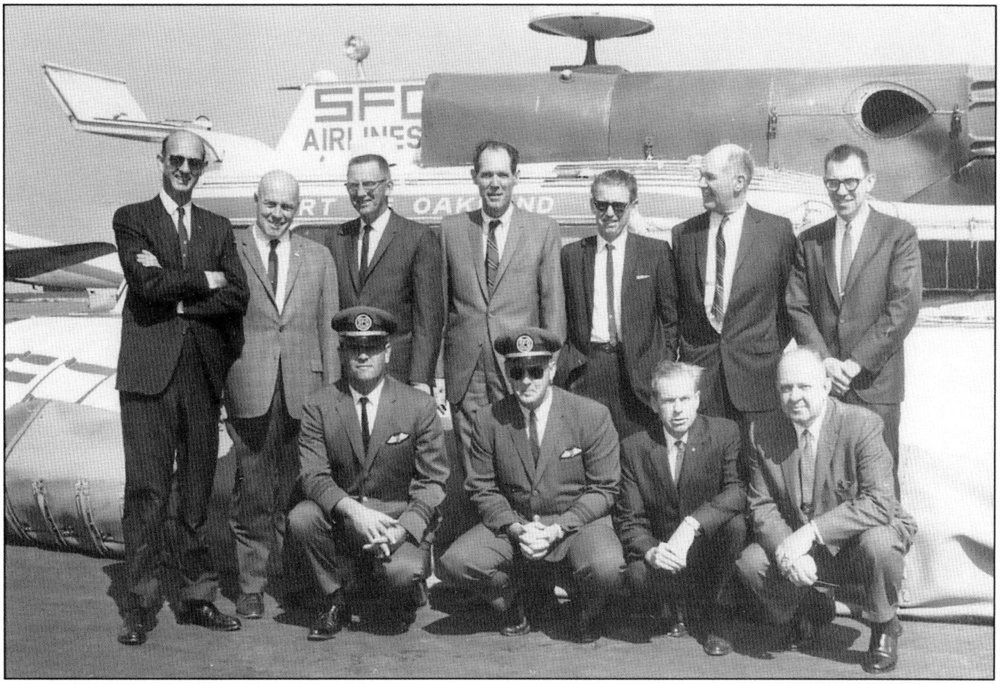

San Francisco–Oakland Airlines experimented with hovercraft service across the bay, and this October 1965 photograph shows the board of directors of the American Aviation Historical Society before boarding a demonstration "flight" on the bay. Board member Larkins is not pictured because he took the photograph. Posing here from left to right are (first row) SFO pilot Ken Vieirra, SFO pilot Gary Richmond, William Riley, and E. T. Smallwood; (second row) John Sloan, Leroy Weber, Walter Jefferies, Roland Bliss, Harry Gann, Willis Nye, and Warren Oberhaus.

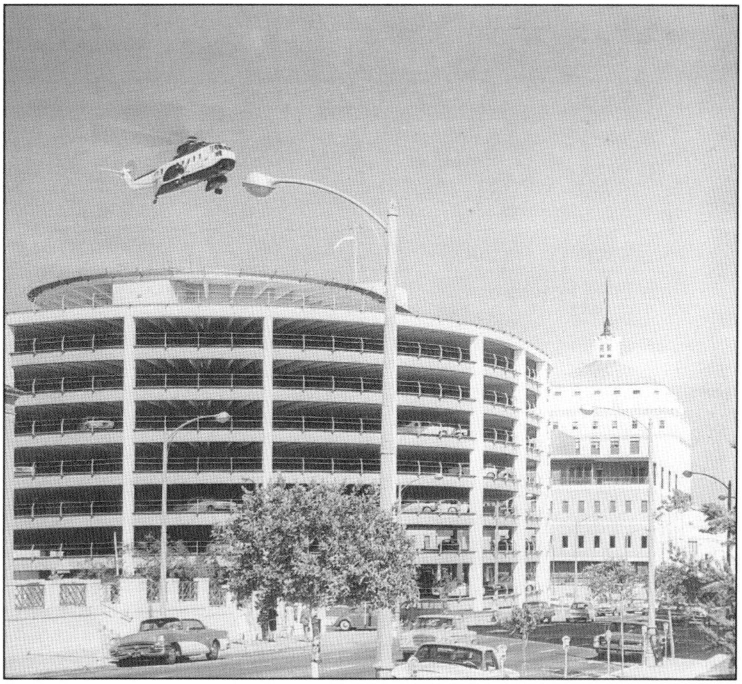

San Francisco–Oakland Airlines built small terminals at the various city locations they served in the Bay Area. The most unusual and spectacular was this one on the top of the automobile garage in downtown Oakland near the city hall.

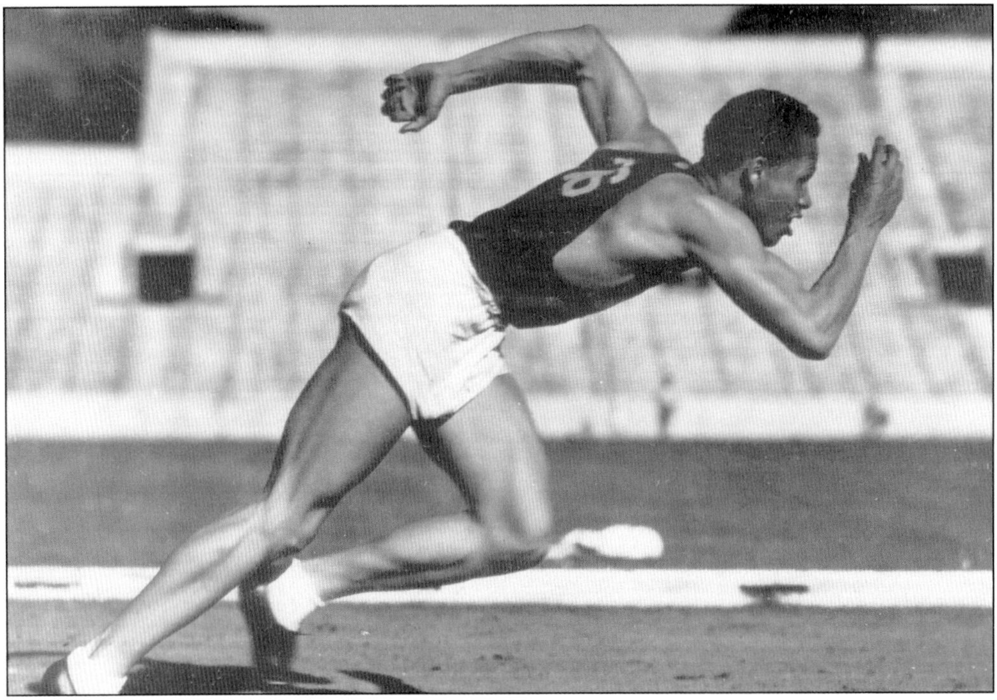

Lt. Col. Archie Williams, USAF (retired), was an engineering graduate of the University of California, Berkeley and was an Olympic champion in the 400-meter race, winning a gold medal at Berlin in 1936. He learned to fly at Oakland, became a civilian flight instructor, and then taught flying and meteorology to the incoming Tuskegee Airmen before going on to fly with the 332nd Fighter Group in Europe, the first black combat unit in the Air Corps in World War II.

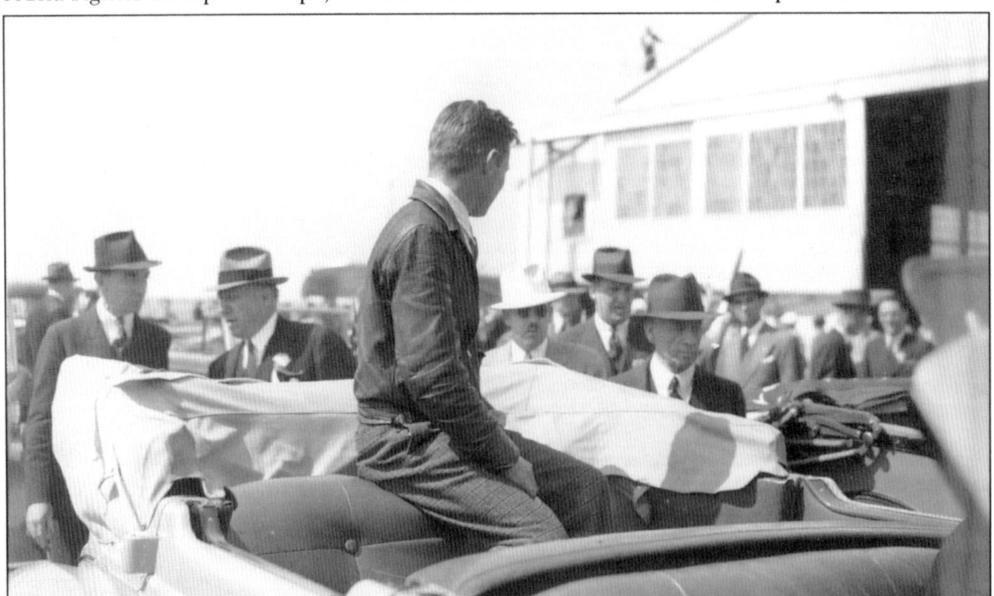

Douglas "Wrong Way" Corrigan is welcomed at Oakland Airport in 1939 after arriving with his Curtiss Robin. The now famous plane, for its solo flight across the Atlantic, was being delivered for exhibition at Treasure Island as part of the Golden Gate International Exposition.

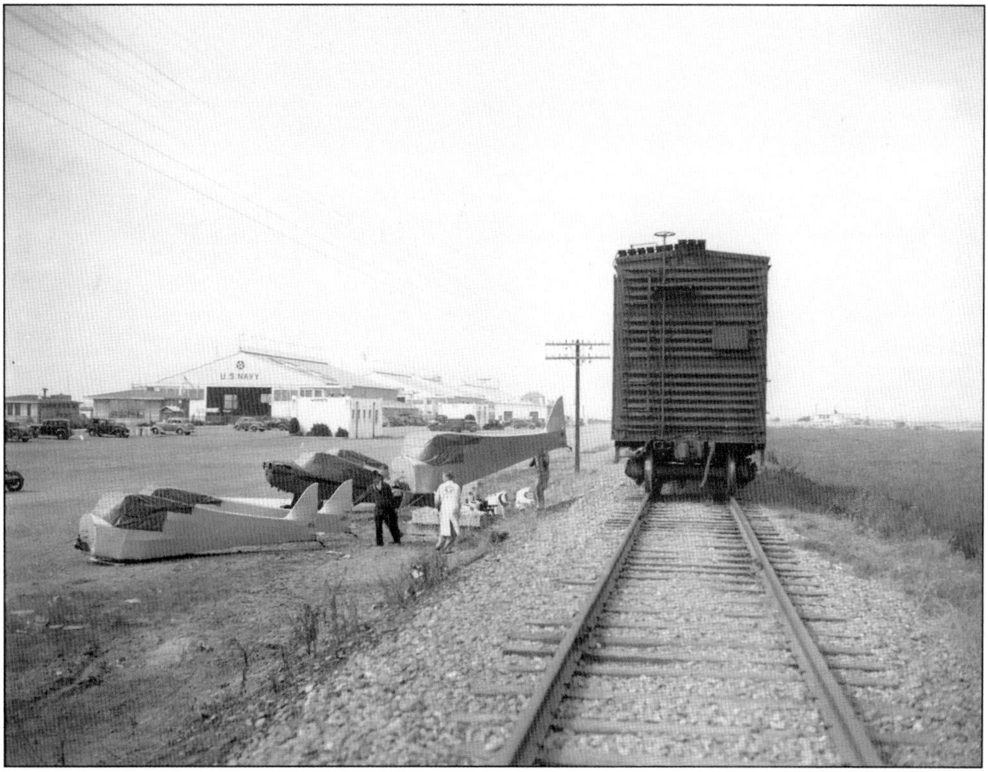

A railroad siding served Oakland Airport, and this photograph shows new Taylorcraft airplanes being unloaded from a boxcar near Hangar 1 on the left.

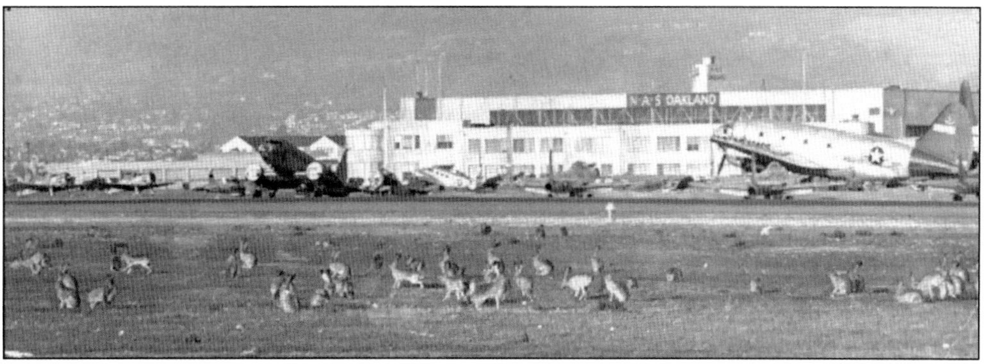

Jackrabbits were abundant at many local airfields, including Oakland Airport prior to the 1960s. This photograph shows many in the foreground with the Naval Reserve Hangar 9 and various aircraft in the background.

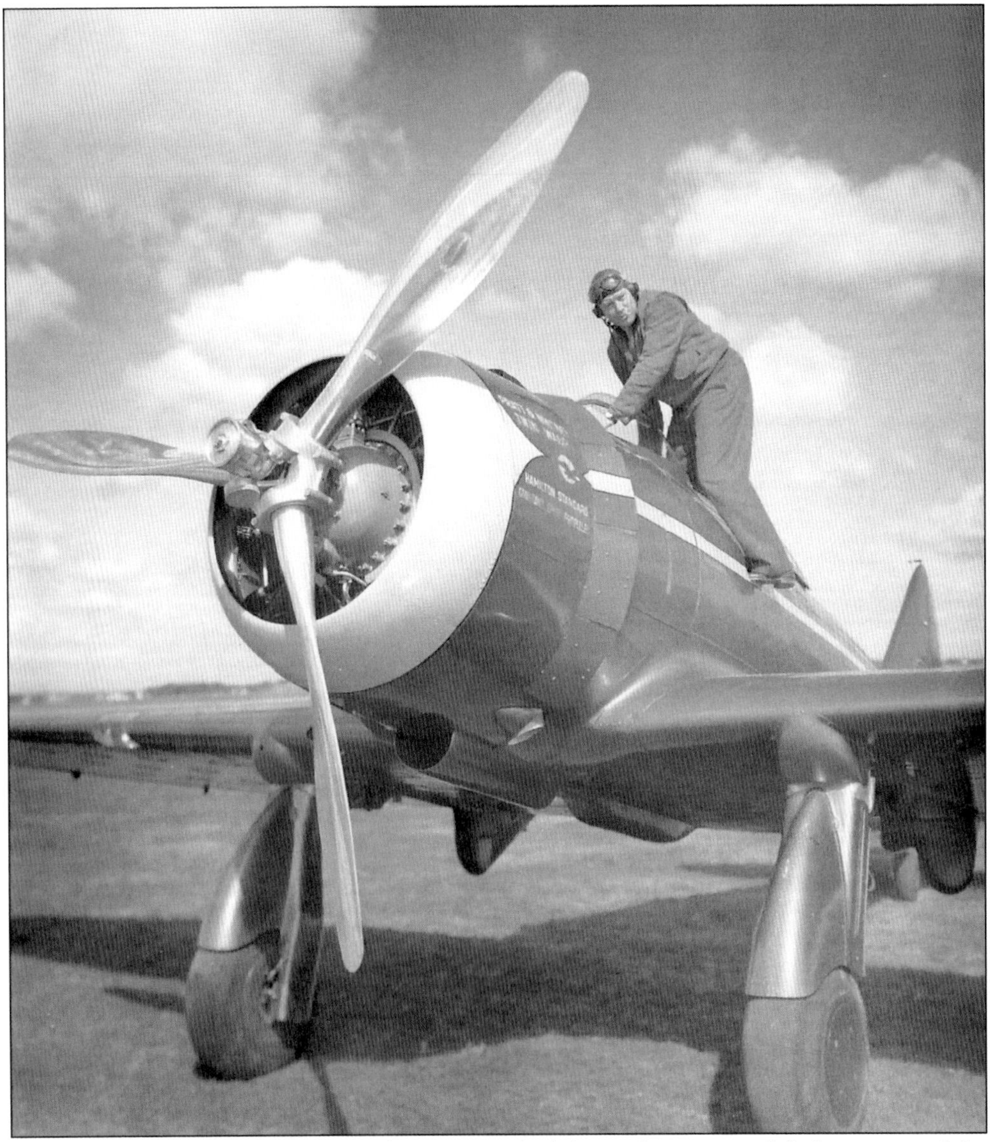

Frank Fuller Jr. poses with his Seversky racer in which he made two record flights as part of the Pacific International Air Races. On May 25, he flew from San Francisco to Seattle in a record time of 2 hours, 31 minutes. On May 28, he returned setting a record of 3 hours, 8 minutes from Vancouver, British Columbia, to Oakland.

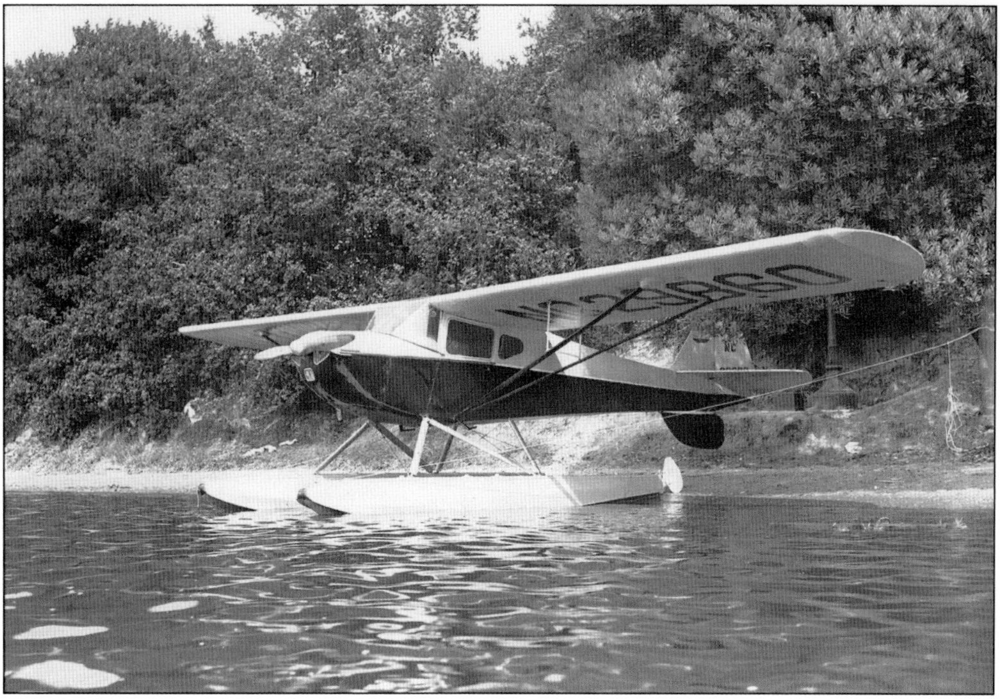

An unusual occurrence took place in Oakland in 1941 when a new Taylorcraft BC12 on floats (NC29860) landed on Lake Merritt. After being tied up on the shoreline in normal seaplane fashion, it stayed overnight and left the next day.

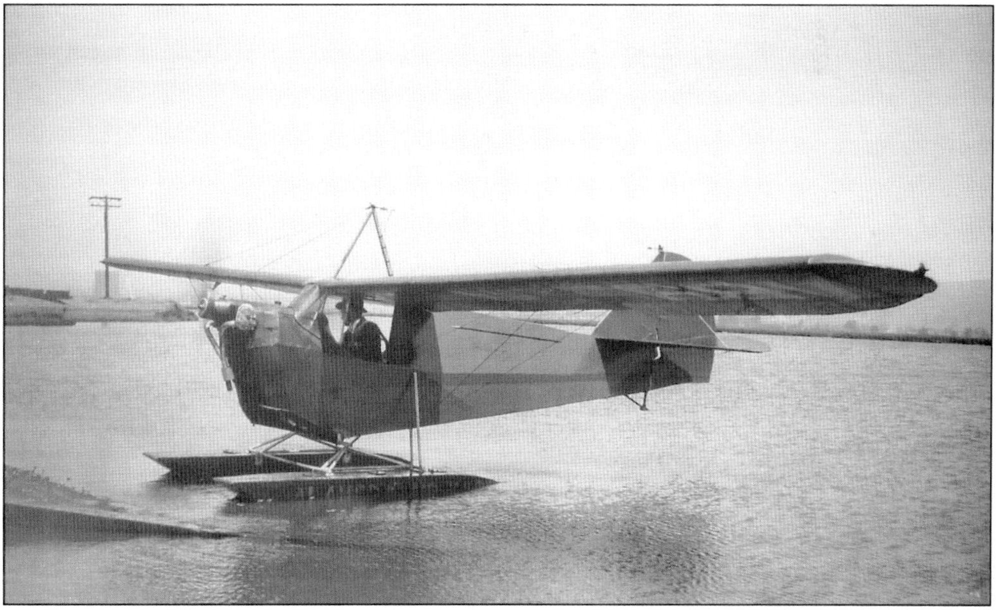

This was not the first time this had happened. Forrest "Iron Hat" Johnson landed his Aeronca C-2 on floats on the lake in the 1930s dressed as Santa Claus for a Christmas celebration.

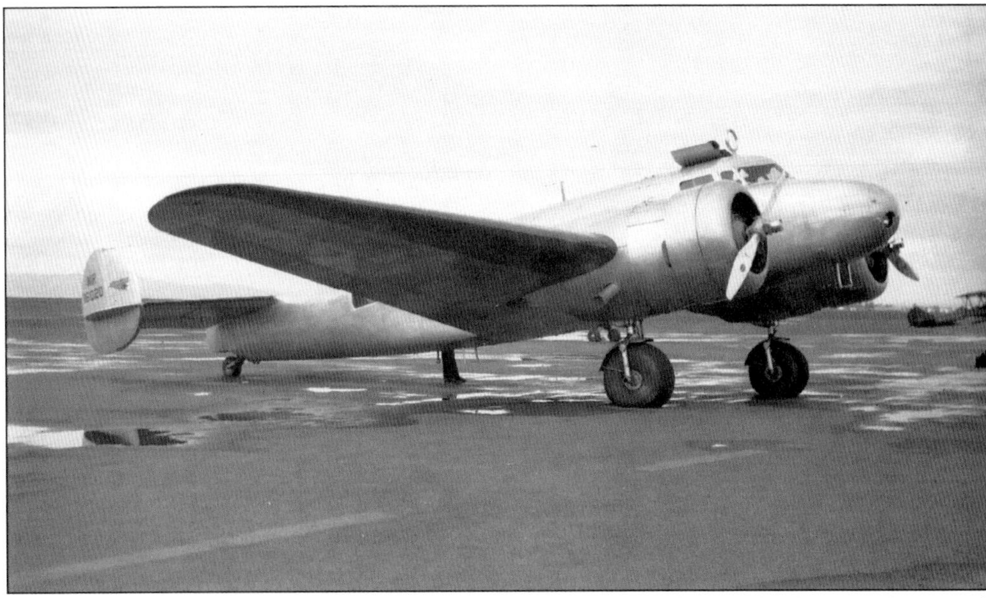

This is Amelia Earhart's Lockheed 10-E (NR16020) photographed at Oakland on Sunday, March 14, 1937. She left on March 17 for Honolulu, Hawaii, for the first leg of her proposed around-the-world flight. After a takeoff accident with a full load in Hawaii, the plane was returned to the factory for repairs. Finally on May 20, 1937, she left Oakland again, flying to Los Angeles before heading east to start the trip again going in the opposite direction.

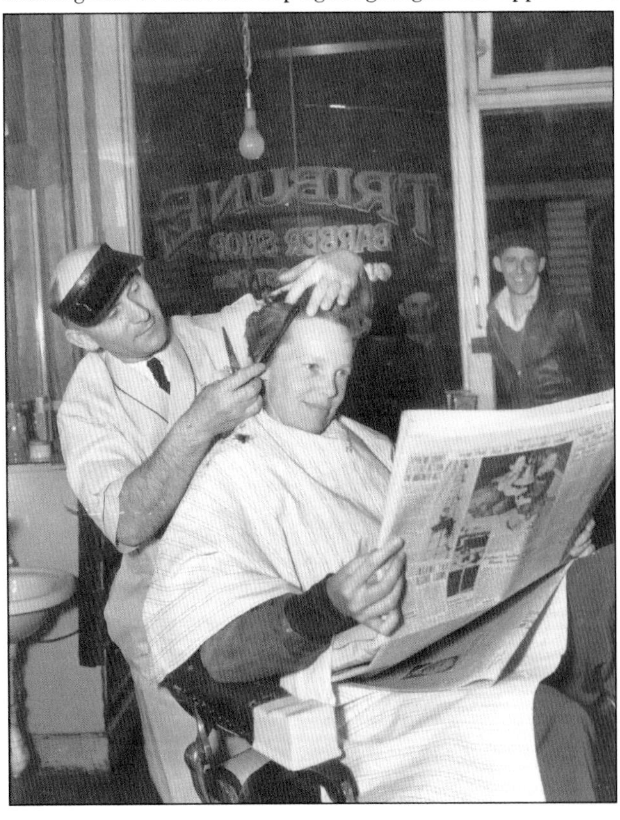

Pictured is Amelia Earhart getting a haircut prior to her March 1937 departure at the barbershop in the Tribune Building in downtown Oakland. Amelia, Fred Noonan, and the Lockheed "Electra" disappeared after leaving Lae, New Guinea, on July 2, 1937. With no trace of them to date, the mystery has resulted in endless stories, books, movies, and television specials.

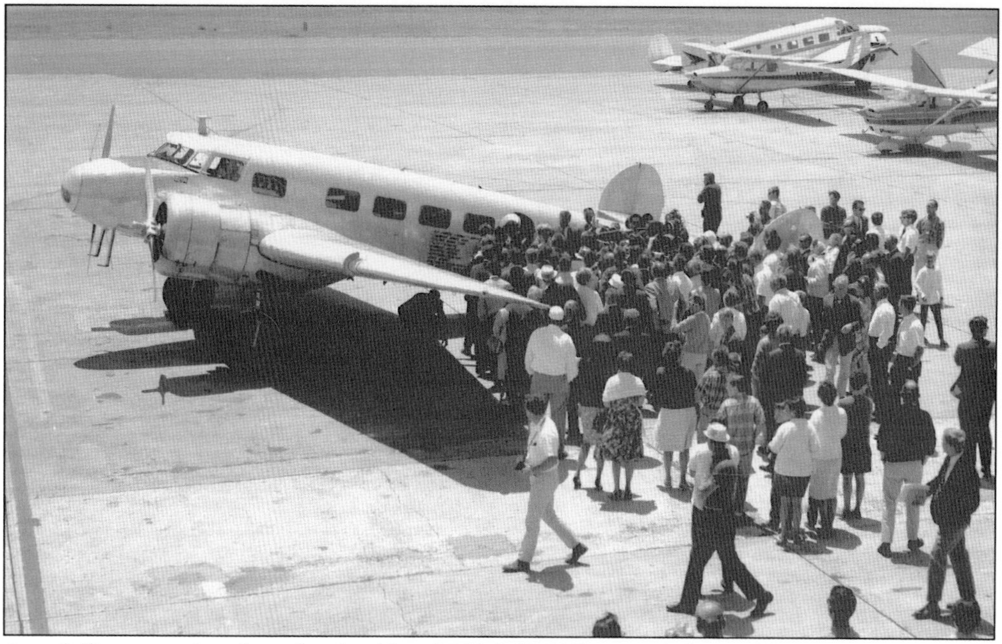

Ann Pellegreno piloted another Lockheed 10E (N79237) around the world, with a crew of three, to re-create Earhart's fatal west-to-east flight in 1937. This photograph was taken upon her arrival back at Oakland on the afternoon of July 7, 1967. To complete the story, it was parked in front of the original airport hotel where Earhart had stayed before her flight.

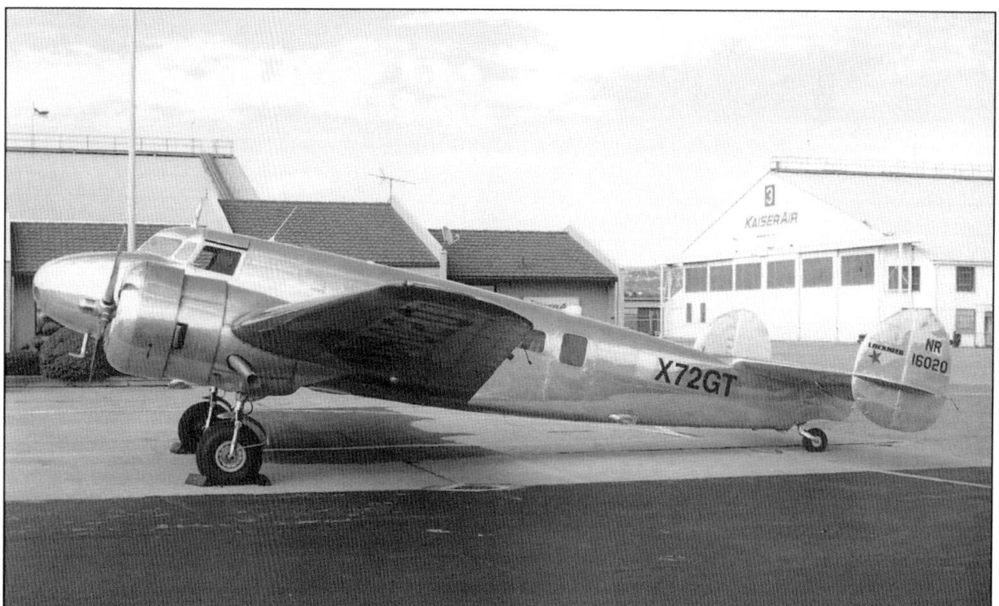

A second Earhart memorial flight was accomplished by Linda Finch and a crew in this Lockheed 10E (N72GT). The photograph shows her plane parked outside the airport executive terminal on May 28, 1997, while she attended a large welcoming dinner at the Western Aerospace Museum.

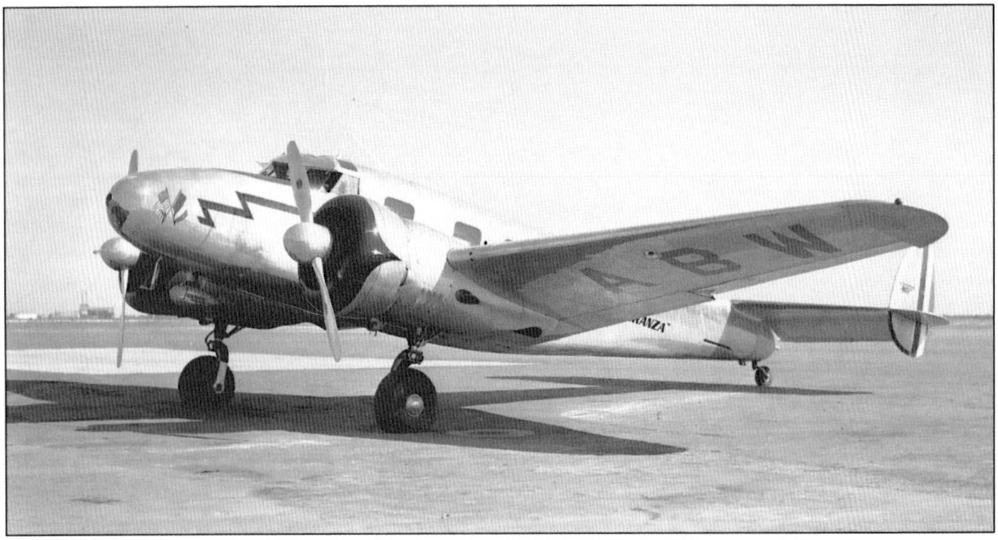

On May 24, 1940, a specially equipped Lockheed 12A (XB-ABW) named *Presidente Carranza* and flown by Major Antonio Cardenas of the Mexican Air Force left Oakland for a goodwill tour of Central and South America. It arrived back in Mexico City on September 13 after covering 20,000 miles.

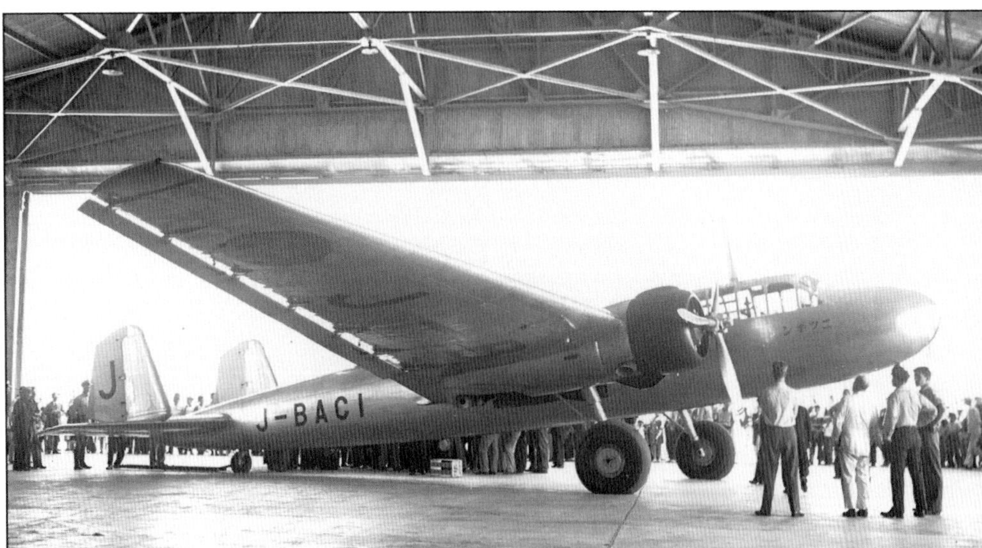

The Japanese Mitsubishi Soyokaze *Nippon* (J-BACI) arrived at Oakland on September 2, 1940, on an around-the-world goodwill flight. Germany's attack on Poland caused major changes in the route, but they arrived back in Tokyo in October after flying 32,846 miles.

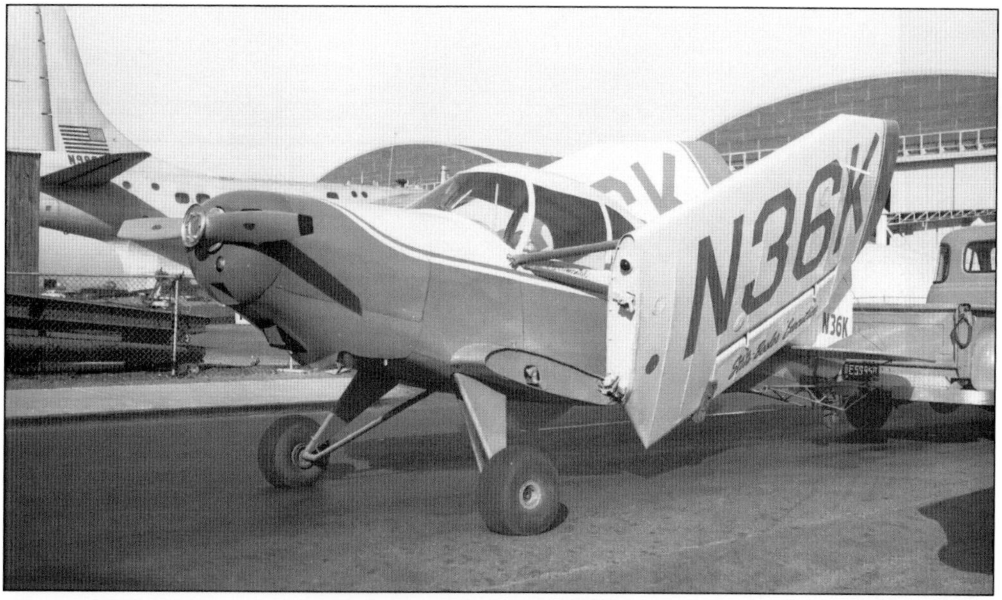

The roadable airplane, a car with wings, never became accepted. A modified version of this idea was the Stits-Besler Executive SA-4A that had folding wings and could be towed by a car. This one (NX36K) was photographed at Oakland Airport in September 1955.

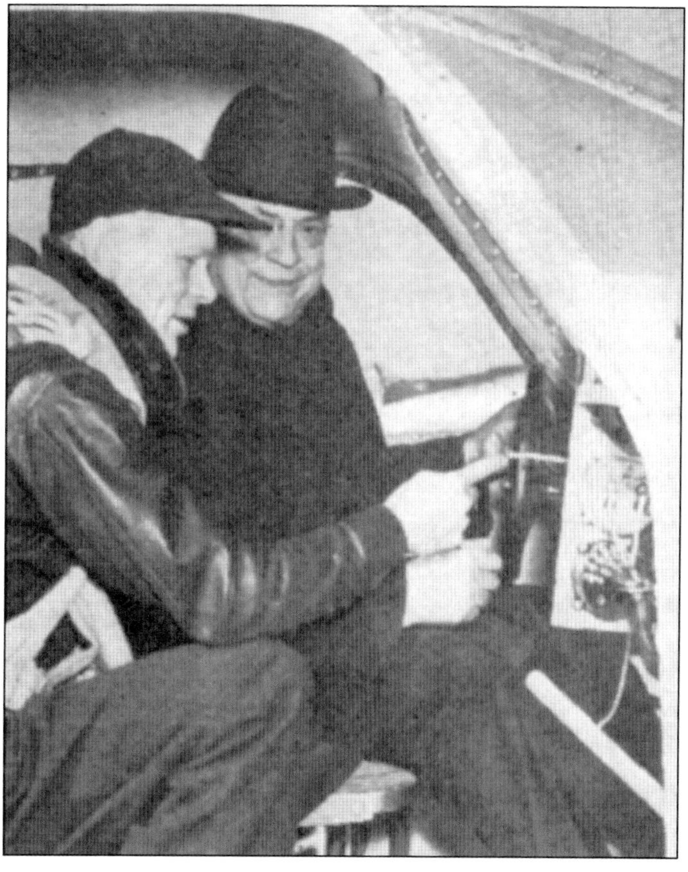

National Advisory Committee for Aeronautics (NACA) test pilot James Nissen is showing Henry Kaiser the operation of the new Kaiser-Hammond two-place safety plane. This was another design aimed at the private pilot that did not get into production.

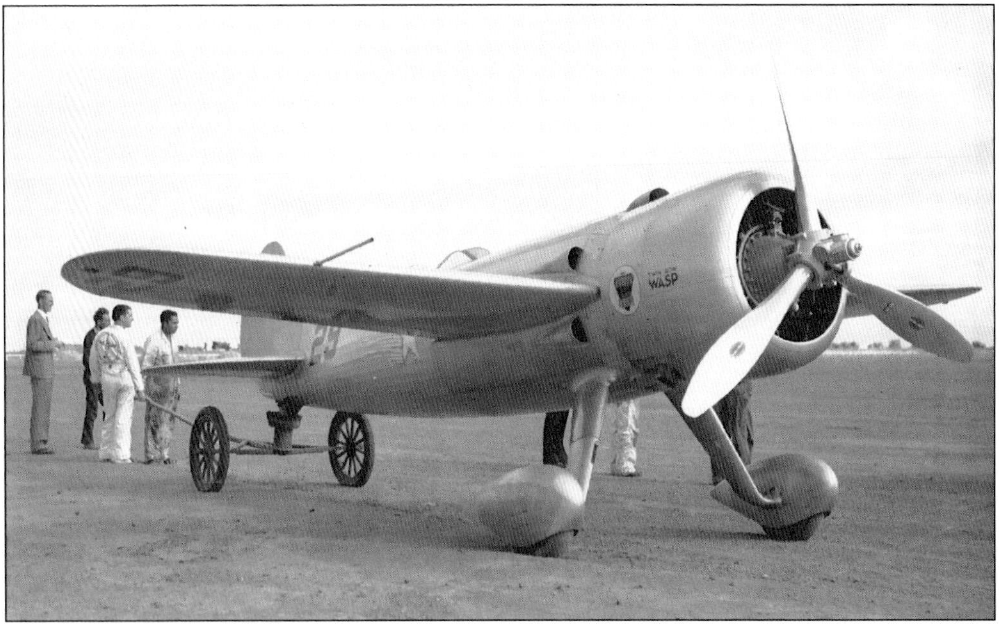

The Air Races at Oakland Airport in May 1938 brought the well-known racers who had flown in the Cleveland National Air Race to this area for the first time. This Laird-Turner LTR-14 (NR263Y) flown by Roscoe Turner came in second in the Golden Gate International Exposition Race at a speed of 265.457 miles per hour. The tail is resting on a dolly for movement by hand.

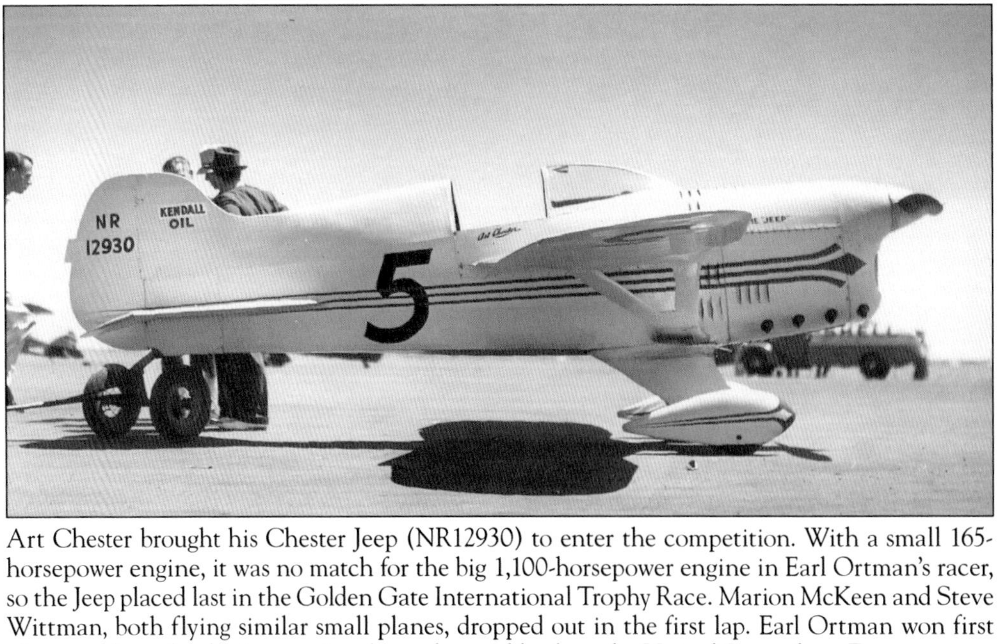

Art Chester brought his Chester Jeep (NR12930) to enter the competition. With a small 165-horsepower engine, it was no match for the big 1,100-horsepower engine in Earl Ortman's racer, so the Jeep placed last in the Golden Gate International Trophy Race. Marion McKeen and Steve Wittman, both flying similar small planes, dropped out in the first lap. Earl Ortman won first place and brought the international speed record back to the United States from France.

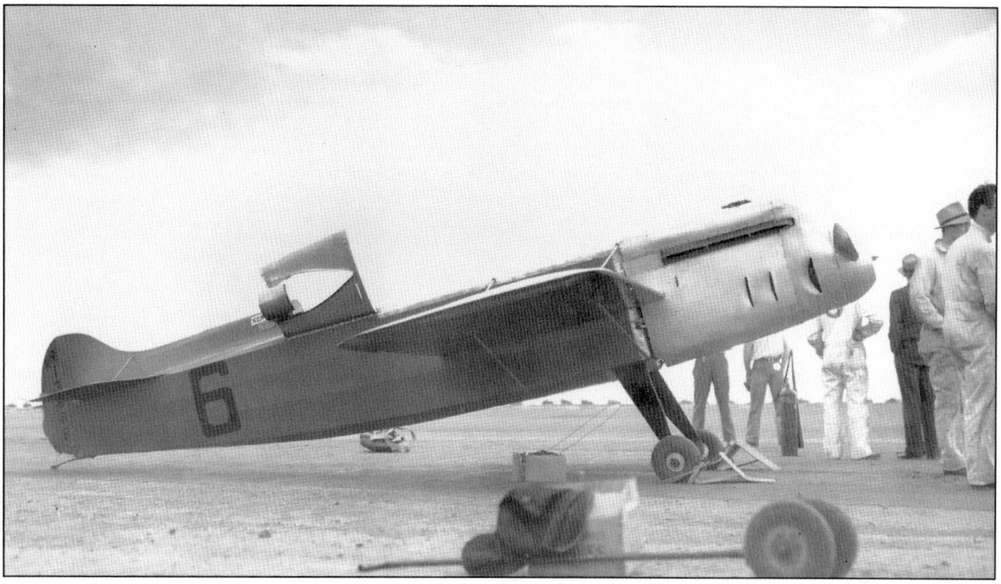

Steve Whitman brought his 1935 Thompson Trophy Racer Bonzo, powered by a big Curtiss D-12 engine, to Oakland and placed third in the Joel Thorne Speed Dash on May 29, 1938.

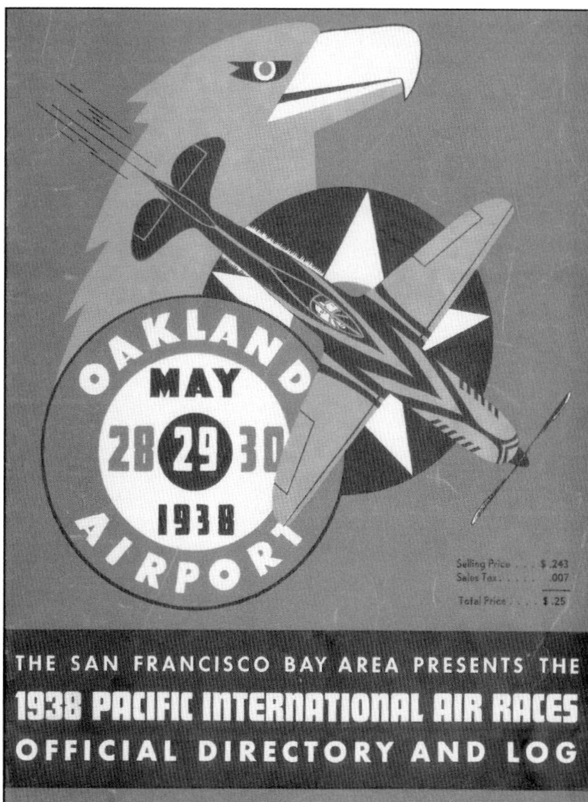

The beautiful red-and-silver program sold for 25¢. The races were sponsored by the International Air Race Association of America, a California nonprofit corporation with George D. Smith as president and James Rowan Ewing as managing director. Most of the well-known pilots and planes from the annual National Air Races at Cleveland took part in this event.

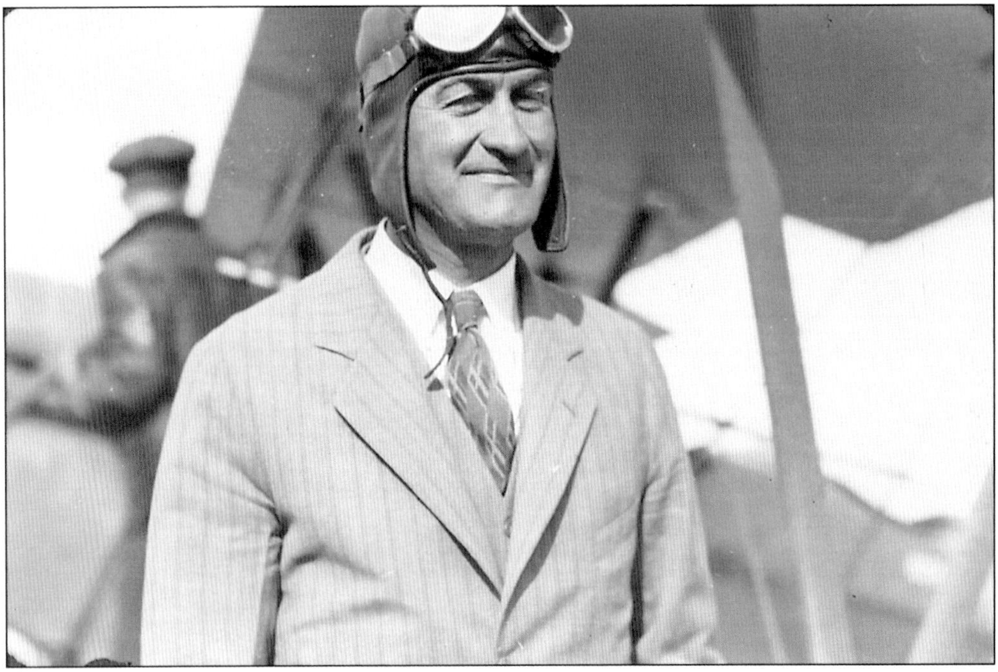

D. C. Warren, who had the early pilot's license No. 2404, formed the D. C. Warren Company at Oakland as the Travel Air distributor for Northern California. R. P. Bowman became his operations manager. During the filming of *Hell's Angels*, they provided some planes for use in Howard Hughes's epic film.

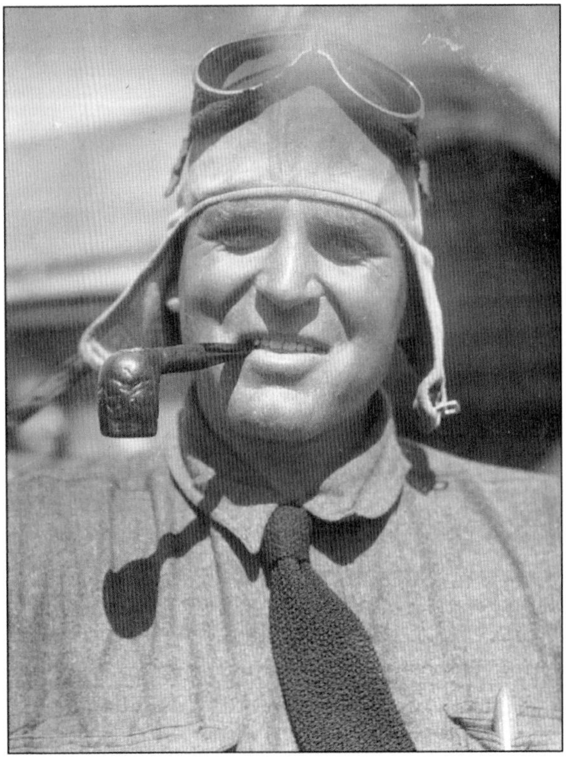

William A. Fillmore learned to fly in the U.S. Army in 1917 and flew for the U.S. Airmail Service in 1919. He became a barnstormer from then until 1925 and in 1927 founded the Fillmore Flying Service at Oakland Airport.

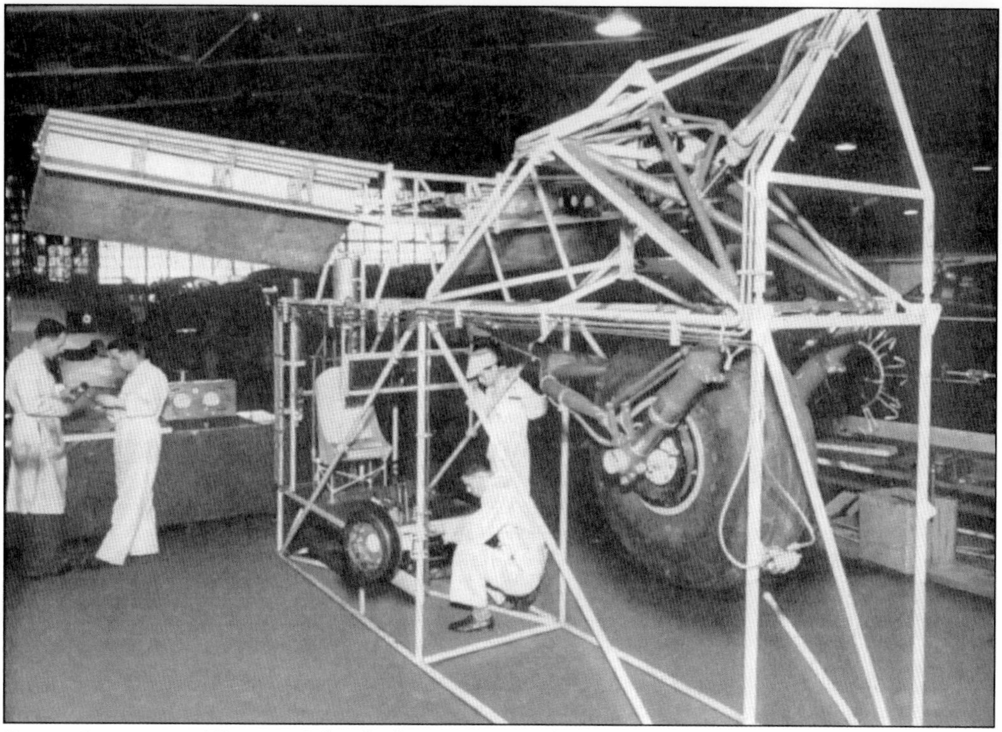

Pictured is a typical Boeing School of Aeronautics classroom showing a full-size operating unit for the Douglas DC-3 landing gear. Boeing School, a division of United Air Lines, was considered the finest school of its kind in the United States.

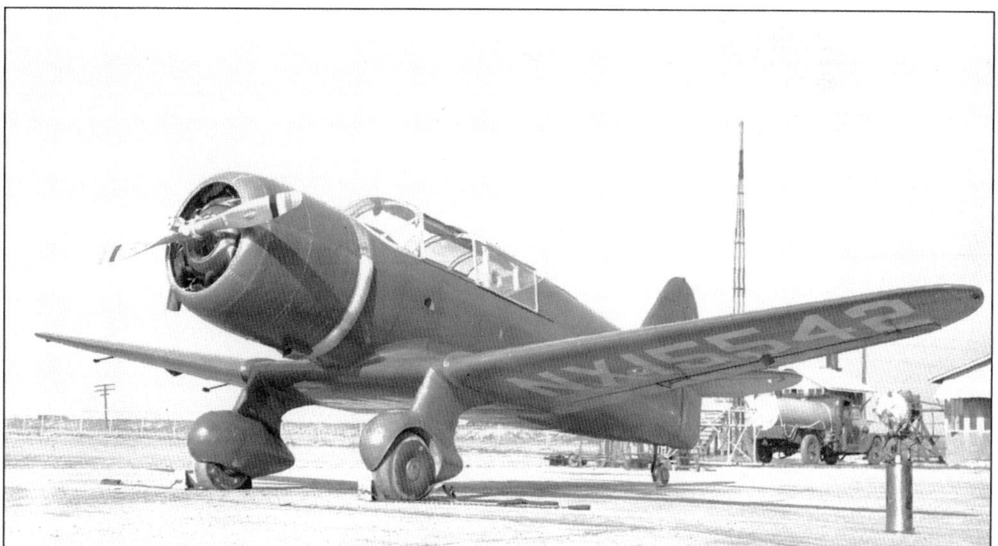

The Boeing School T-5 (NX15542), designed by instructor John Thorpe, was a major project in 1939 that allowed the students to design and build an all-metal airplane. Boeing test pilot Eddie Allen came down from Seattle for the initial flights. It was later modified into the T-6 with tricycle gear and a different engine.

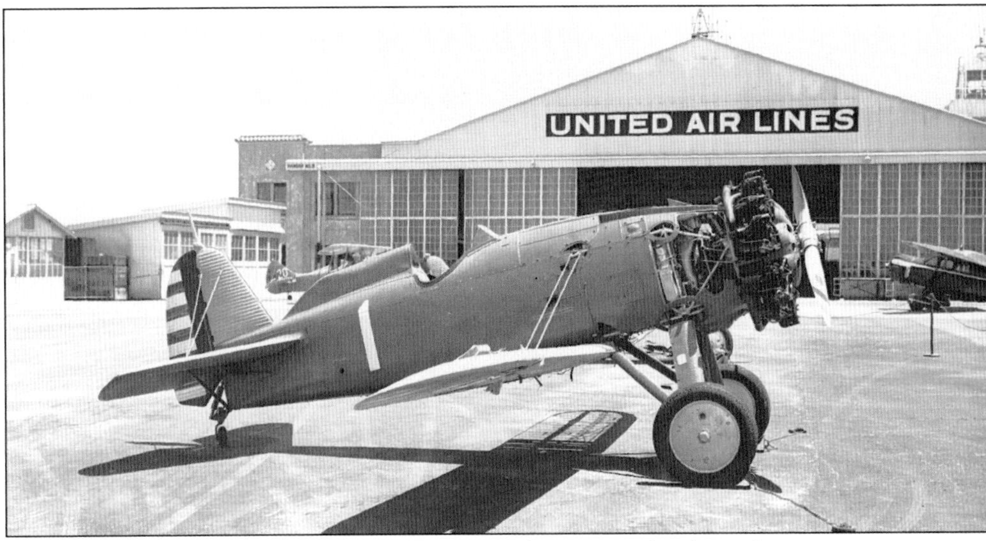

A former Army Air Corps Boeing P-12E presented an unusual sight with its top wing removed as well as the fabric from the lower left wing. This was one of the planes provided to the Boeing School students for practical experience. A Boeing School Waco UPF-7 is in the left background, and a Stinson SR-10J can be seen in the right background in front of Hangar 5.

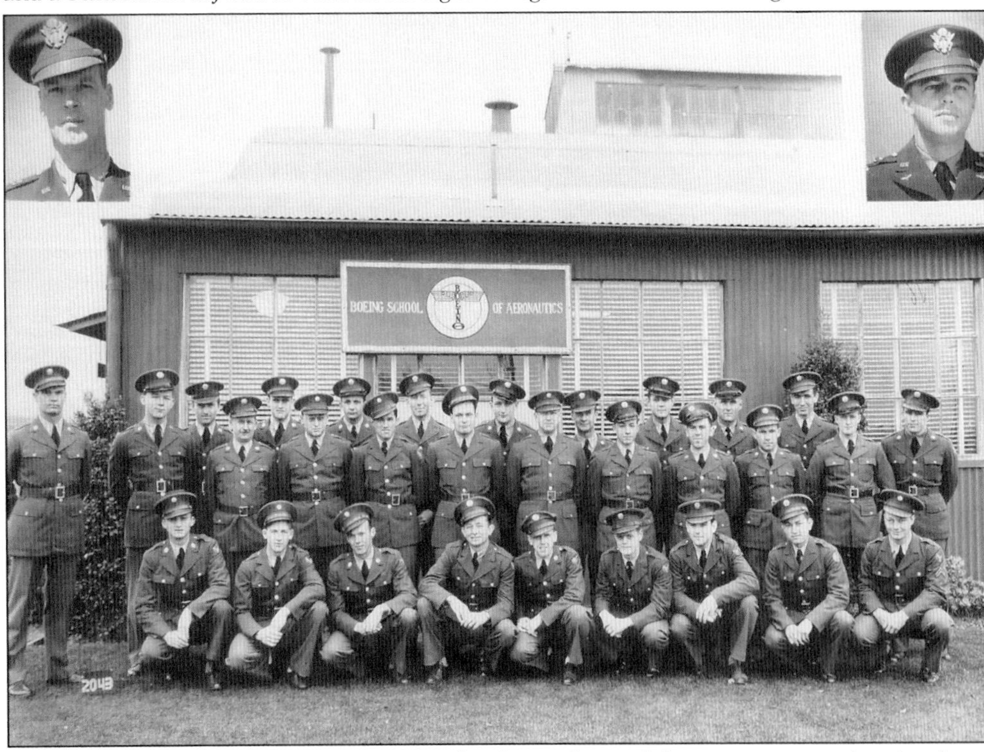

With the start of World War II, Boeing School was changed from a private trade school to a military operation, and an enlarged aircraft mechanics course was limited to AAF enlisted men. This photograph shows Class 20-43 that graduated on March 1, 1943. The officers in charge, Maj. John Roberts Jr. and Capt. George Johnston Jr., are pictured in the upper left and right respectively. Twelve of the students were from Texas.

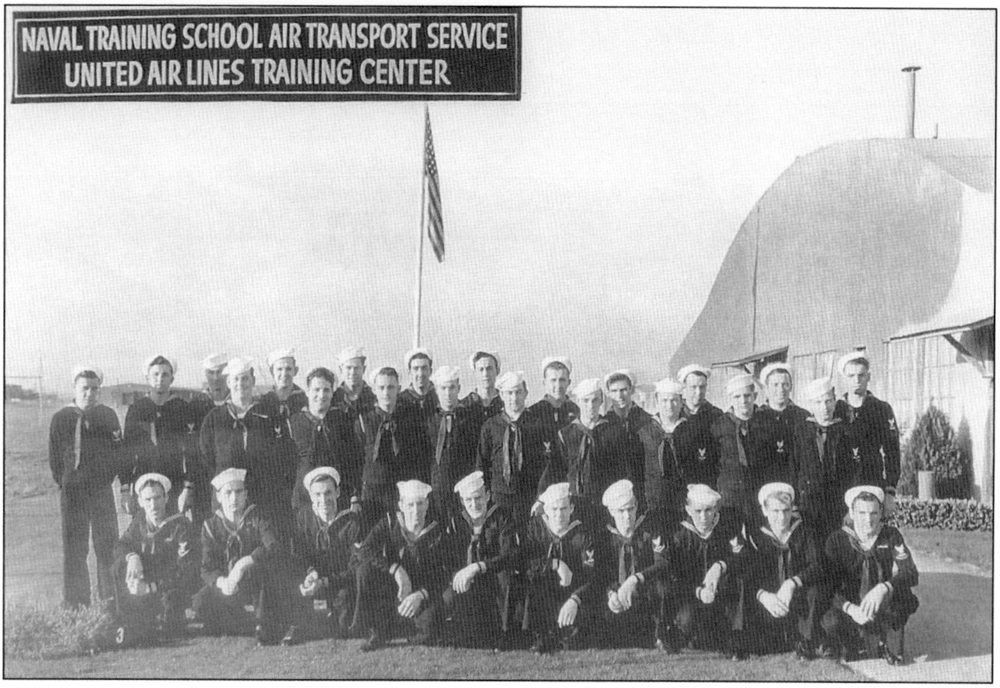

Training was also provided for the navy, in this case for the Naval Air Transport Service. By this time, later in the war, the military training was operated by a division of United Air Lines. The camouflaged building in the right rear is now the Oakland Aviation Museum.

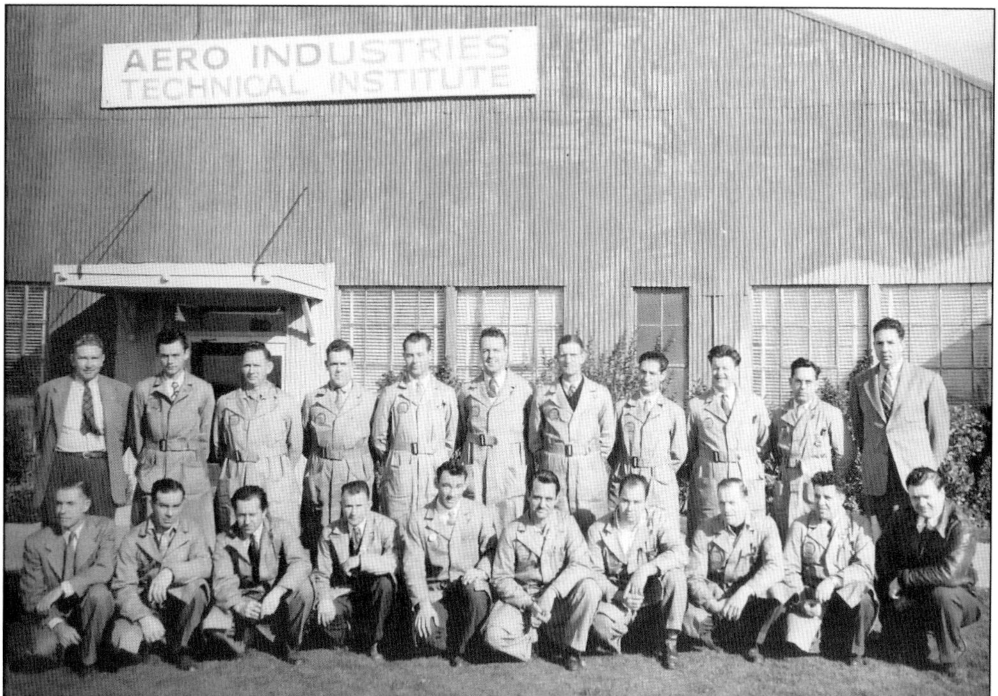

After the war was over, the building was taken over by the Aero Industries Technical Institute and became a private school. This photograph shows the school's instructors in front of the building.

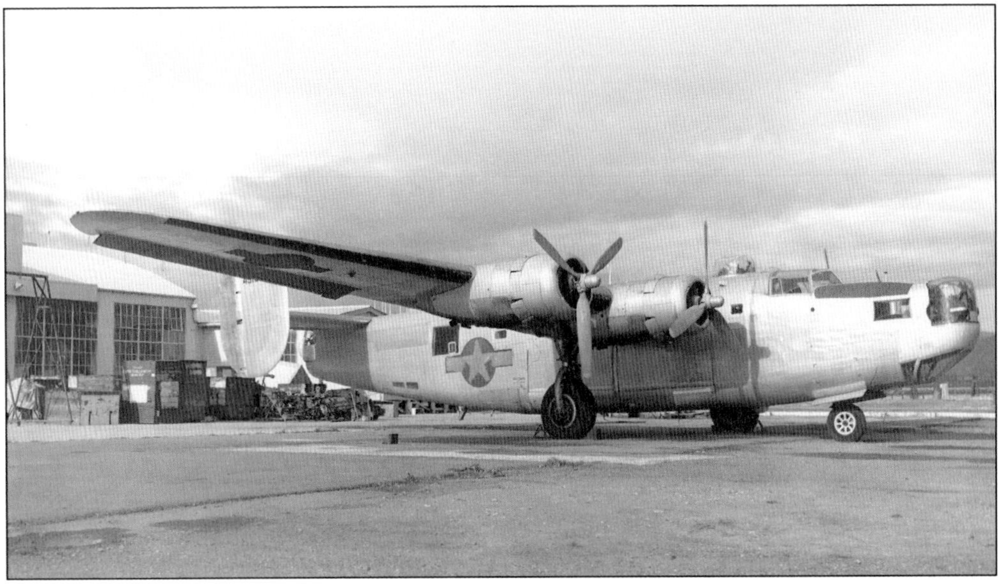

On May 2, 1946, an almost new war surplus Ford-built B-24M (44-51556) was flown in for the use by the students. Four other combat planes joined it at the school—a Republic P-47G, a Bell P-39Q, a North American A-36A, and a Vought F4U-1.

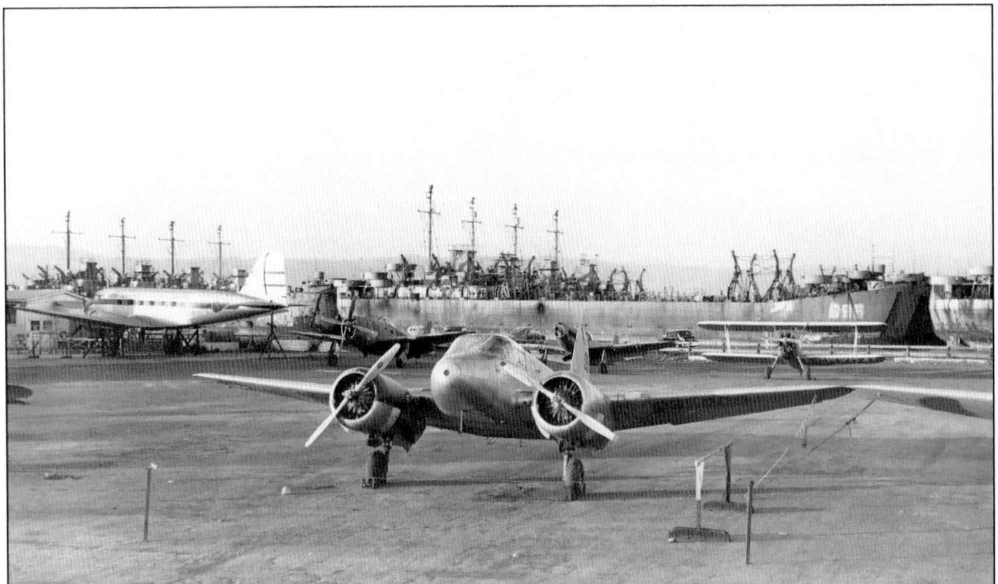

The school also had a Beech AT-10 for instruction, seen in this exotic photograph of the view behind the school. An old Douglas C-33, the P-47, the A-36A, and a PT-17 are lined up in front of a group of war surplus navy LSTs tied up in the Airport Channel in June 1946.

Four

Military Operations, Nonscheduled Airlines, and Supplemental Carriers

Every military service has had formal operations at Oakland. On August 1, 1928, the Oakland Naval Reserve Aviation Unit was established, beginning a 33-year history of naval aviation on the field. Arrangements were made with the city for the navy to use the runway and park two planes, rent free, for one year. At the expiration of this lease, a new one allowed the use of one half of a hangar and 11,200 square feet of parking area. A seaplane ramp was added in 1932, and Naval Reserve Aviation Bases (NRAB) Oakland took over all of Hangar 3. In 1933, Oakland was rated the best in the nation out of 15 such units. In 1932, a Marine Corps Reserve aviation unit was established with Livingston Steadman as the first commanding officer. Clyde Sunderland became chief of their photography unit as the only photographer's mate in the entire Naval Reserve. Officers from NRAB Oakland who were captured on Wake Island included Lt. Cmdr. Winfield Scott Cunningham; Lt. John Kinney, USMCR; and Lt. Hubert Freuler, USMCR.

In November 1941, the Naval Reserve moved into their new facility in Hangar 9. The flight training program was given considerable impetus in 1942 when the secretary of the navy approved a plan to increase navy pilot training to 2,500 aviation cadets per month. As a result, preliminary flight training was moved to the Naval Reserve aviation bases, including Oakland. Due to the war, this was moved from Oakland to Livermore by November 1942. After the war, the reserve unit was reestablished at NAS Livermore before returning to Oakland. During the Korean War, NAS Oakland became the largest naval reserve air base in the country.

During World War II, Oakland became a major marshaling facility for dispatch of military aircraft to the Pacific and included both U.S. Navy and Army Air Corps units. NRAB Oakland was changed to Naval Auxiliary Air Station (NAAS) Oakland in the fall of 1942 and then changed to NAS Oakland in January 1943. In 1946, the new California Air National Guard began with one quarter of Hangar 28 and three borrowed planes before moving to Hayward Airport.

After World War II, Oakland became a large center for nonscheduled and supplemental air carriers, including the three largest companies: Transocean Air Lines, World Airways, and Trans International Airlines. Oakland became one of the largest aircraft overhaul and maintenance operations in the country when the Aircraft Engine and Maintenance Company (AEMCO) processed thousands of aircraft.

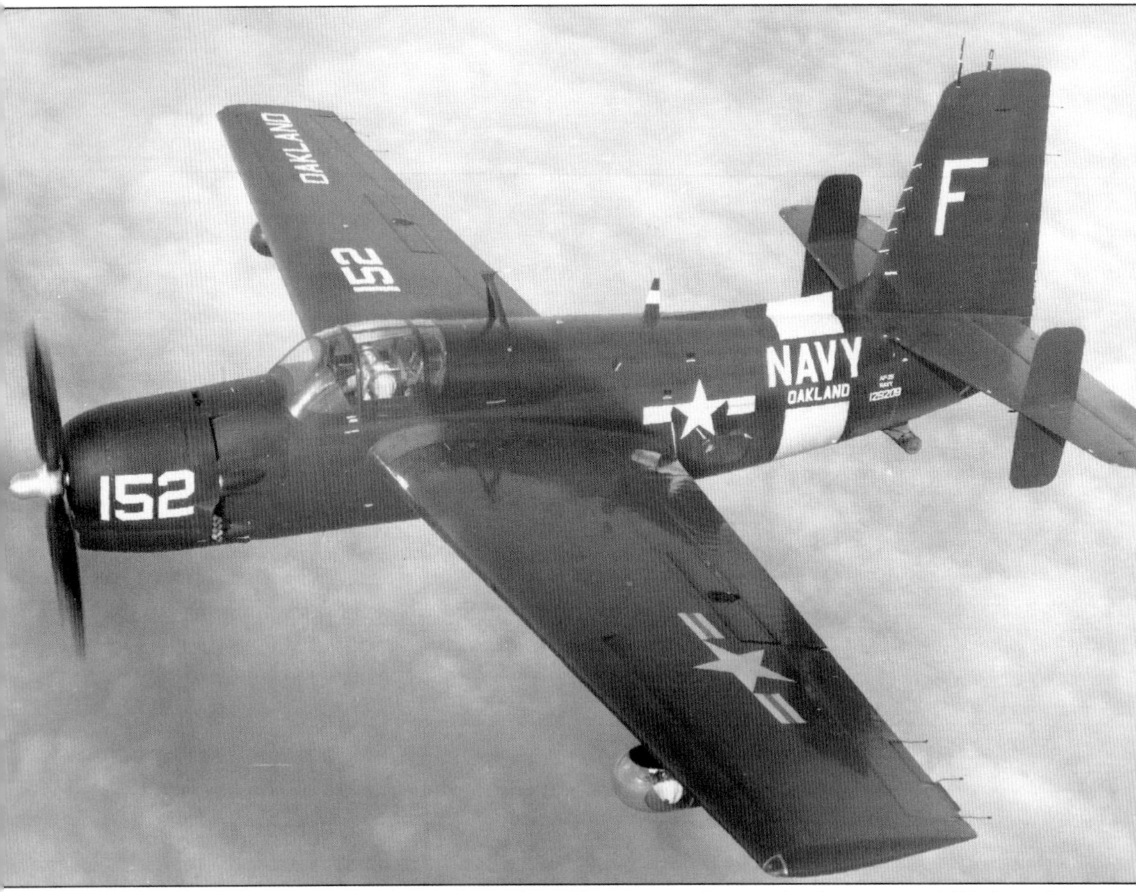

By 1953, the old TBM Avengers were replaced by a newer design, the Grumman AF-2 Guardian. This photograph shows Oakland's F-152 (129209), an AF-2S, flying over the bay. Oakland flew both versions of this plane: the AF-2S (Submarine Attack) and the AF-2W (Submarine Search).

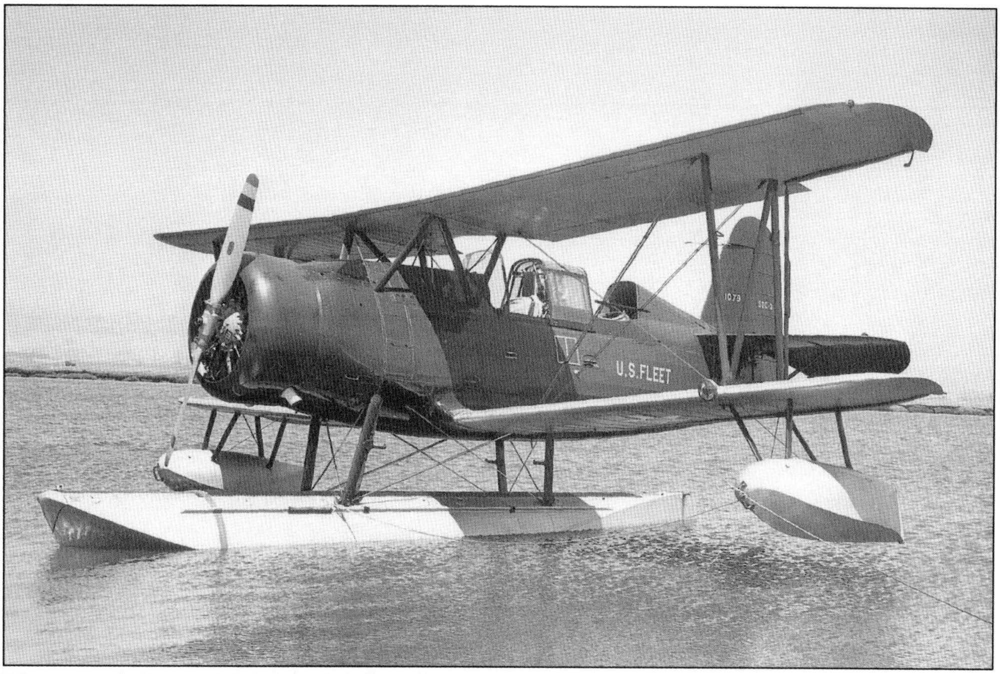

This special Curtiss SOC-3 (1079) flag plane was assigned to the commander in chief of the U.S. Fleet and made a rare visit to Oakland in June 1939. The photograph shows it in the Airport Lagoon near Hangar 5. Many battleship- and cruiser-borne SOCs visited NRAB Oakland before World War II.

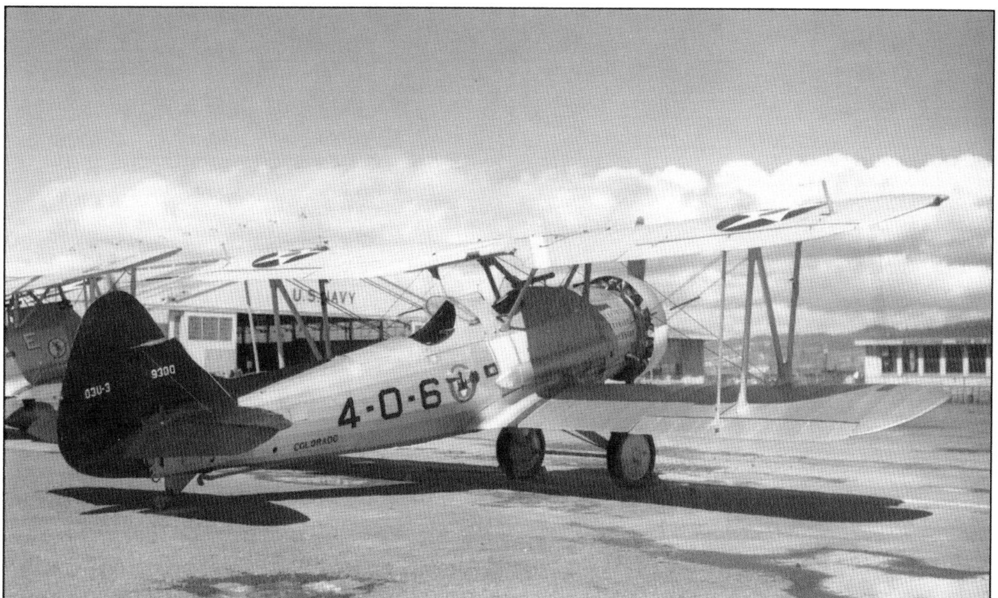

This Vought O3U-3 (9300) from the battleship USS *Colorado* in 1938 is representative of the U.S. Fleet aircraft that visited Oakland on a regular basis. The Naval Reserve aviation base provided extensive service for active-duty cross-country training flights. Weekend visitors included such types as the Great Lakes BG-1, Martin BM-1, Northrop BT-1, Vought SB2U-1, and the new Douglas TBD-1. Hangar 3 can be seen on the left and the exhibit building on the right.

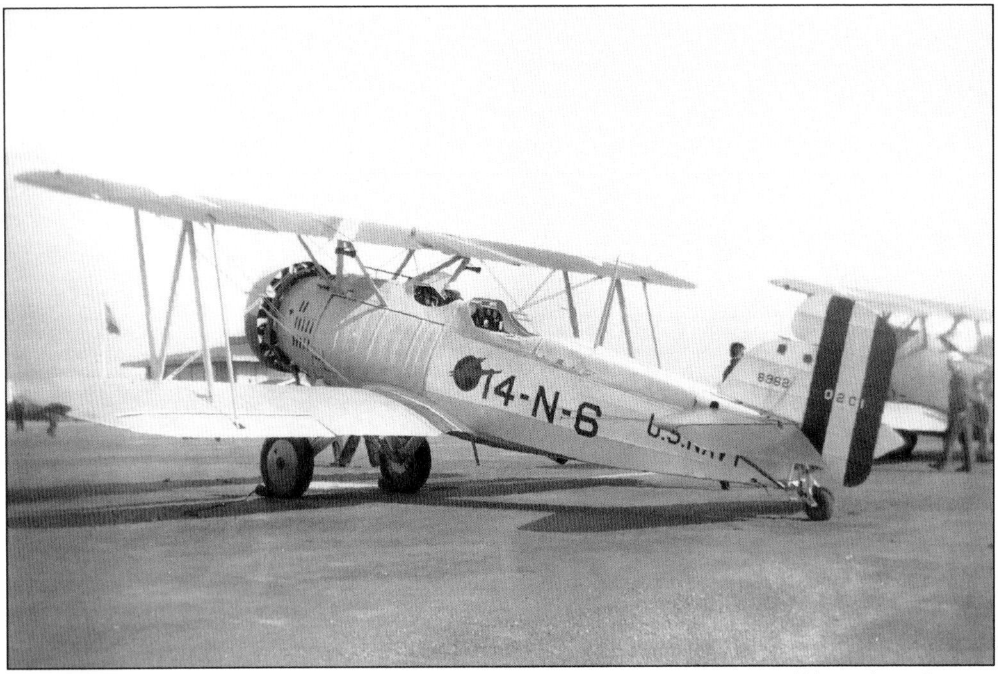

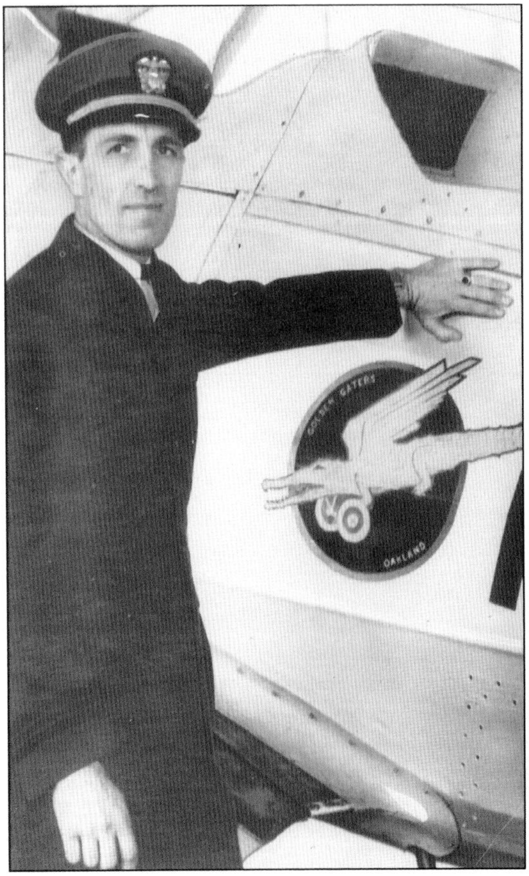

The Curtiss O2C-1 Helldiver (8962) was the first combat type assigned to the Naval Reserve at Oakland. This 1936 photograph shows the early VN-14RD12 squadron markings (Heavier-than-Air, Training Squadron 14, Reserve, 12th Naval District) that were replaced by a simple plane number. The name was made famous by the popular motion pictures *Hell Divers* and *King Kong*.

Lt. Cmdr. Francis B. Connell, USNR, the first commanding officer of NRAB Oakland, stands next to the "Golden Gator" insignia on a Curtiss O2C-1. The alligator-on-wheels insignia was a reference to the squadron's proximity to the Golden Gate. Naval Reserve Aviation Unit Oakland was formed in August 1928 with one consolidated NY-1 primary trainer.

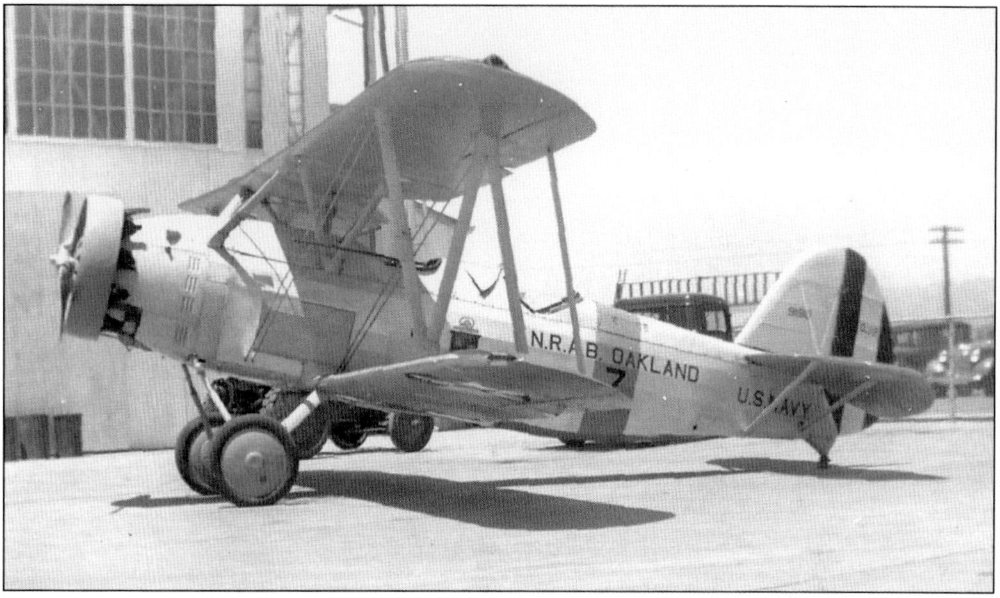

This photograph of Berliner-Joyce OJ-2 (9190) is rare because it shows the name "N.R.A.B. Oakland," which was on the sides of these planes for a short time in 1936. This was soon replaced by just a simple number. This plane was a former fleet observation plane operating from the light cruiser USS *Marblehead* CL-12.

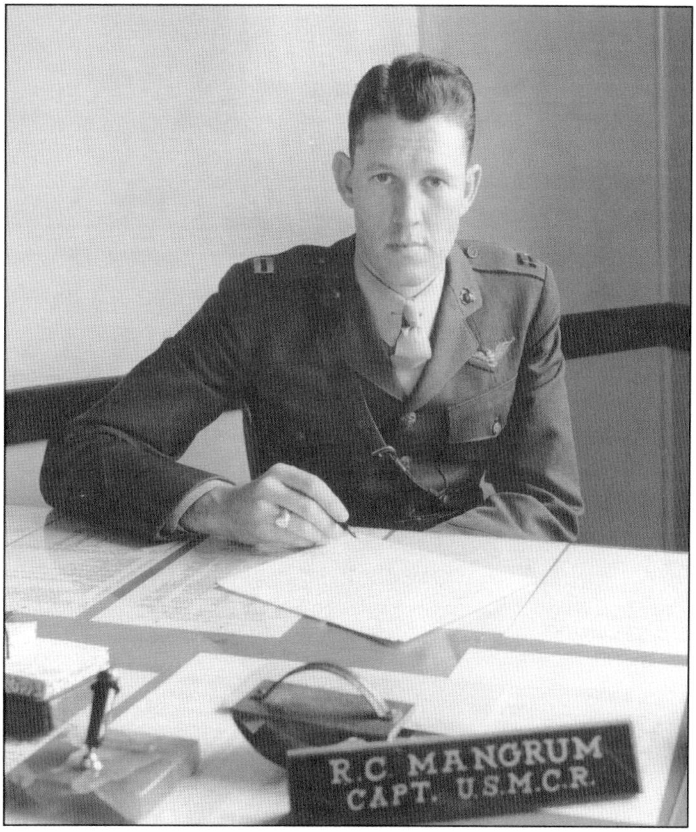

Capt. Richard C. Mangrum, USMC, was executive officer of NRAB Oakland and in charge of the Marine Corps units. The U.S. Navy and Marine Corps Reserve pilots flew the same airplanes during drill periods but were organized in separate navy and Marine Corps squadrons, re-designated VS-15R and VMS-8R in 1937. Mangrum became a lieutenant general and assistant commandant of the Marine Corps before retiring in 1965.

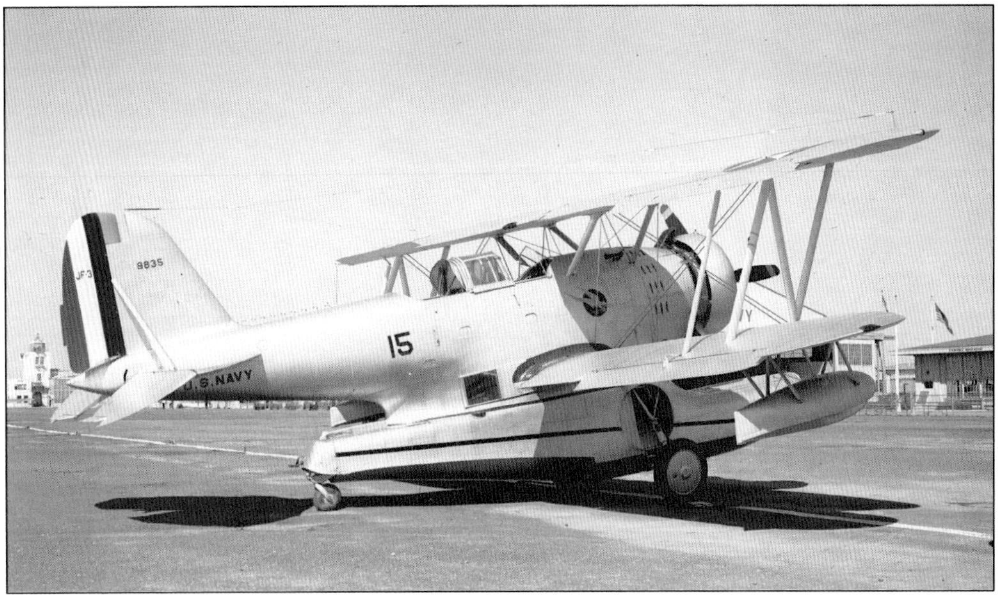

Each Naval Reserve air station situated near water was assigned an amphibian for rescue efforts. This Grumman JF-3 (9835), shown here in November 1940, replaced an earlier Loening OL-8. A Grumman J2F-2 was also assigned to Oakland during 1938–1939.

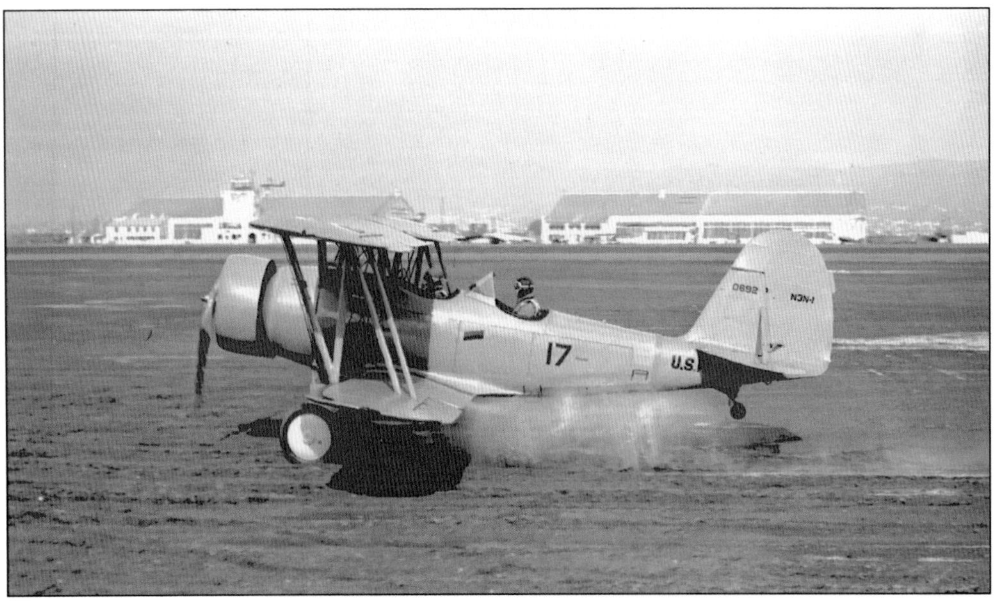

The primary purpose of NRAB Oakland, other than reserve training, was to provide preflight elimination checks to prospective aviation cadets. The Naval Aircraft Factory N3N-1, such as this one (0692) shown taking off during the annual inspection in 1940, was used for this purpose.

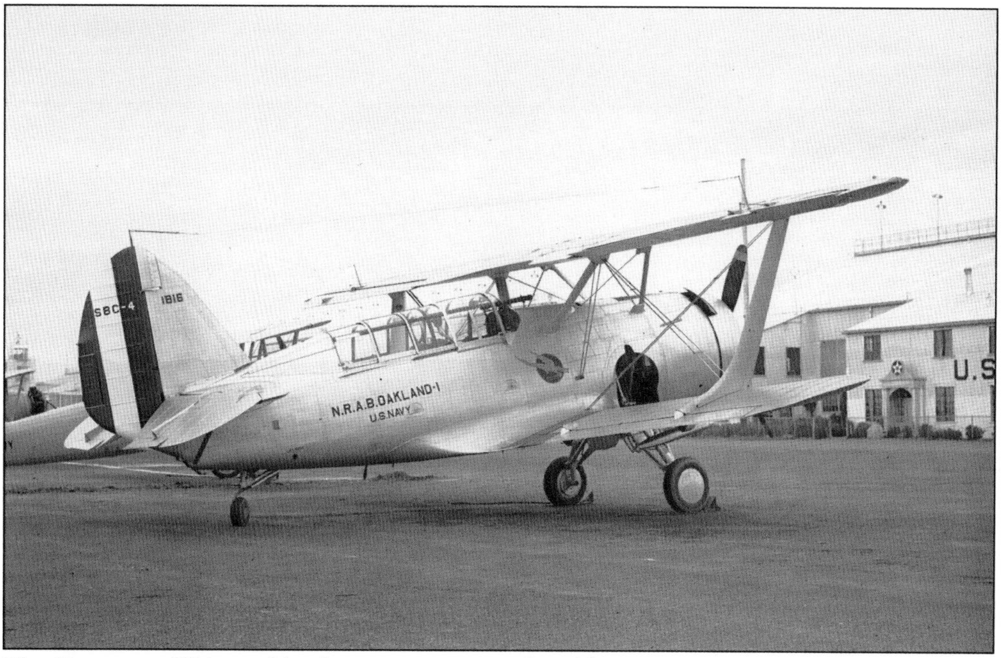

The Grumman SF-1s used by the reserve were replaced by newer Curtiss SBC-4s in 1940. This photograph of SBC-4 (1816) in December 1940 is unusual because of the name on the side instead of a single aircraft number. Hangar 3, used exclusively by the Naval Reserve, is in the background. Most SBC-4s were taken away from the reserves to be sent to France via Canada but were too late to be delivered before the German occupation.

Two enlisted men are shown at NRAB Oakland in 1940. Jay Wright (left) spent his life in aviation after service in World War II. Eugene Valencia (right) went on to become a naval aviator during the war, becoming the third-highest ranking navy ace with 23 victories.

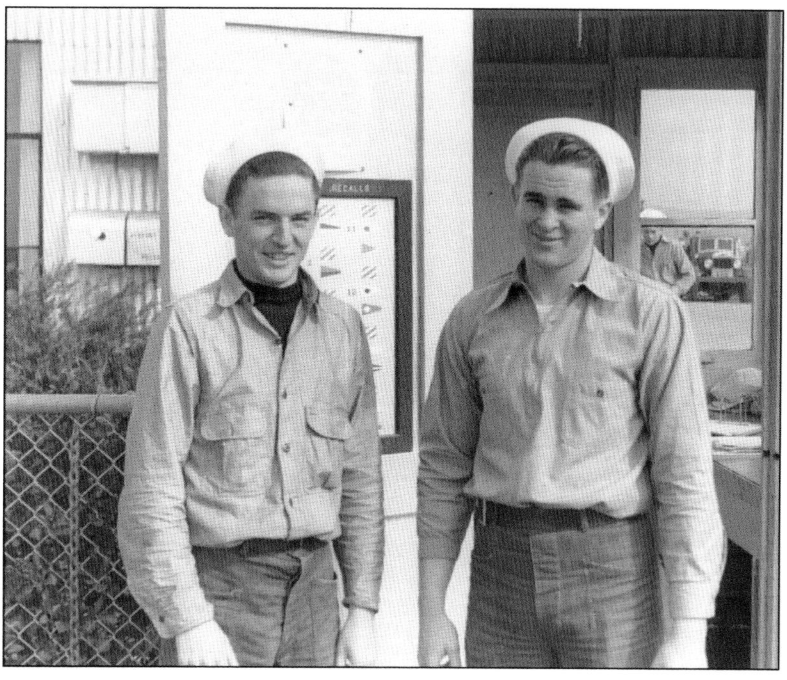

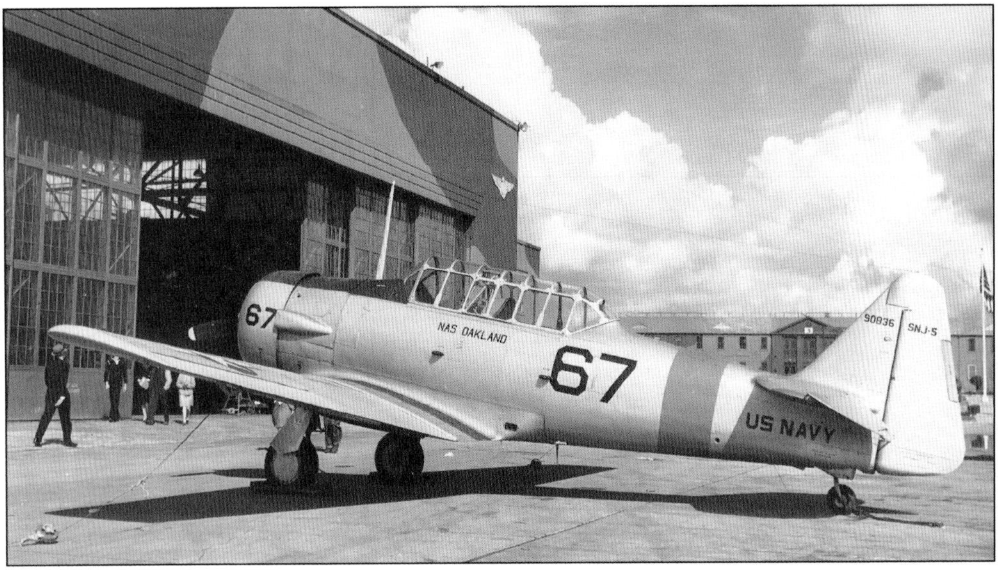

This photograph of the North American SNJ-5 trainer (90836) is different because it shows the name of the air station on the side and the World War II camouflage remaining on the reserve hangar in February 1947. Oakland had an SNJ-2 before the war and SNJ-4s, 5s, and 6s after the war.

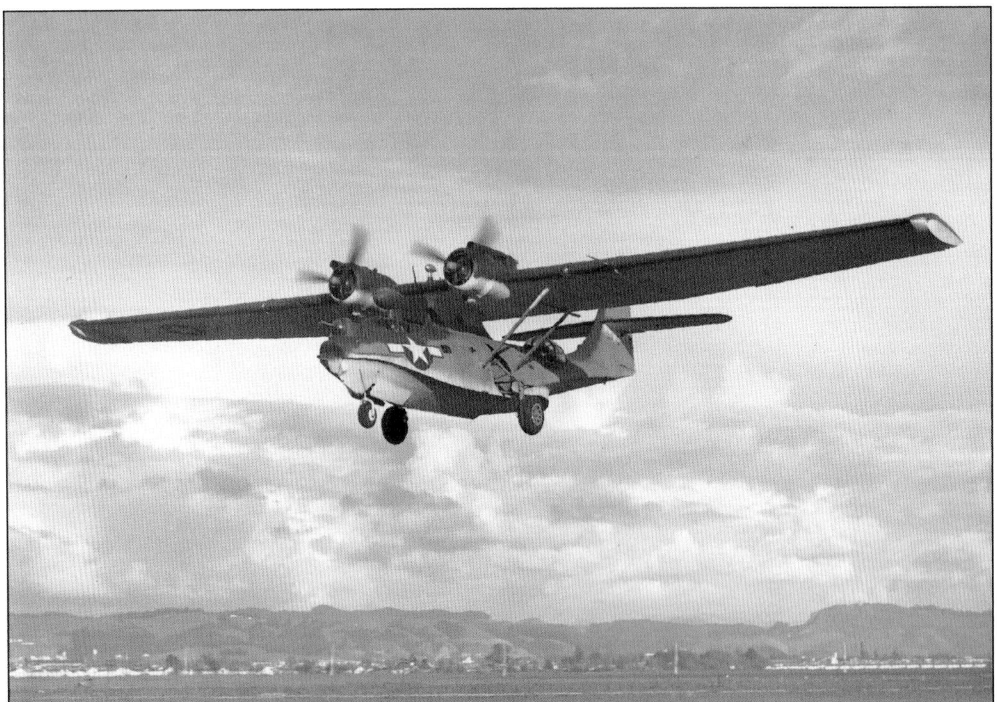

A Consolidated PBY-5A patrol bomber amphibian is shown landing at Oakland in February 1947. These were assigned to Reserve Squadron VPP-51. The aging World War II amphibians were replaced shortly after by newer Lockheed PV-2 Harpoons.

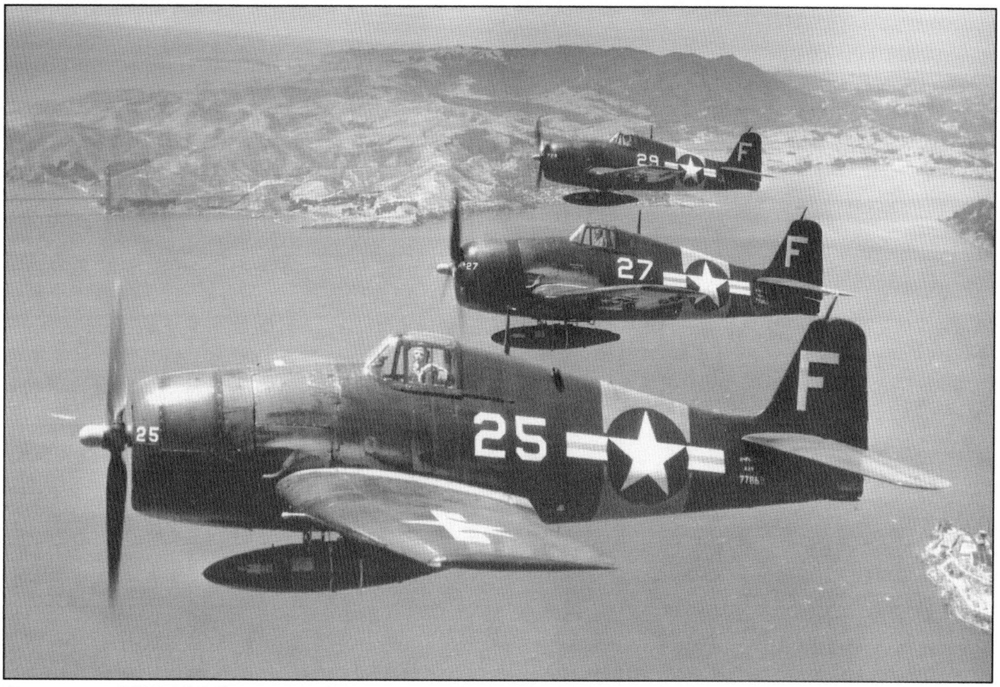

Grumman F6F-5 Hellcats are shown over San Francisco Bay with the Golden Gate Bridge on the left and Alcatraz Island on the right. The F6F was the standard fighter in the Naval Reserve in the immediate postwar period. In December 1949, Oakland had 61 of them in service with Reserve Squadrons VF-61, 62, 76, 97, and 98, and VMF-141.

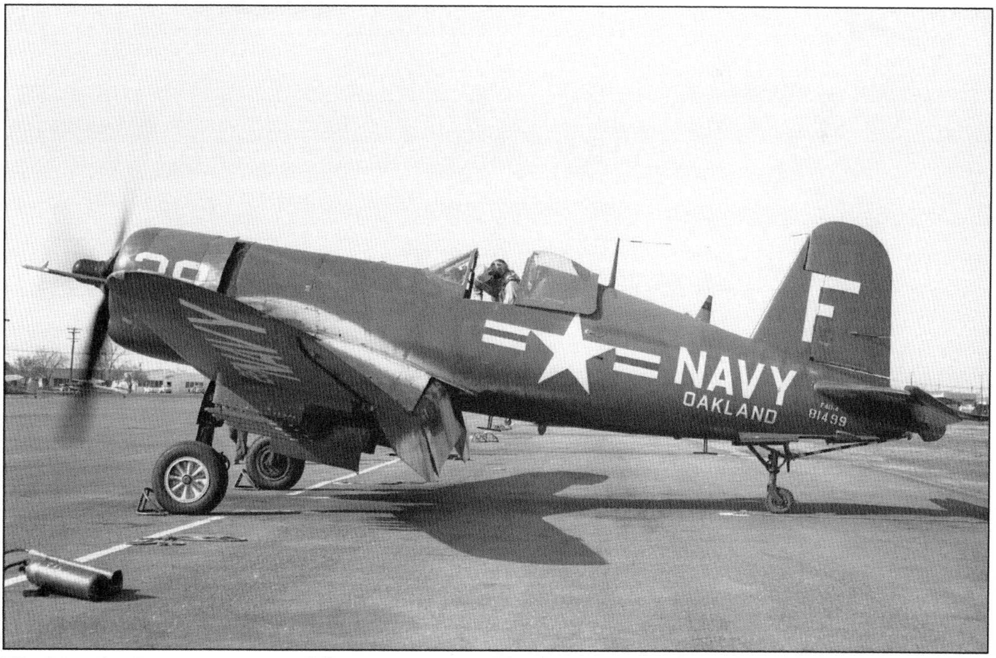

The Vought Corsair was one of the types operated by the reactivated Oakland reserves at Livermore Airport in January 1946. The early Goodyear FG-1Ds were replaced by the later Vought F4U-4s by 1948. This one (81499) was photographed at Sacramento in February 1955.

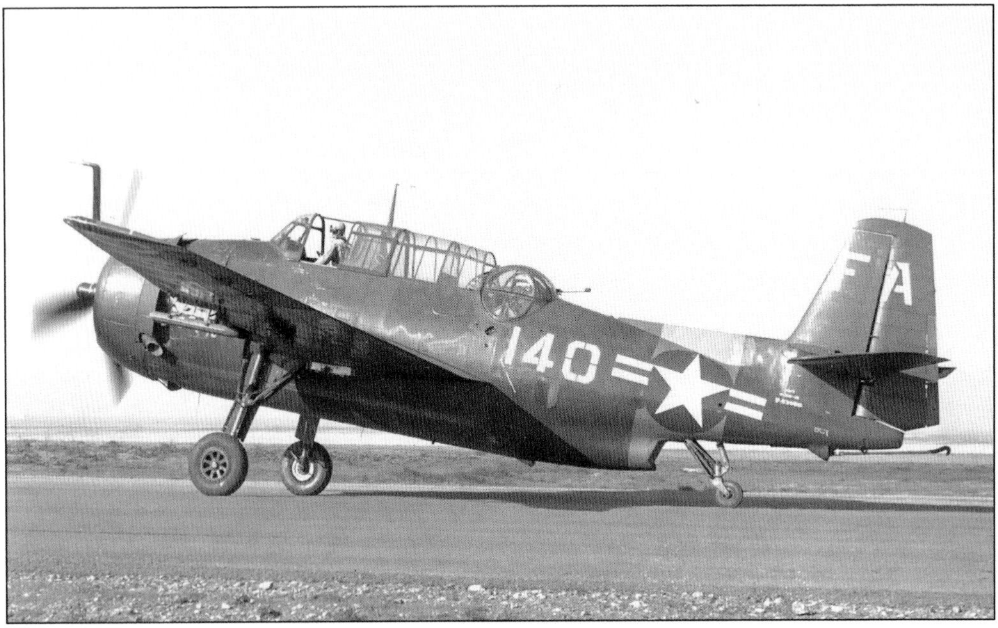

Every reserve base in the United States at the end of the war had General Motors TBM-3 torpedo bombers in service. Here Oakland's FA-140 (53060) is ready to take off at Oakland in January 1948. The tail code letters for Oakland had been changed from a single "F" to two letters denoting Oakland and the type of squadron, such as "A" for attack.

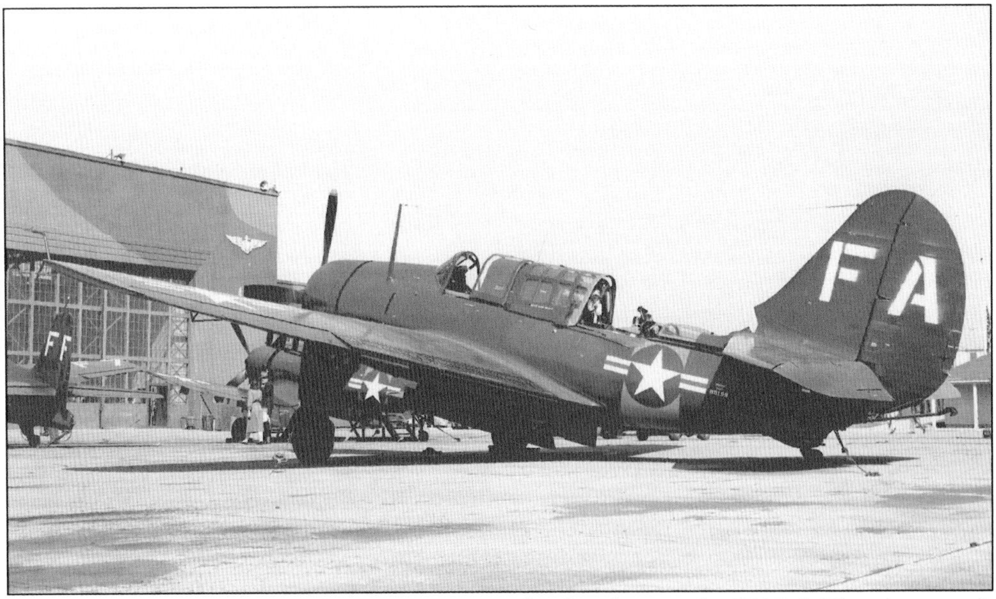

The final improved version of the postwar Curtiss dive bomber was the SB2C-5. This photograph of Navy 89198 demonstrates the top section of the rear fuselage folded down to allow the use of the machine guns in the rear cockpit. Note the World War II camouflage on the NAS Oakland Reserve Hangar that was still in place when this photograph was taken in October 1947.

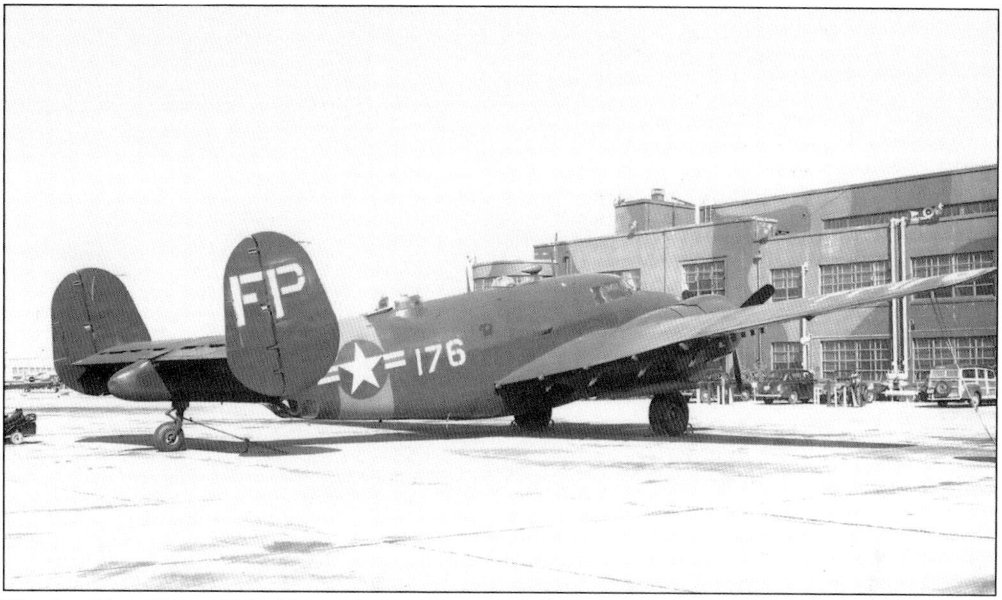

The Lockheed-Vega PV-2 Harpoon was the patrol plane type used by the reserves between the PBY and the P2V. This photograph of Oakland's FP180 (37214) was taken on Navy Day, October 23, 1947. By the end of 1949, six were in use by NAS Oakland. The squadron designations VP-ML-57 and VP-ML-72 were for Patrol-Medium-Land.

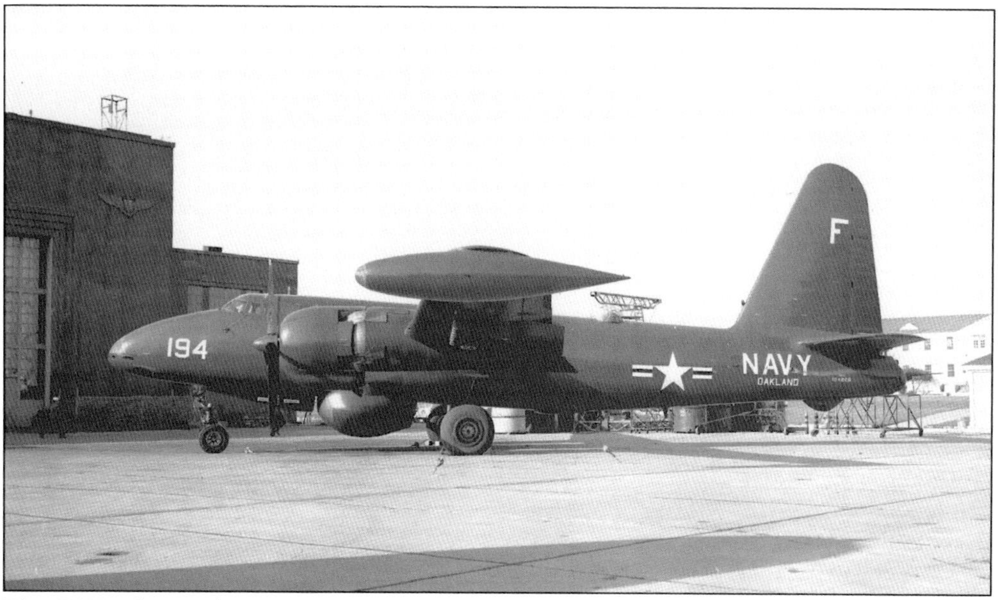

This P2V-4 (124226) was one of the first Lockheed Neptunes to be assigned to the Oakland reserve. This one was photographed in April 1954 when the tail codes were a single letter for the air station (F for Oakland). By this time, Naval Reserve squadrons had been renumbered in the 800 series, with Oakland assigned VP-872 and VP-876.

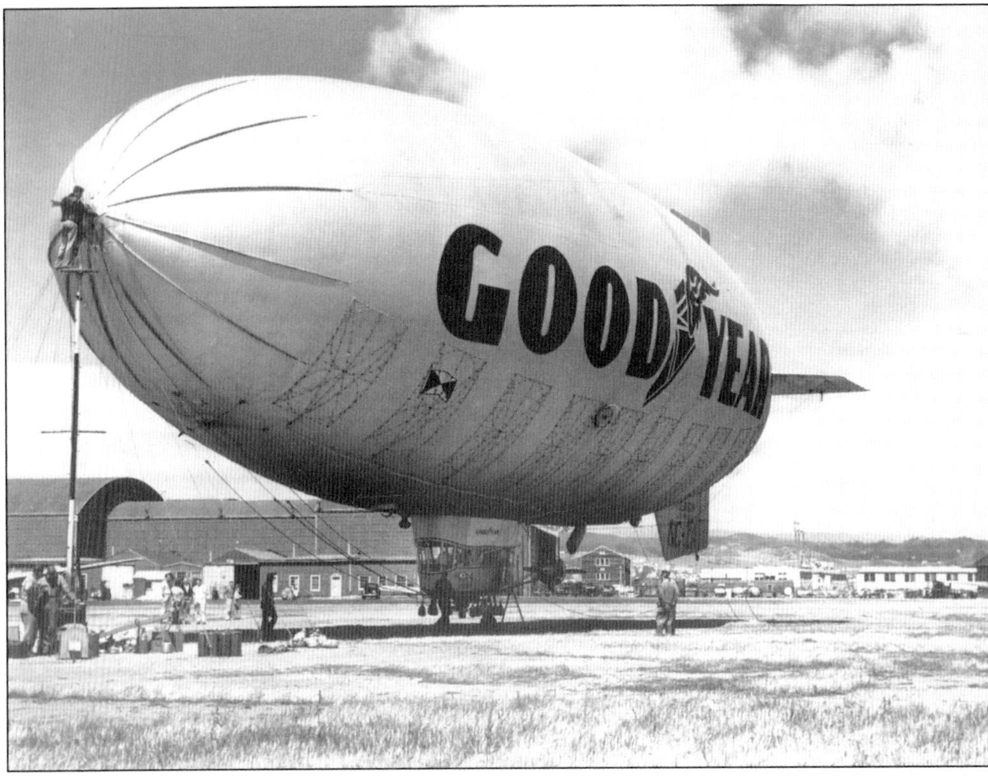

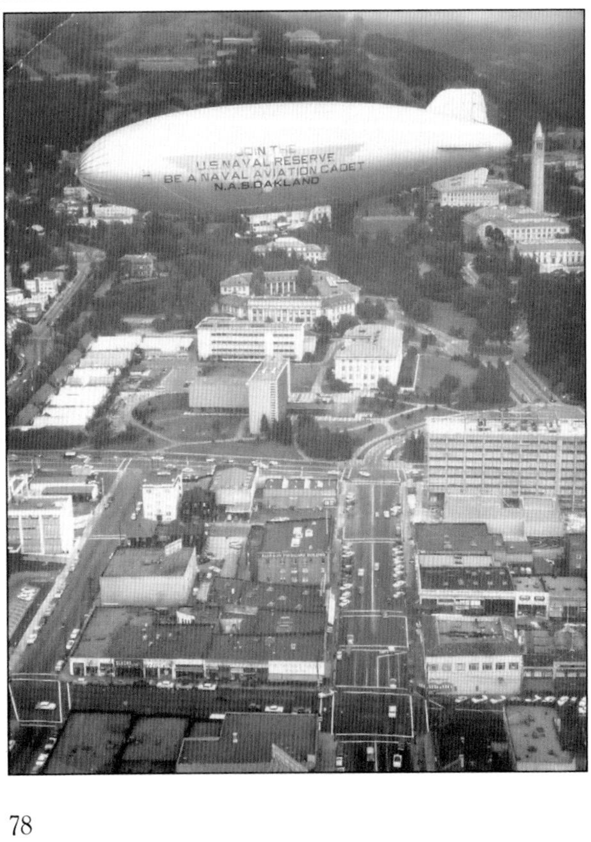

The Goodyear Blimps flew in and out of Oakland before and after the war. Those lucky enough to get a ticket from their Goodyear tire dealer were given a ride in the 1930s. This photograph shows one moored at North Field with the old World War II hangars in the background.

The same size blimp was developed for navy use during the war for antisubmarine patrol. Navy Reserve Squadron ZP-871 (Lighter than Air) flew one after the war at Oakland from 1952 to 1958. This photograph shows it flying over Berkeley and the University of California campus. It was used as a slow, low-flying billboard, with the words "JOIN THE U.S. NAVAL RESERVE, BE A NAVAL AVIATION CADET" on the side.

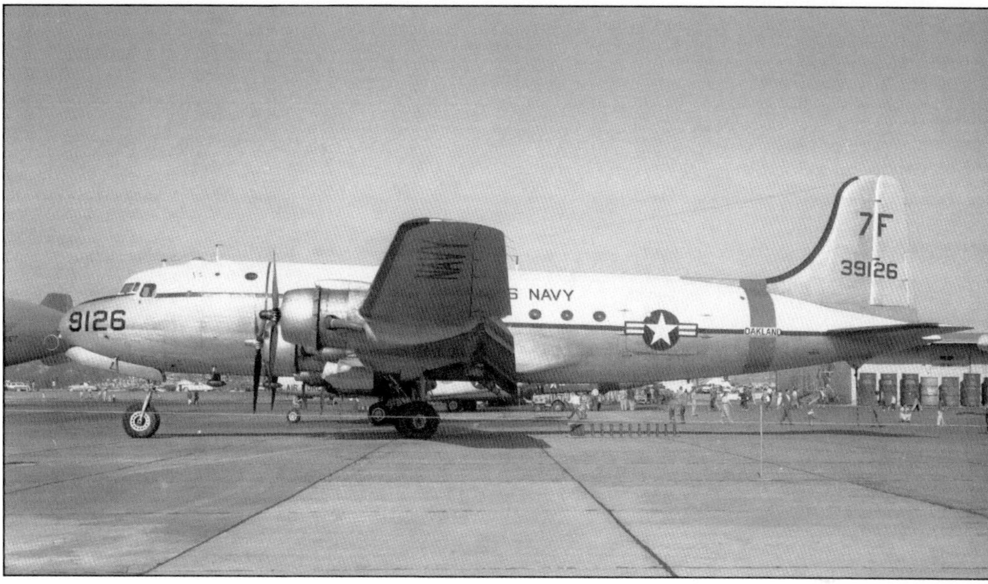

The reserves at NAS Oakland had Transport Squadrons VR-871, 872, 873, and 874 flying World War II Douglas R5Ds (the navy version of the AAF C-54) from 1954 to 1965. This R5D-2 is parked in their area at the north end of North Field, and the reserve blimp can be seen on the left.

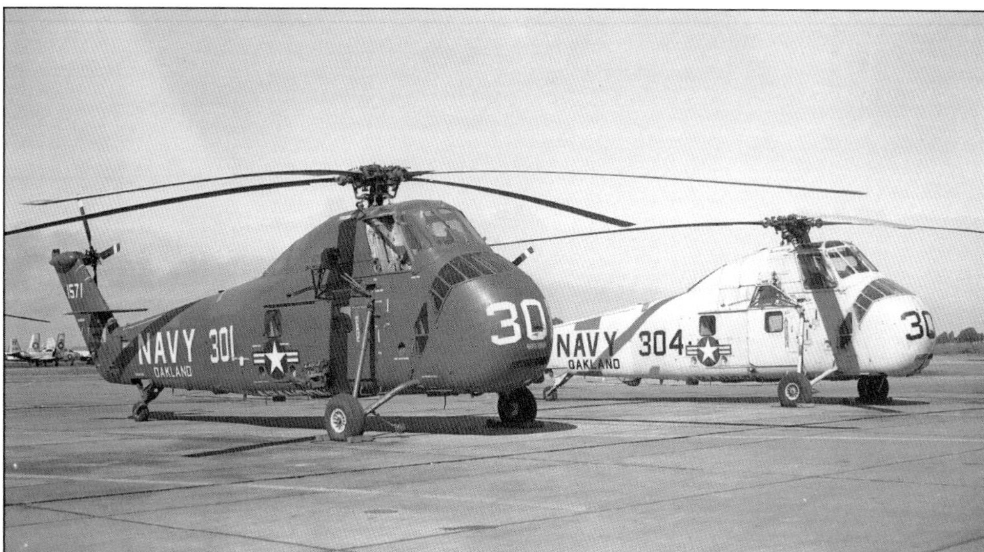

The era of the helicopter in the reserves was ushered in with the Sikorsky HSS-1. This September 1959 photograph shows two different paint schemes. The 301 (141571) is seaplane gray, and the 304 (138485) is white. Reserve antisubmarine squadrons HS-871 and HS-872 operated at NAS Oakland from 1958 until they moved to NAS Alameda in 1961.

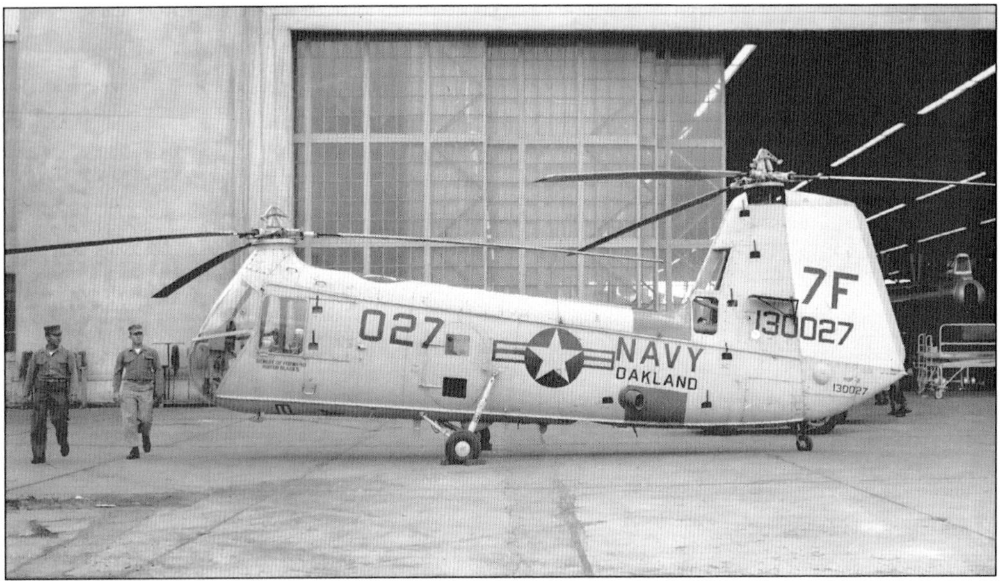

Another helicopter type flown by the Oakland reserve was the Piasecki HUP-2. This photograph of 7F-027 (130027), taken in September 1957, shows the change in tail codes to two characters. The "7" indicated a naval air station, and "F" remained as "Oakland."

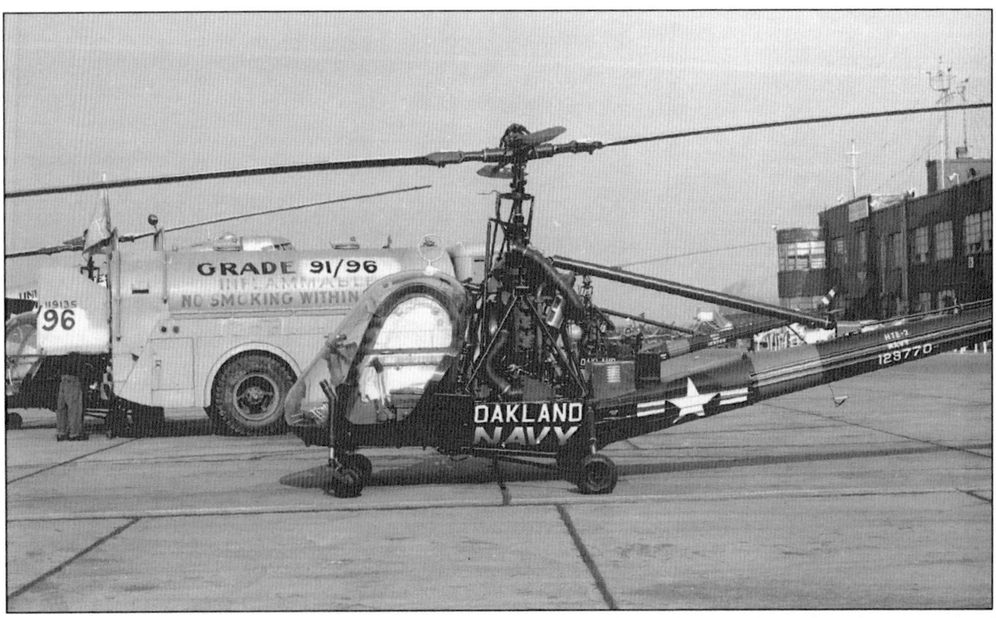

The lesser-known helicopter type used by the reserves was the Hiller HTE-2. This photograph of Navy 129770 from Squadron HU-871, taken in November 1952, shows three of them being fueled in front of the naval reserve hangar. Oakland flew HTE-2s from 1952 to 1955.

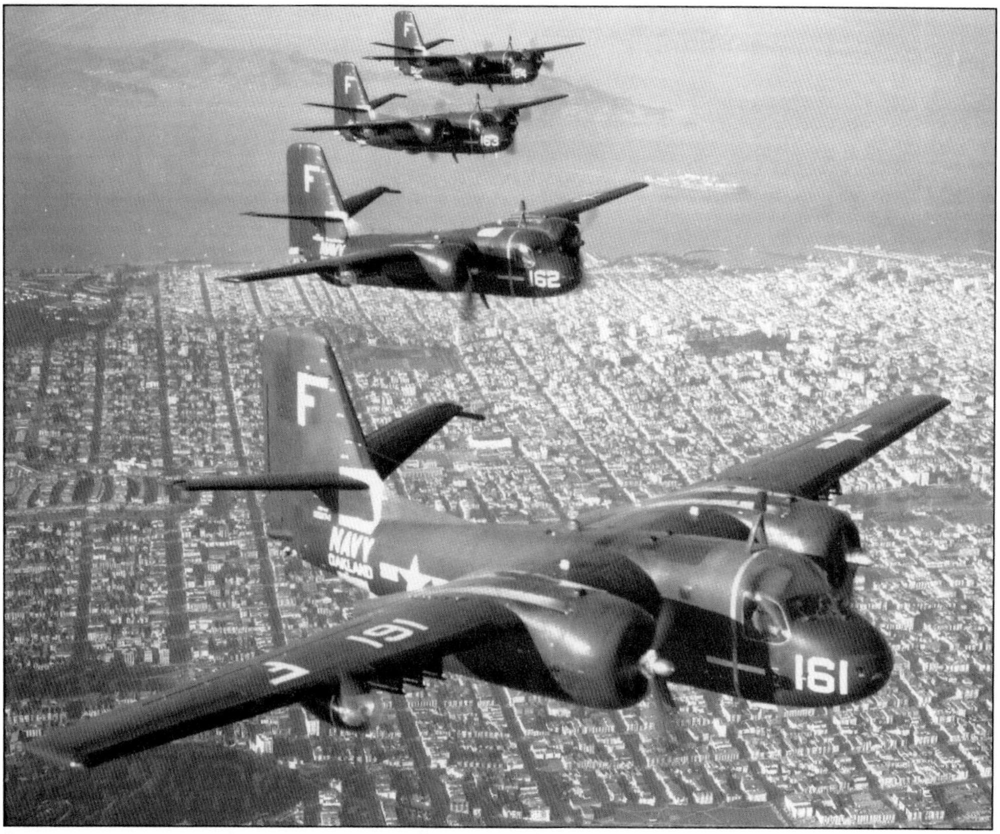

Reserve scouting squadrons were eventually equipped with Grumman S2F antisubmarine Trackers. This dramatic U.S. Navy photograph shows four S2F-1s in left echelon formation over San Francisco in 1956 with the early dark blue colors. Starting in 1957, this was changed to white with high visibility international orange for safety throughout the Naval Reserve.

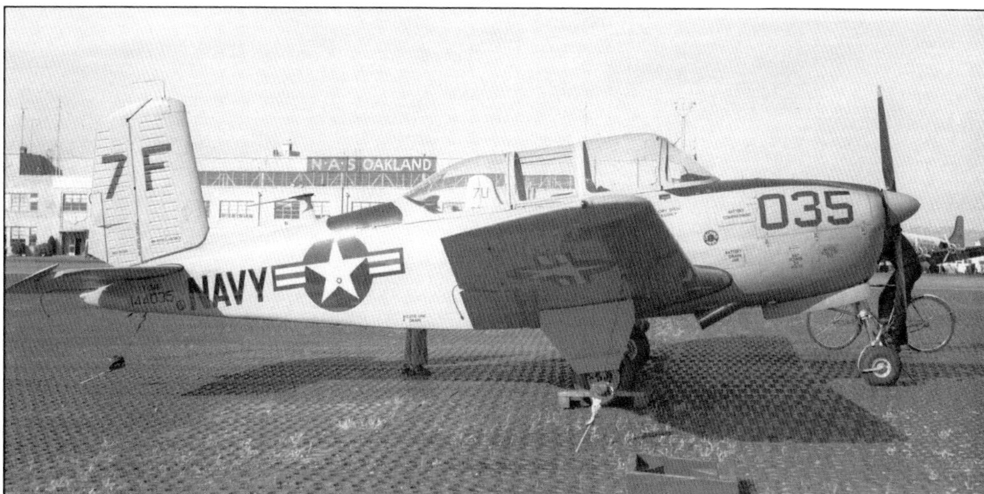

Several Naval Reserve bases had a Beech T-34B, such as this 7F-035 (144035), to give familiarization rides to college students and other prospective candidates to recruit for naval aviation. This one was at Oakland in September 1957.

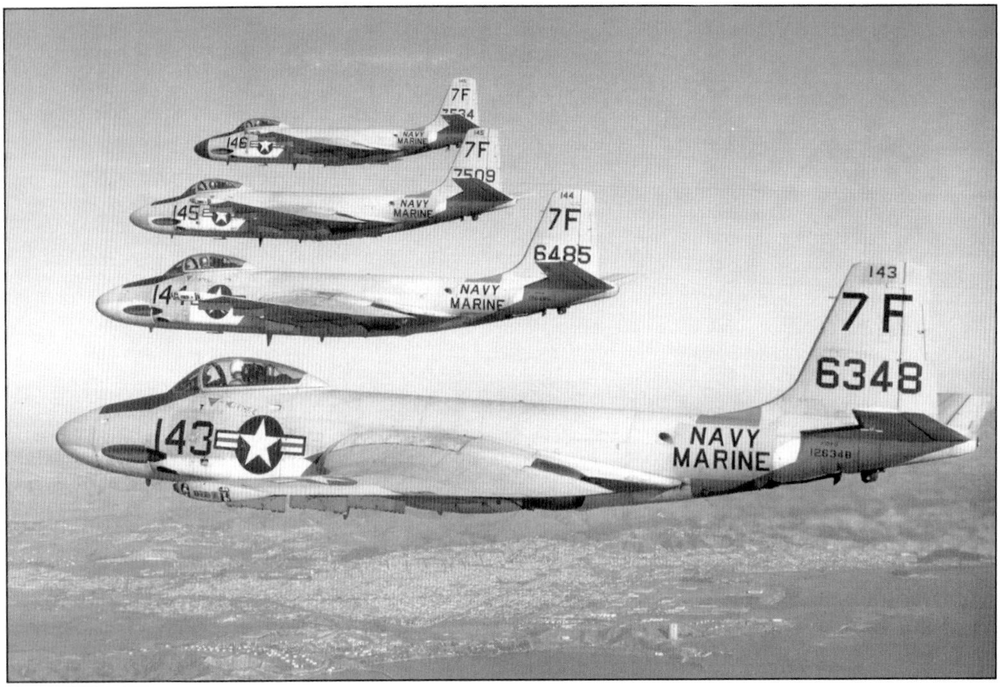

The second jet fighter type after the FJ-1 (see cover photograph) to be used by Oakland was the McDonnell F2H Banshee, starting in 1956. This shows four of Oakland's F2H-4s in flight over the Bay Area in 1959. It was the last jet type to be flown by NAS Oakland, as the base was closed on June 30, 1961. Most of the aircraft had been moved to NAS Alameda by March of that year, and the reserves continued to fly at their new location.

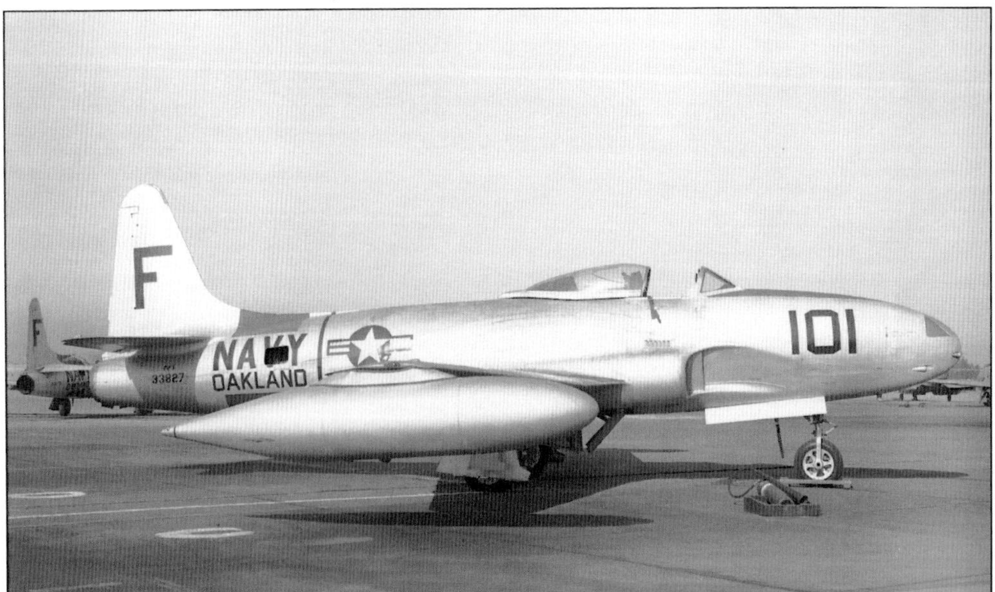

The navy operated some of the single-place USAF F-80Cs, first as model TO-1 and later as the TV-1. This photograph shows Oakland's TV-1 (33827) in September 1955. Oakland also had some of the two-place Lockheed TV-2s (USAF T-33A) in 1958.

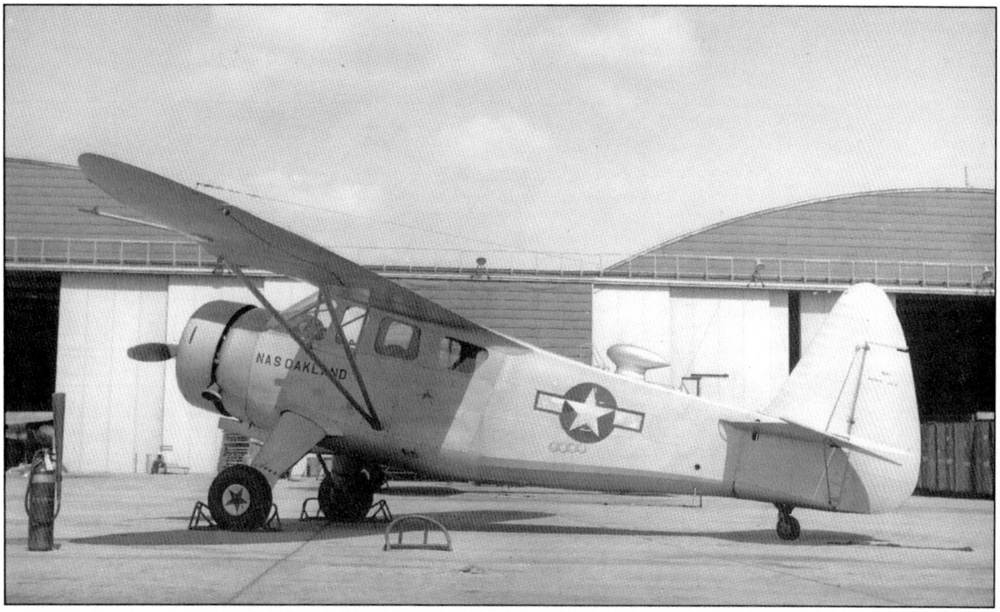

During the time that Naval Air Transport Service (NATS) was operating, there was an active-duty Naval Air Station Oakland. They had small utility planes for their own use, and this Howard GH-3 (44998) was one of them in April 1946.

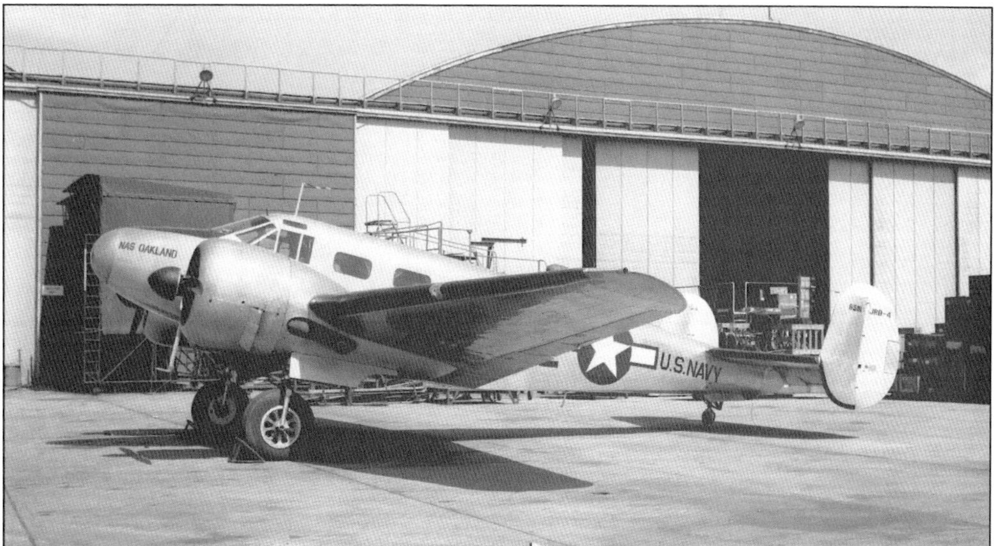

Oakland also had this larger twin-engine Beech JRB-4 (85111) utility-transport for staff use in April 1946. There was no connection between this plane and the Naval Reserve, and it carries the name "NAS Oakland" on the nose. The prewar Oakland reserve was reformed at NAS Livermore in January 1946 and did not return to Oakland until the end of that year.

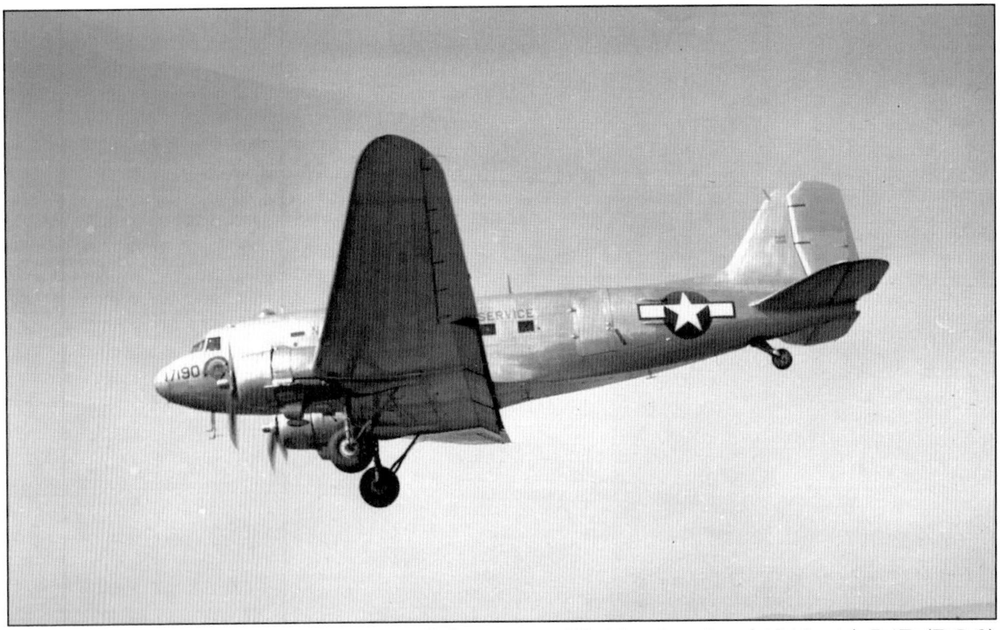

The Naval Air Transport Service was still flying out of Oakland in April 1946 with R4D (DC-3) and R5D (DC-4) aircraft. This is R4D-5 (50821) of Transport Squadron Three (VR-3) coming in for a landing.

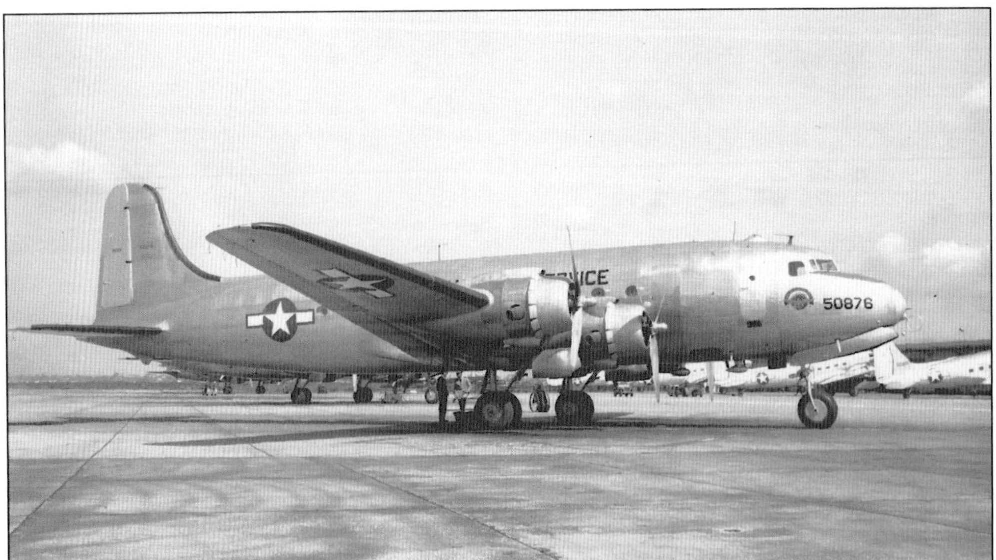

This Douglas R5D-2 (50876) is at the head of a line of other R5Ds and the NATS Douglas R4Ds can be seen to the right. This is at the NATS operational base at the north end of the old airport, now called North Field.

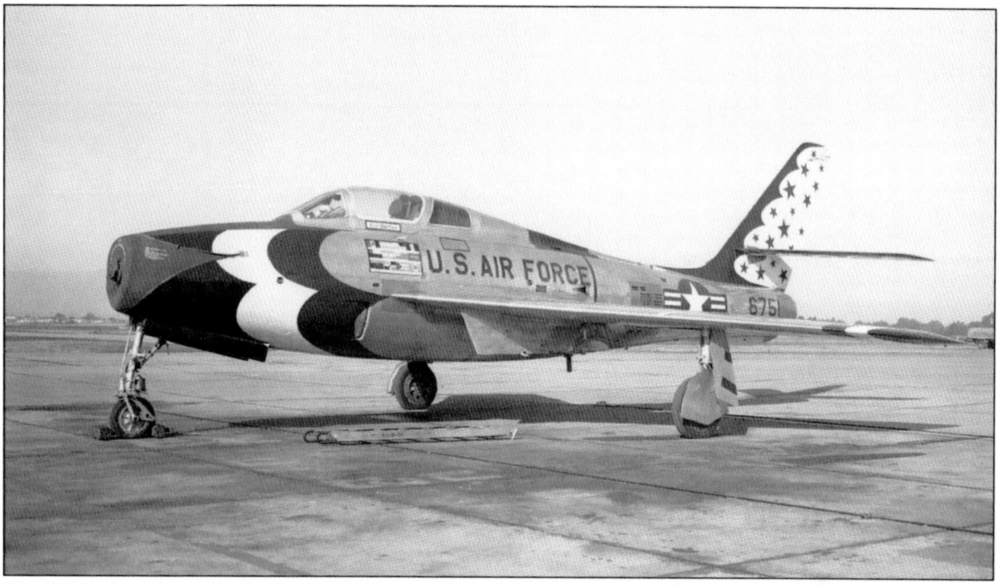

The U.S. Air Force flight demonstration team, the Thunderbirds, performed at the Oakland Air Show in September 1955. This is Republic F-84F (52-6751) flown by Capt. Paul Ross; it has the flags of the 12 countries the team has performed in outside the United States.

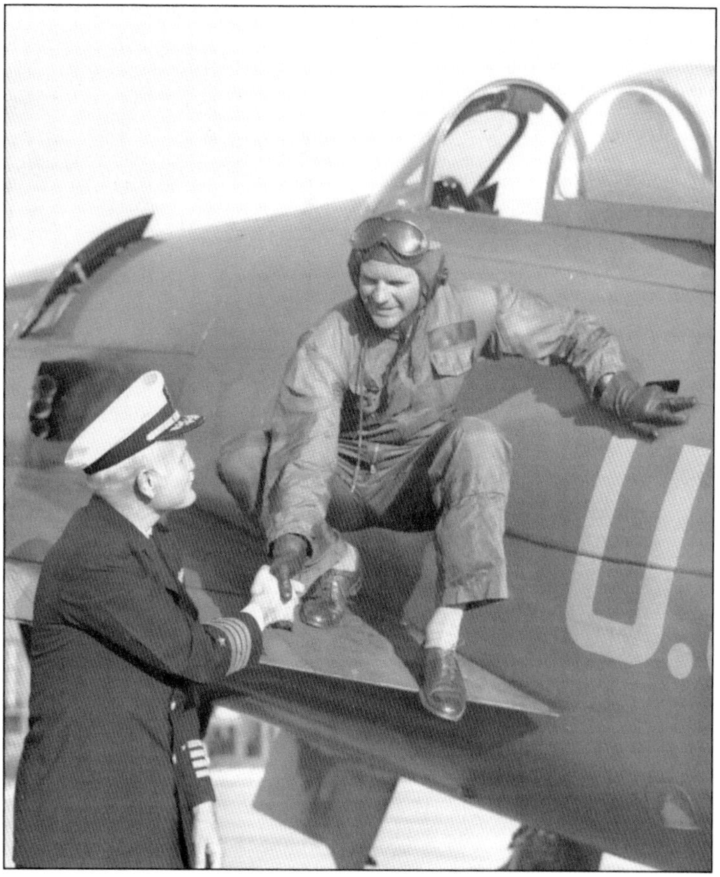

The commanding officer of NAS Oakland welcomes Cmdr. Roy "Butch" Voris upon his arrival with the Blue Angels, the Navy Flight Demonstration Team, on October 9, 1946. Oakland was one of the first cities to see them fly the new Grumman F8F-1 Bearcat fighters.

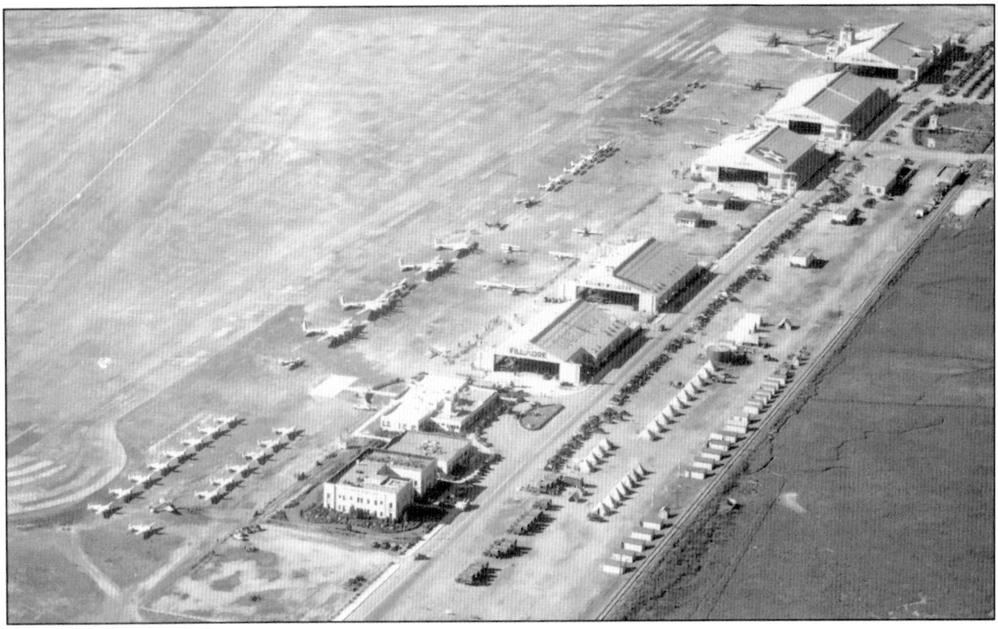

The Army Air Corps came to Oakland in January 1940 for maneuvers with 16 Curtiss P-36As, 3 Boeing Y1B-17s, a Douglas B-18, and a Northrop A-17. Their trucks and 26 tents can be seen in the lower right on the street side of the airport. The small buildings creating the row are permanent airport structures and not part of the army encampment.

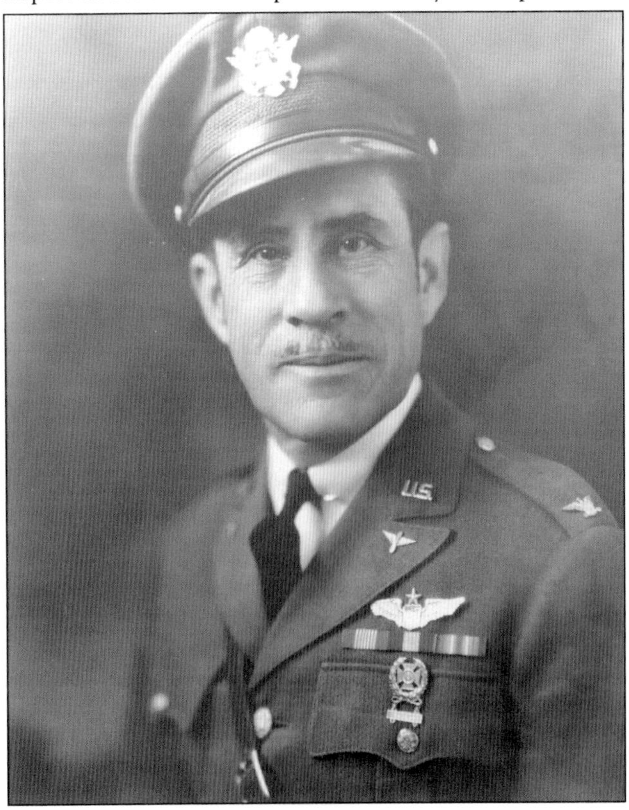

This shows Col. (later Gen.) Clarence L. Tinker, Army Air Corps command pilot. During the critical period in 1934 when the Army Air Corps was suddenly given the duty of flying the airmail, he commanded the Oakland–Salt Lake City–Cheyenne route with headquarters at Oakland Airport. Due to his alertness and ability, there were no serious accidents on that route.

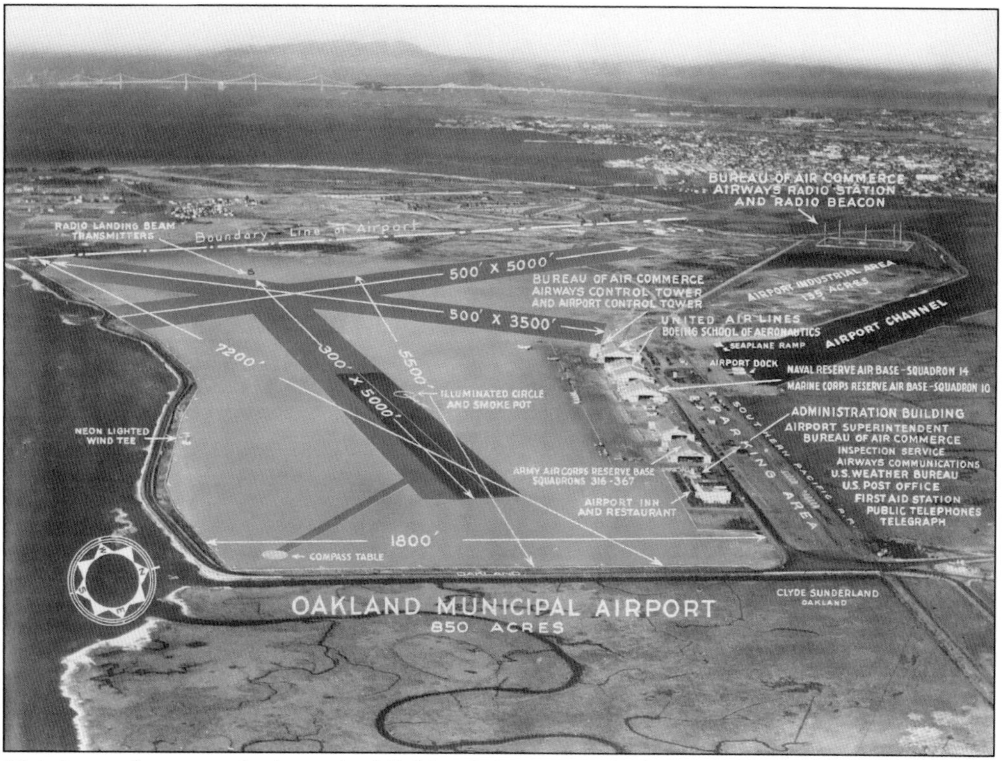

This is another retouched aerial of Oakland Airport with the runways added and additional information lettered on the photograph. This 1940 image is the first to show the Army Air Corps Reserve in Hangar 1 with Squadrons 316 and 367. The perimeter road on the left borders the airport and the bay.

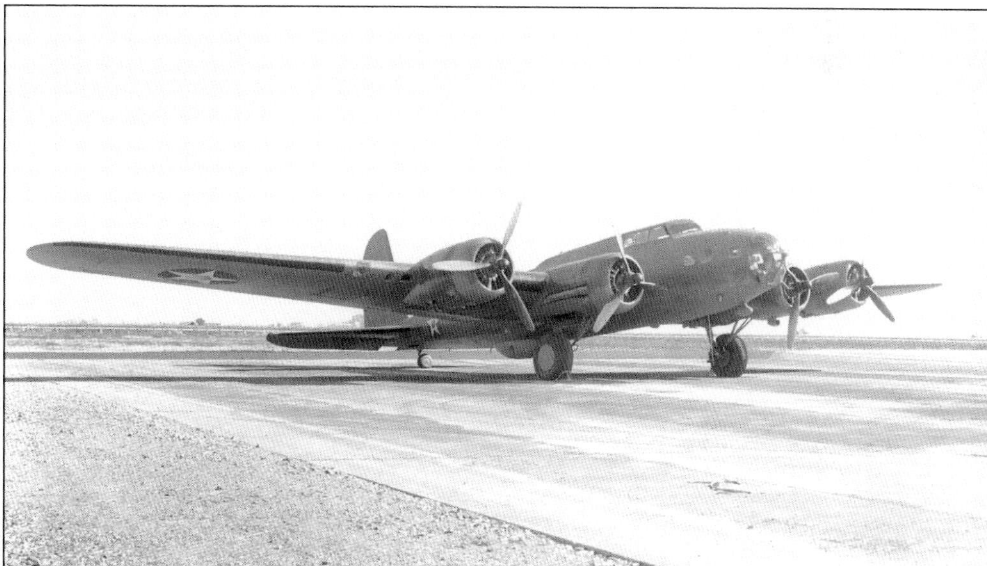

The war in Europe was brought home to people at Oakland Airport in the summer of 1941 when this Boeing B-17C arrived in war paint. This was long before the mass production of the well-known B-17G.

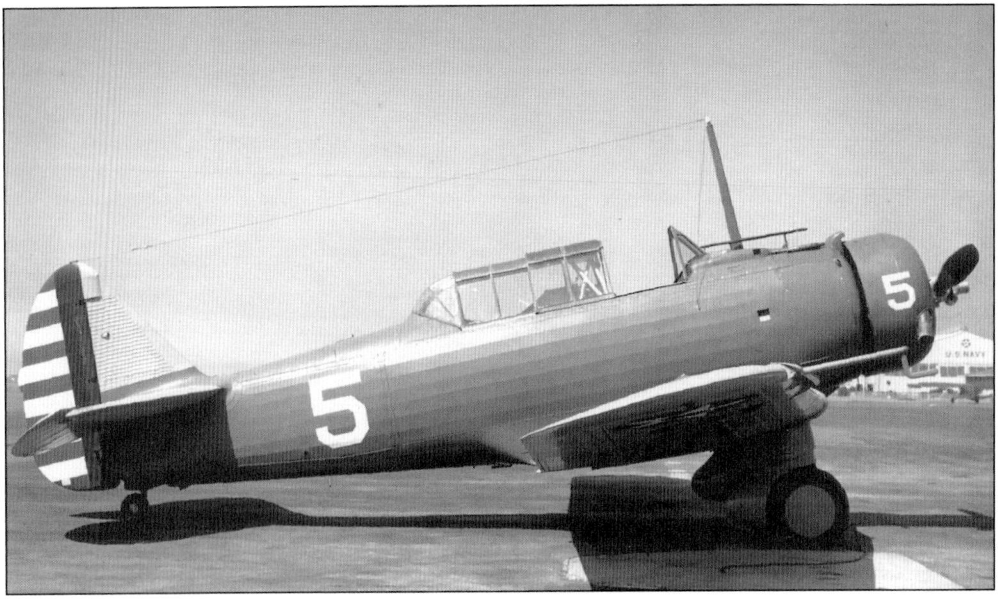

Starting in 1938, the Army Reserve unit was allocated new North American trainers. This BT-9C (38-232) was No. 5. These basic trainers were fully equipped, and it was all serious business. So the pilots looking for something fun to fly competed for the few Boeing P-12E fighters that were also assigned to the Oakland reserve unit.

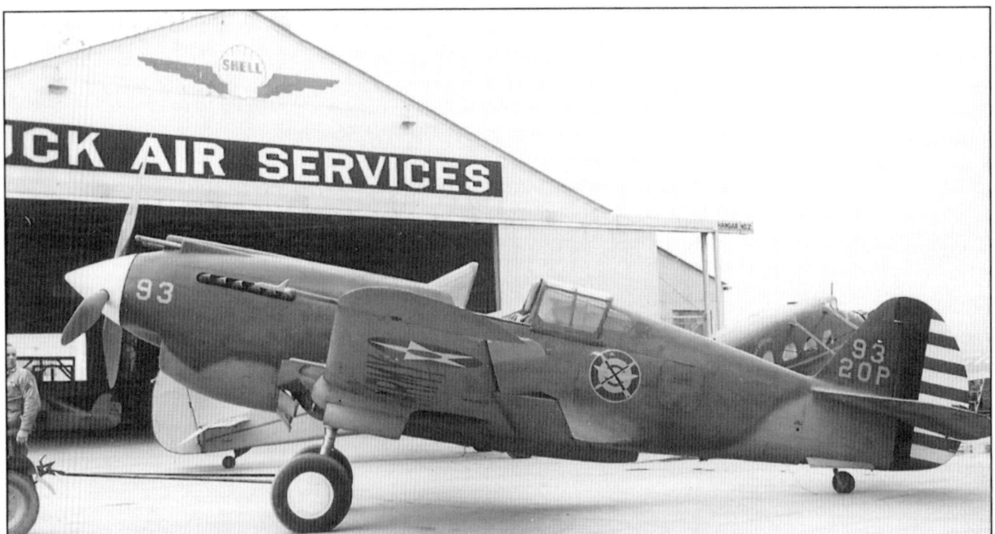

This new Curtiss P-40 from the 55th Squadron of the 20th Pursuit Group is being towed out of the Army Reserve Hangar in the summer of 1941. Active-duty Army Air Corps planes as well as National Guard planes would visit Oakland because it was an Air Corps Reserve squadron with minor service. Duck Air Service's Stinson A trimotor is in the right rear behind the P-40.

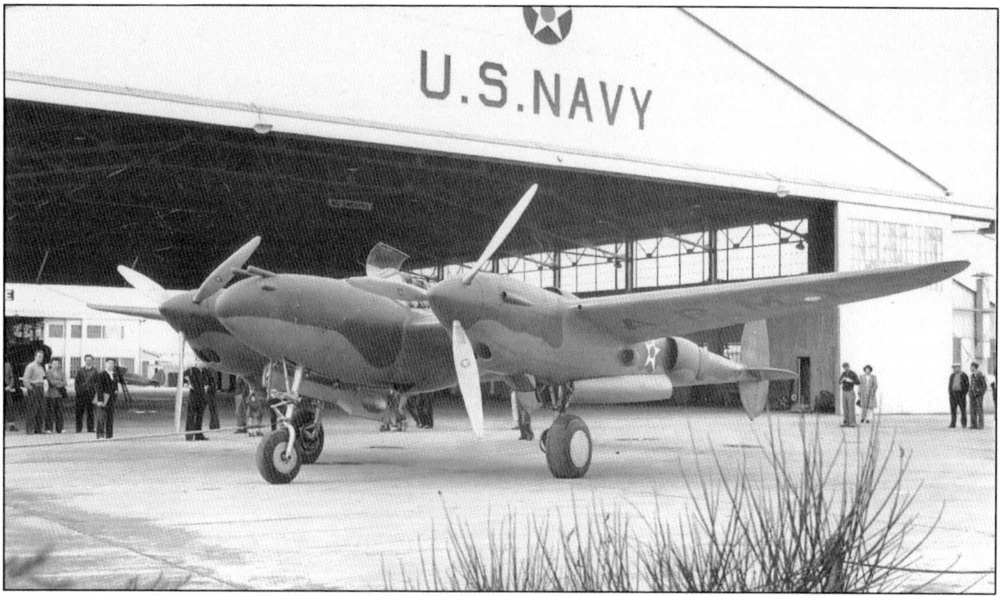

The most exciting visitor in late 1941 was this Lockheed P-38D of the 51st Pursuit Group because very few people had ever seen a P-38. It arrived on November 15, 1941, from March Field and is shown being towed out of Hangar 3 the next day. Because of its security status, it was locked in the Naval Reserve Hangar overnight.

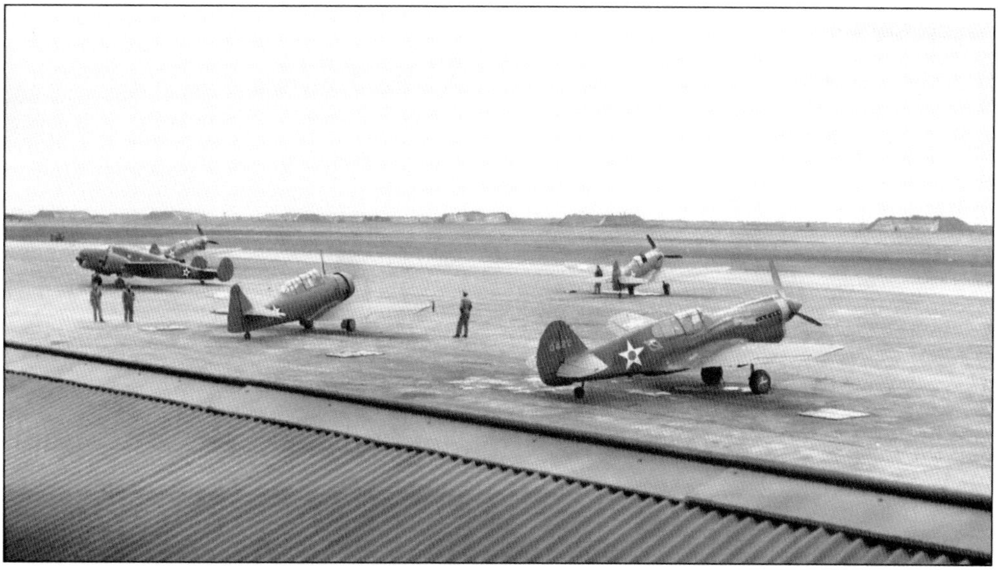

A rare photograph shows Oakland Airport on combat status after being taken over by the Army Air Force in December 1941. Six dirt revetments can be seen on the horizon together with two Curtiss P-40Es. The three planes in the foreground, from left to right, are a Beech C-45, North American BT-14, and a Curtiss P-40E.

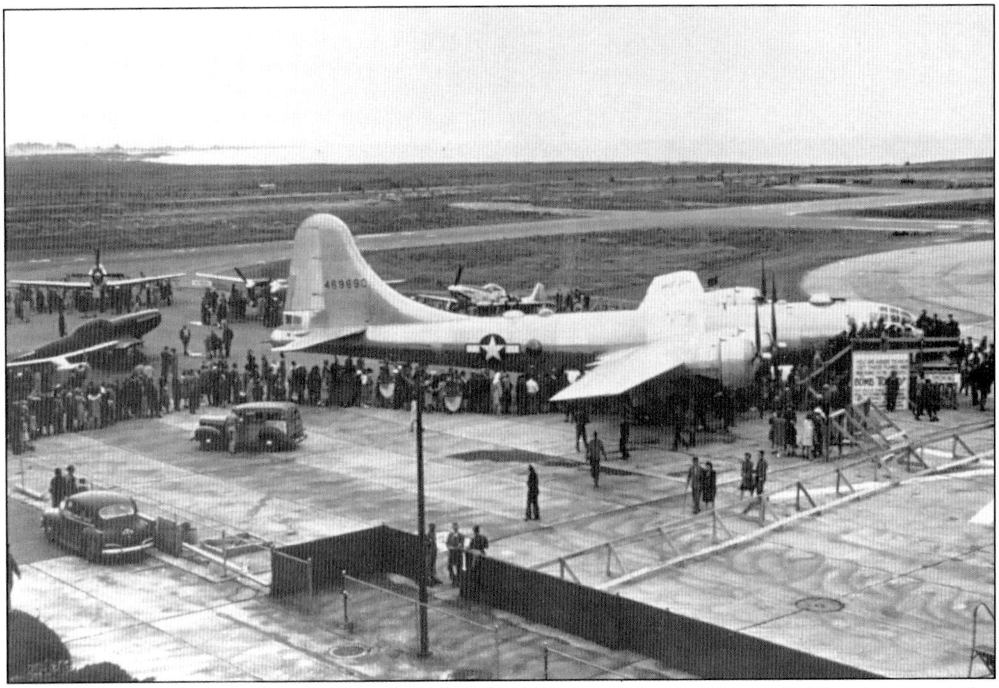

Another rare sight was this Boeing B-29 (44-69690) on public display in 1945 to promote the sale of war bonds. Behind it on exhibit are a P-47, a P-38, and a P-51. B-29s did not operate out of Oakland Airport.

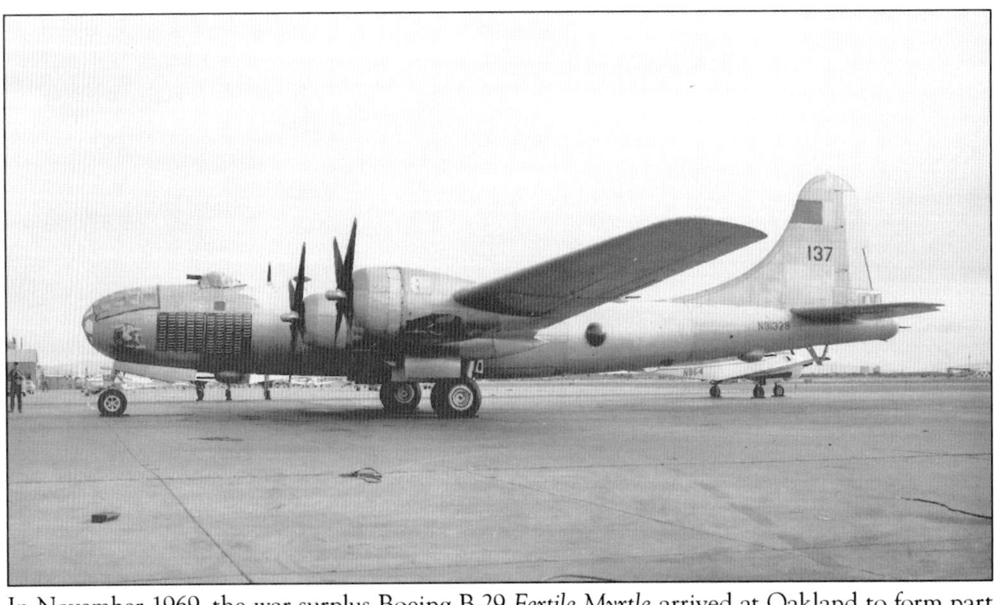

In November 1969, the war surplus Boeing B-29 *Fertile Myrtle* arrived at Oakland to form part of the new American Air Museum Society, founded by Ralph Johnson, William Patrick, John Viano, and Arthur Stagg. Its history included carrying Chuck Yeager in the Bell X-1 rocket plane in October 1947.

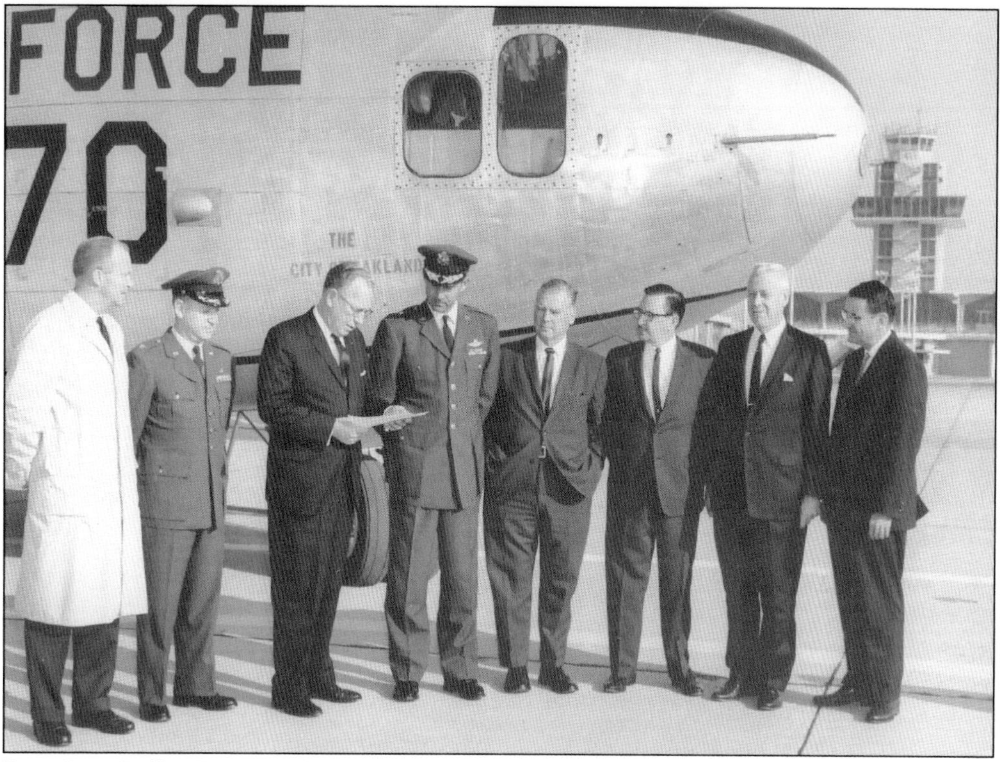

Brig. Gen. Rollin B. Moore (center)—commanding officer of the 349th Troop Carrier Wing, Air Force Reserve, at Hamilton Field—is surrounded by officials of the Port of Oakland and Oakland Airport in 1959 as a proclamation is read naming of one of their Fairchild C-119s the *City of Oakland*.

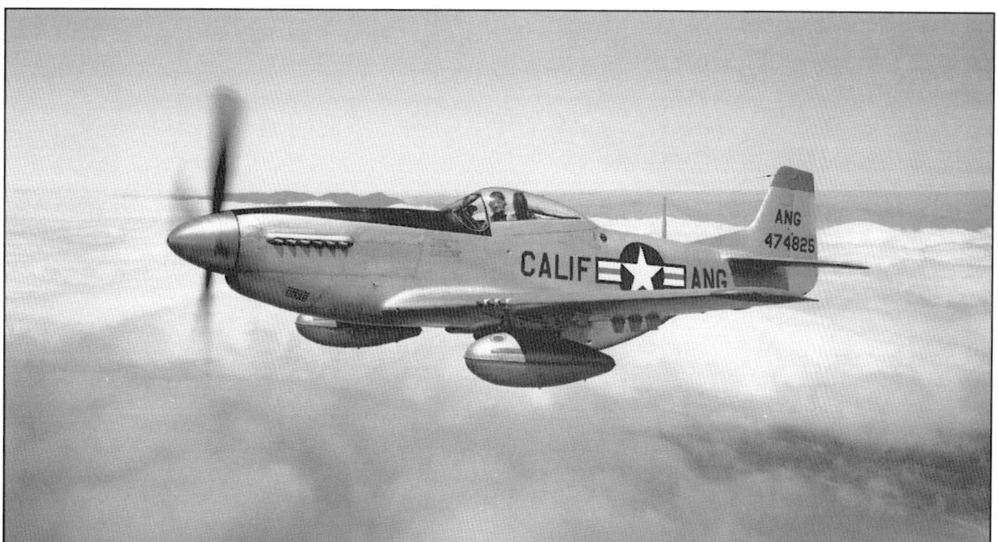

Brig. Gen. John Felton Turner of Oakland was the commanding officer of the 144th Fighter Wing, California Air National Guard, in June 1951 when this posed photograph of him flying a North American P-51D was taken by coauthor Larkins. Another view appears in the book *San Francisco Bay Area Aviation*.

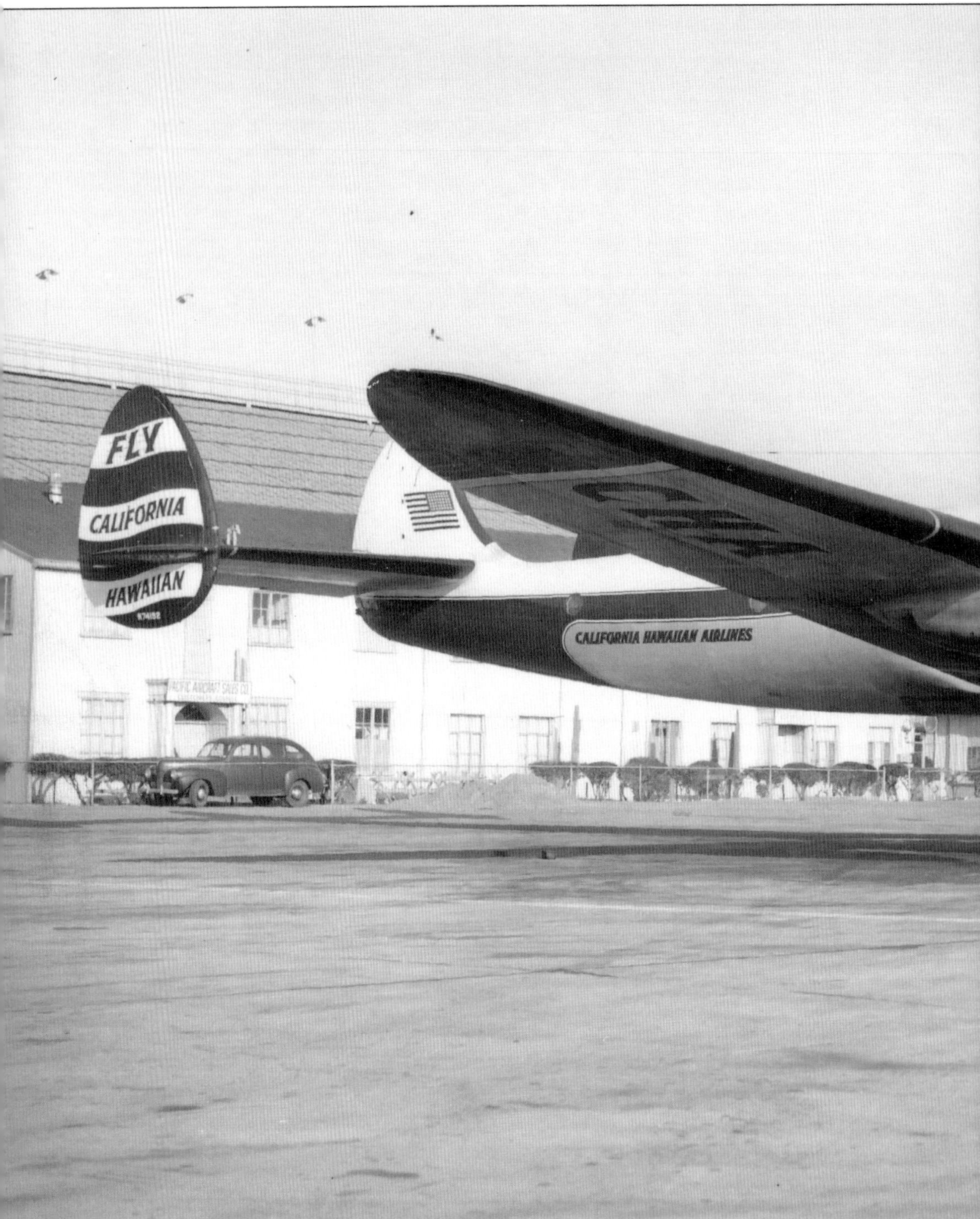

California Hawaiian Airlines was founded by Col. Charles Sherman at Burbank, California, as part of his larger Air Transport Carriers organization. The first plane was this Lockheed 049 Constellation (N74192), shown here running up its engines in front of Hangar 3 in February 1953. This was an example of the use of surplus World War II planes, this one being the former

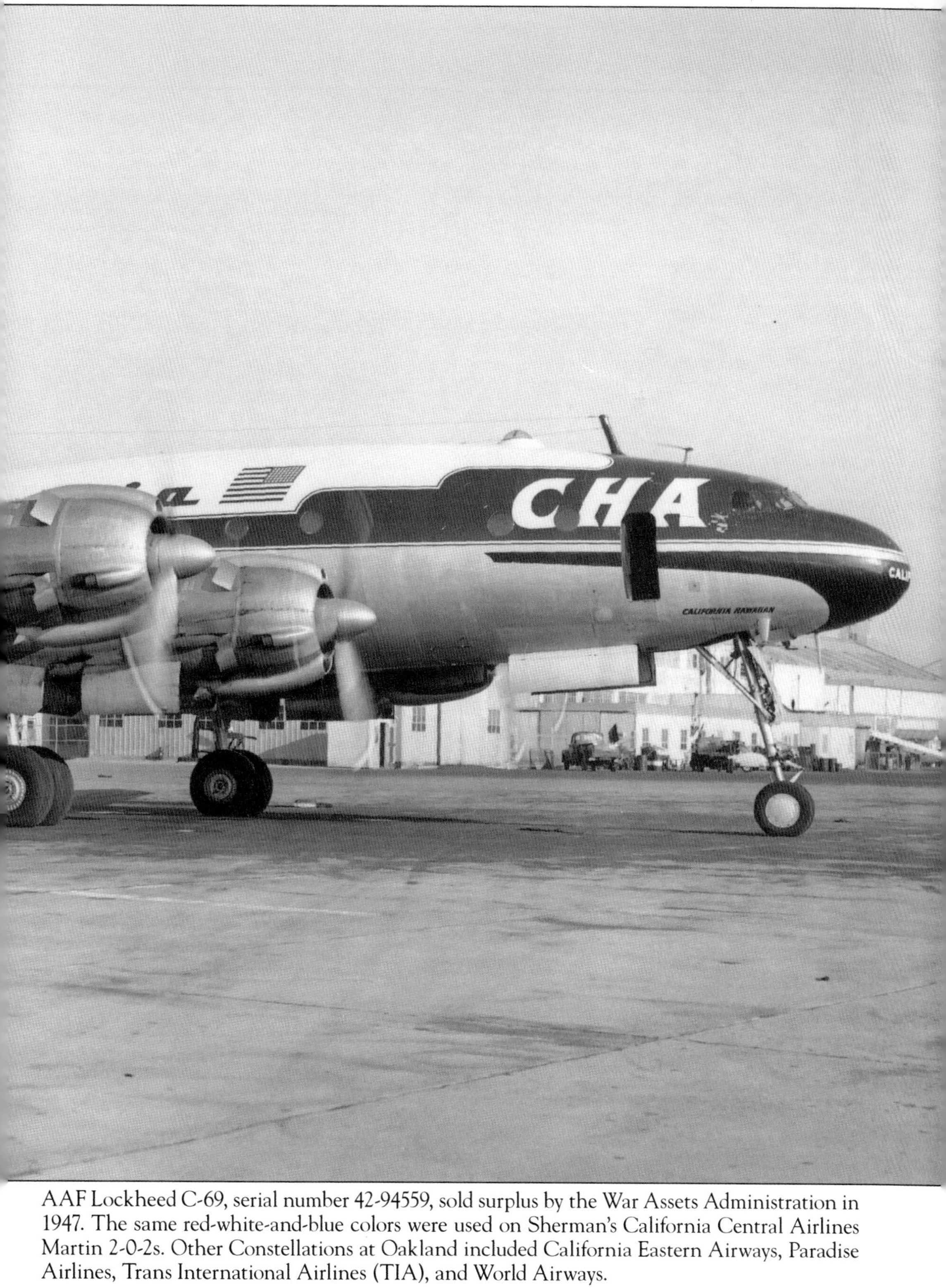

AAF Lockheed C-69, serial number 42-94559, sold surplus by the War Assets Administration in 1947. The same red-white-and-blue colors were used on Sherman's California Central Airlines Martin 2-0-2s. Other Constellations at Oakland included California Eastern Airways, Paradise Airlines, Trans International Airlines (TIA), and World Airways.

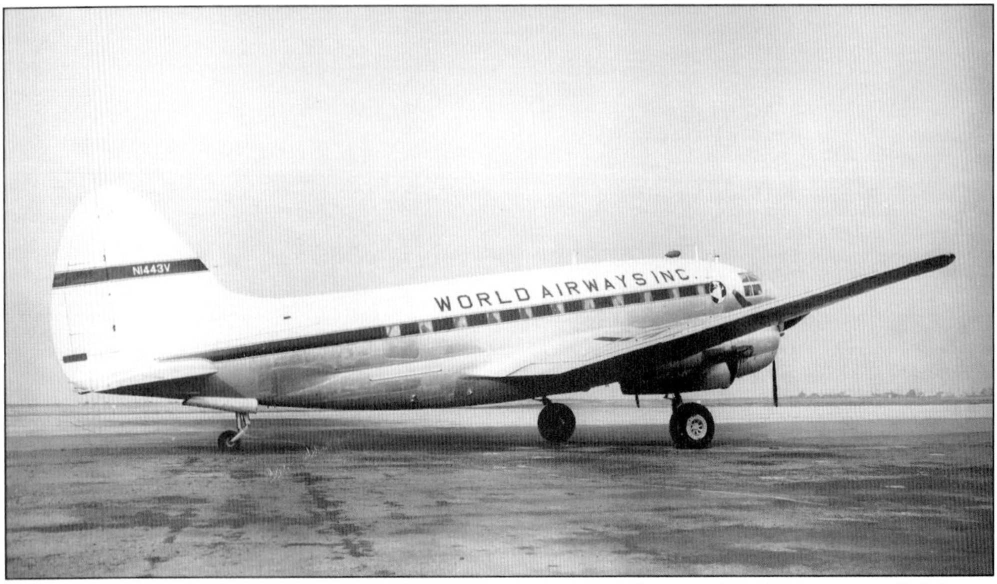

World Airways started in New Jersey with two Curtiss C-46Fs. This one, N1442V, came to California with the purchase of the airline by Ed Daly and is seen at Oakland in August 1953. At least 48 nonscheduled companies flew C-46s at Oakland, including AAXICO, Aero Coach, Air America, Air Cargo Express, Air Services, ATA, All-American, American Air, Arctic-Pacific, Argonaut, AAT, California Air Freight, Capitol, Caribbean-American, Central, and Coastal Cargo.

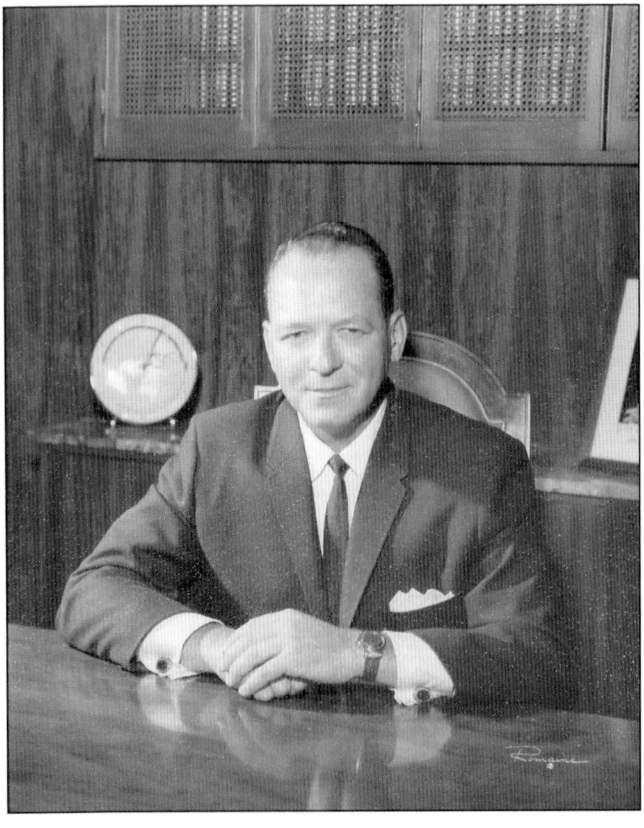

Edward J. Daly built a small two-plane company in New Jersey into a worldwide intercontinental cargo and passenger airline with extensive Military Air Transport Service contracts for military personnel and cargo as World Airways. He retired as president in 1982 after 36 years managing the expanding airline.

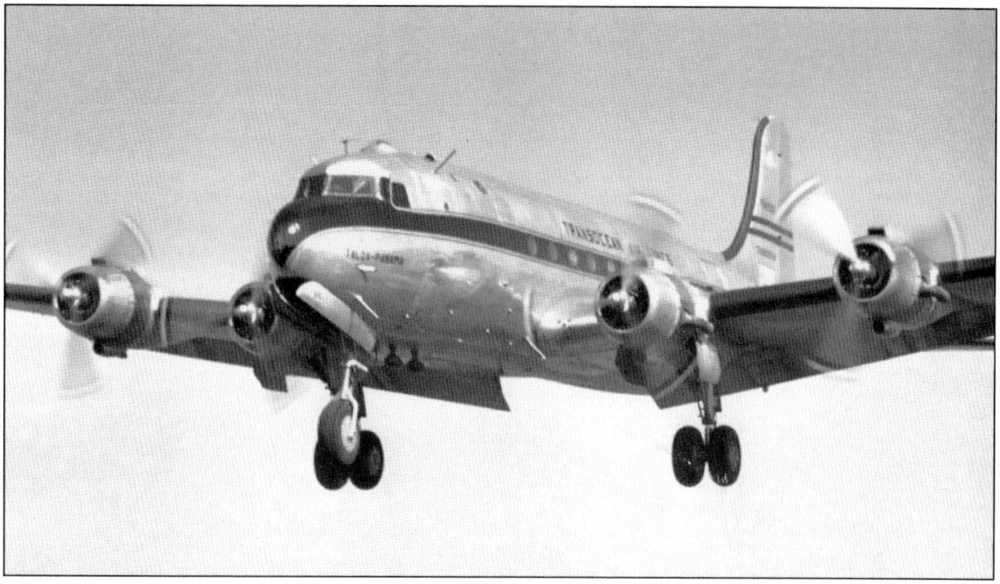

Pictured is Transocean Airlines Douglas DC-4 (N 90915) *Taloa-Panama* landing at Oakland in March 1951. Transocean, also known as TALOA, flew 68 different DC-4s and one DC-6B during its existence.

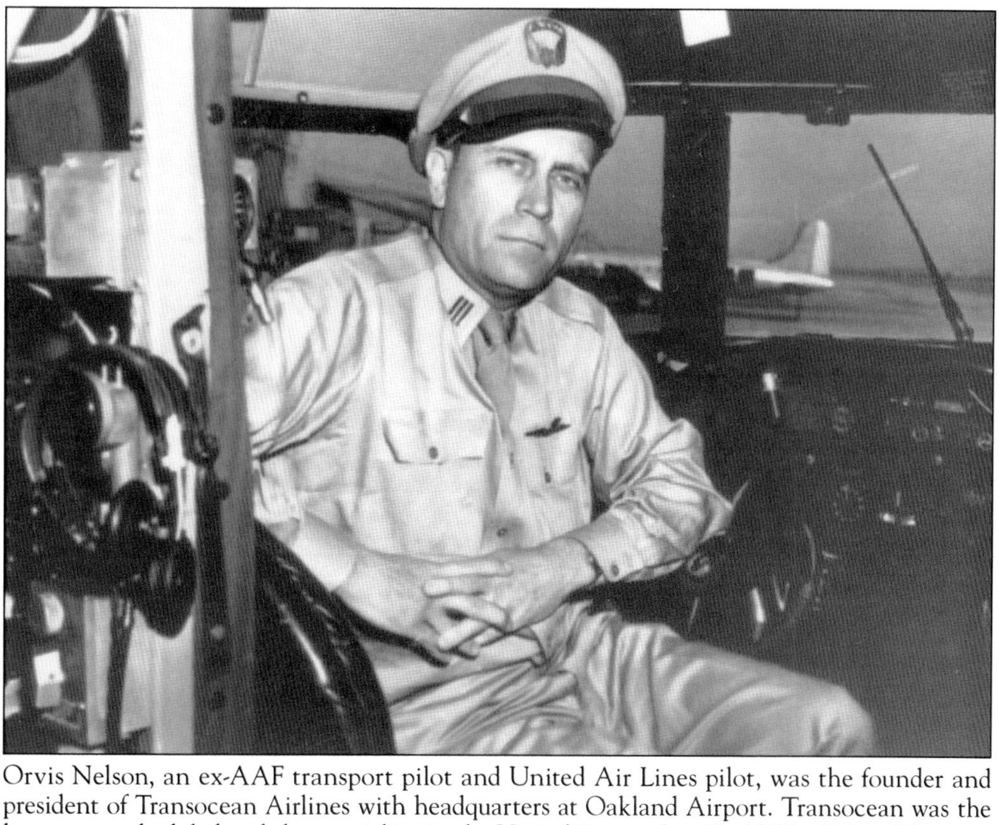

Orvis Nelson, an ex-AAF transport pilot and United Air Lines pilot, was the founder and president of Transocean Airlines with headquarters at Oakland Airport. Transocean was the largest nonscheduled and charter airline in the United States after World War II. In addition to flying all over the world, the company operated several subsidiaries, including a flight school.

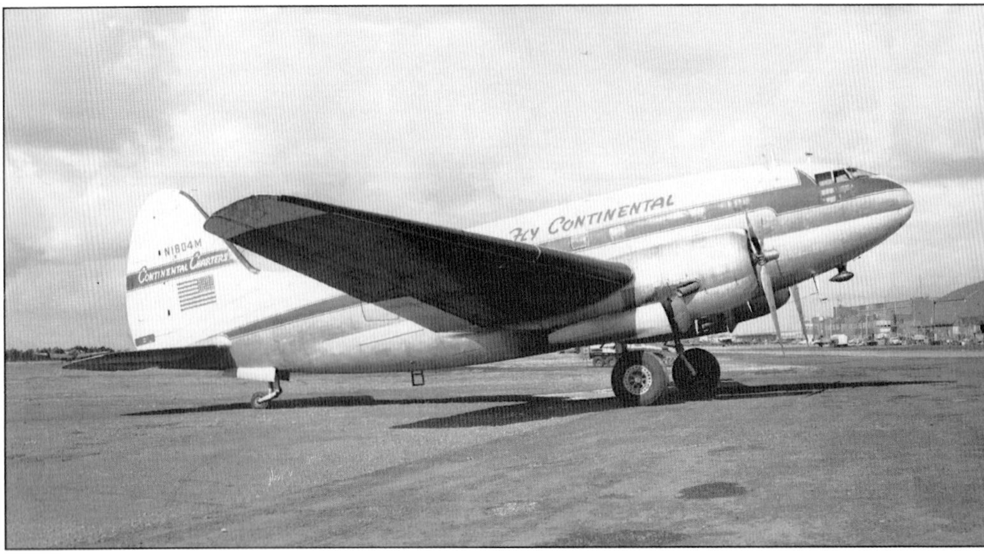

Continental Charters of Miami was one of at least 48 nonscheduled companies that flew C-46s into Oakland in the early 1950s. Others were Conner, Economy Aircoach, Federated, GHEZZI, Golden State, Lake Central, Los Angeles Air Service, Meteor, Miami, Mid-America, Modern, Orion, and Peninsular Air Transport.

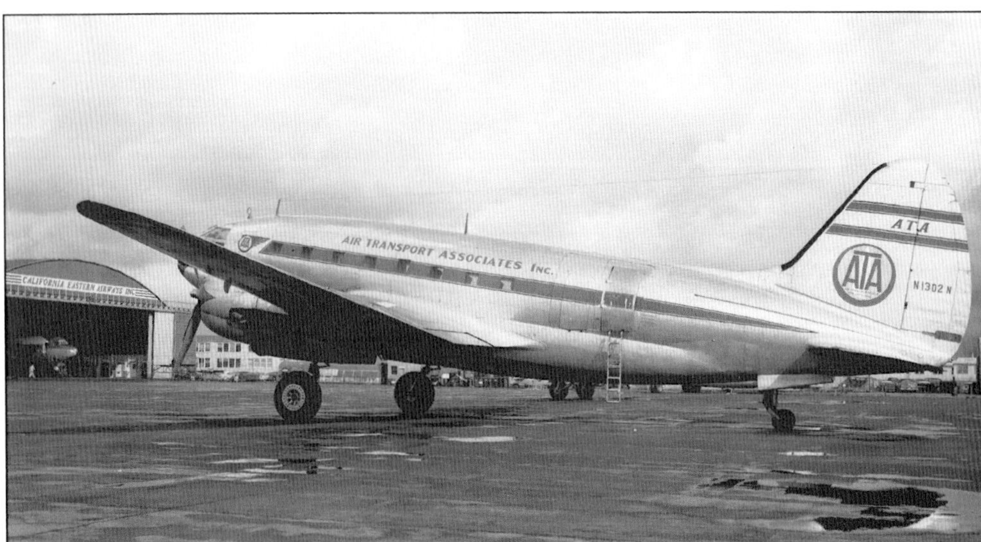

C-46F (N302N) of Air Transport Associates (ATA) from Seattle is pictured in November 1952. Others were Regina Cargo, Resort, Riddle, SSW, Skycoach, Sourdough, South East, Southern, Trans Caribbean, Trans Global, Transocean, Unit Export, U.S. Aircoach, U.S. Airlines, and Viking.

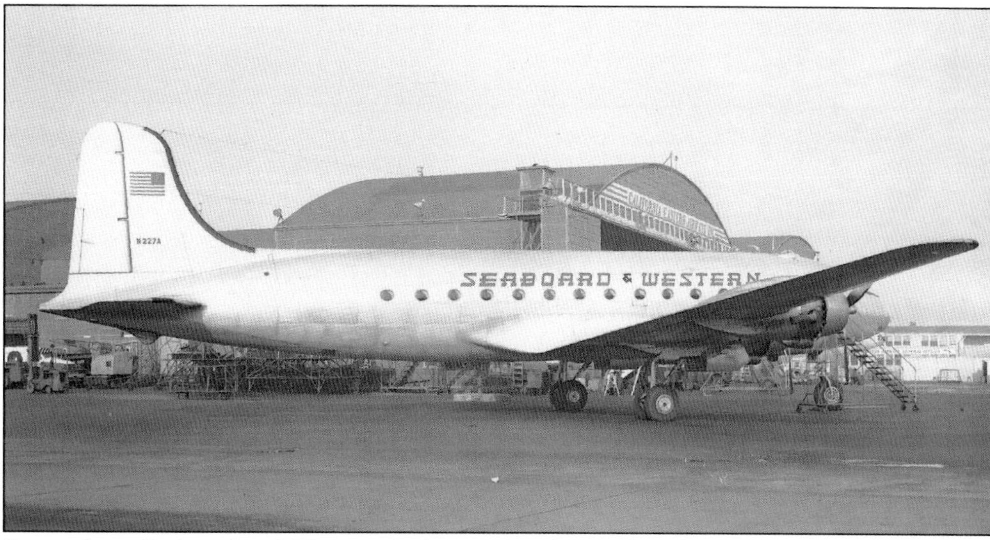

Pictured is a Seaboard and Western Airlines DC-4 (N227A) in front of the California Eastern Airways hangars in November 1953. The plane, a surplus C-54B, was on lease from California Eastern and had been previously operated by Cruizero do Sul in Brazil.

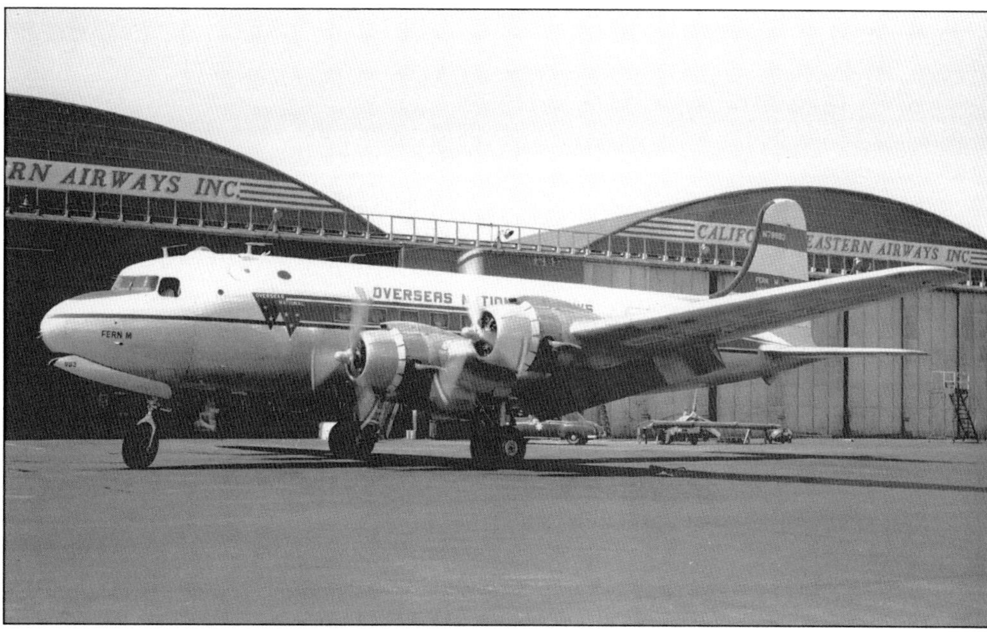

This photograph shows one of the Douglas DC-4s of Overseas National Airlines (ONA) running up in front of the California Eastern hangars in 1952. This one, N79993, was named *Fern M.* ONA was a large passenger charter carrier with additional military contract operations.

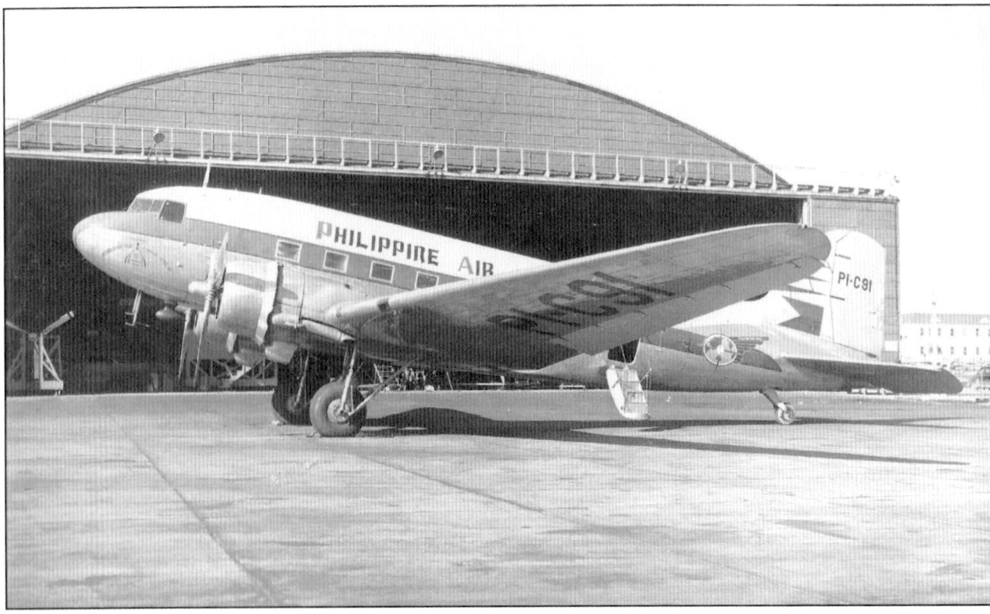

California Eastern and others did overhaul and maintenance work for several airlines. This DC-3 (PI-C91) of Philippine Air Lines (PAL) is ready to return after some work and a fresh paint job. PAL also had DC-4s at Oakland in 1947–1948. Another overhaul was for a DC-4 of AVENSA Venezuela in 1953.

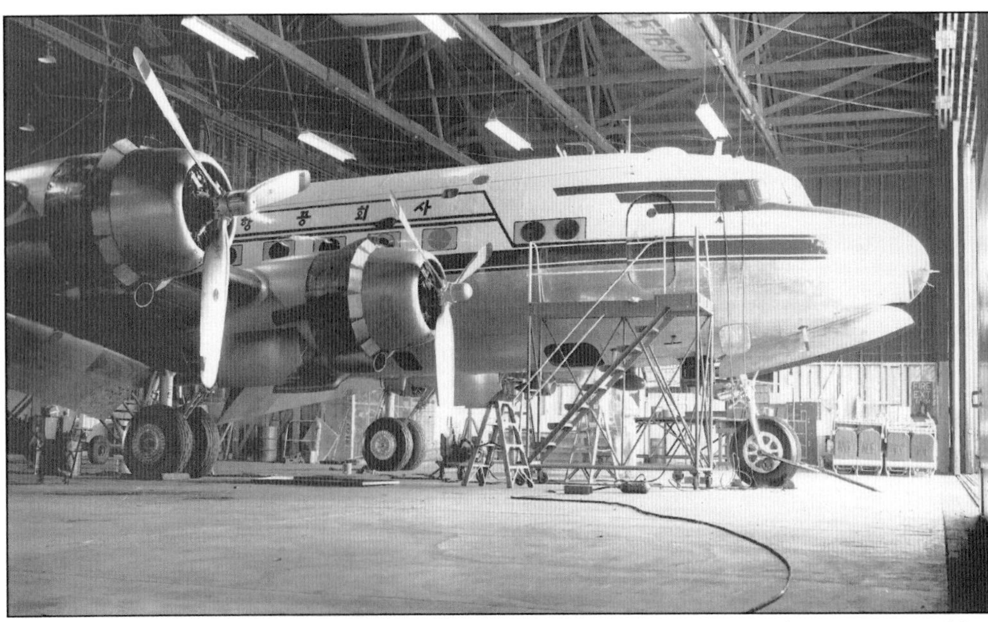

After a complete overhaul and painting, a California Eastern Airlines Douglas DC-4 was sold to Korean National Airlines. The airline name was in English on the left side and Korean on the right side as shown in this photograph ready for delivery in October 1953.

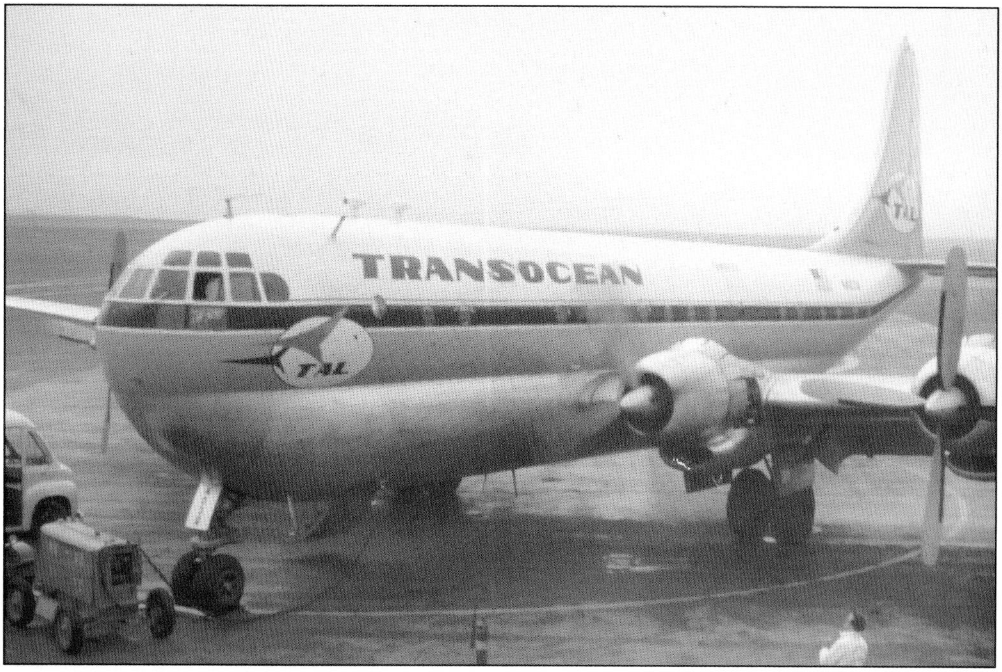

Transocean's Boeing 377 (N403Q) is ready to load at the new Oakland Terminal. It has the last TALOA logo—TAL on the nose—before the airline went out of business as a result of its inability to buy new jet transports and receive government approval for worldwide airline routes in competition with the long-standing companies, such as Pan American Airways.

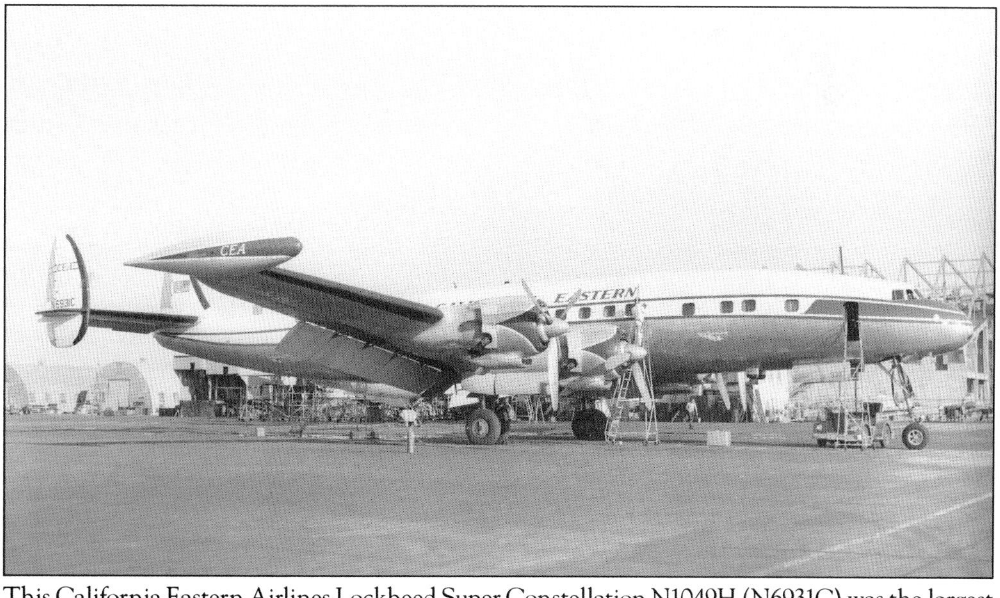

This California Eastern Airlines Lockheed Super Constellation N1049H (N6931C) was the largest type of transport plane to be operated from Oakland by an irregular carrier. This photograph was taken in September 1957. Another 1049H, owned by Dollar Lines, was at Oakland in 1959 for overhaul after being leased to the German airline Lufthansa.

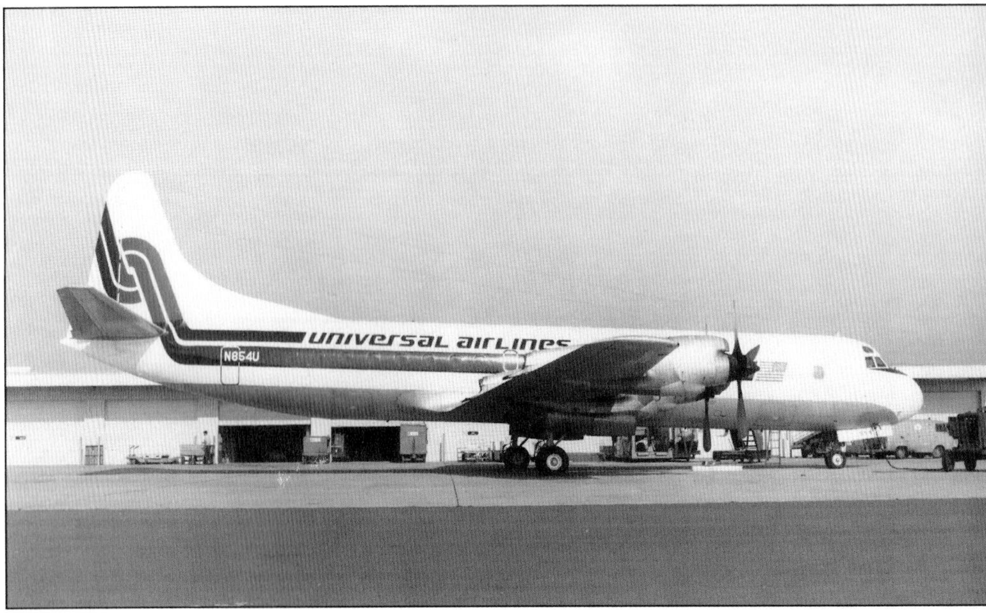

This Lockheed Electra (N854U) of Universal Airlines is an example of the introduction of the turboprop airliner to Oakland. This photograph was taken in February 1971 at the far end of North Field. The first jet service to serve Oakland was a TWA Convair 880 on June 1, 1963. The inaugural flight was from Oakland to Chicago with Robert Murphy, vice chairman of the Civil Aeronautics Board (CAB), and 60 passengers aboard.

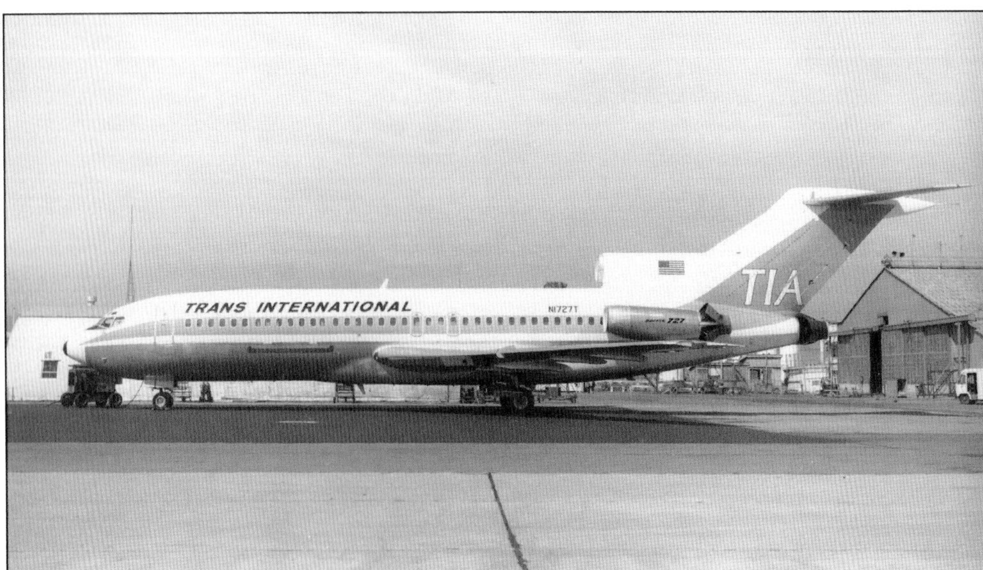

A Trans International Airlines Boeing 727 (N1727T) is pictured at Oakland in August 1968. Hangar 5 can be seen in the background on the right. TIA was a large worldwide cargo and charter passenger service at Oakland with additional military contract flights. Aircraft types in addition to the 727 included the Boeing 747, Lockheed Constellation, Douglas DC-8, and DC-10.

Five

A New Airport in the Modern Era

Trans International Airlines was founded by Kirk Kerkorian, who in 1960 bought Los Angeles Air Service and later changed the name to Trans-International Airlines. TIA was acquired by Transamerica Corporation in San Francisco in 1968, with its headquarters at Oakland Airport. In 1976, TIA bought Oakland-based Saturn Airways to become the largest nonscheduled airline in the world, and the name was changed in October to Transamerica Airlines. This was the third time a nonscheduled airline based at Oakland became the largest in the word, following Transocean and World.

The Oakland Air Route Traffic Control Center that had been established at Oakland in July 1936, on the second floor of the old control tower, moved to Fremont in 1960. In June 1961, San Francisco and Oakland Helicopter Airlines started their scheduled service covering the Bay Area, with Mike Bagan as president. The airline's best year was 1969, when it carried 320,000 passengers and had 100 flights per day.

In 1960, a 10,000-foot jet runway as well as a new passenger terminal topped with a 10-story control tower were constructed on fill behind a 4.5-mile dike adjacent and to the south on the bay side of old North Field. The new part, called South Field or Oakland Metropolitan International Airport, was dedicated in September 1962 at a cost of $20 million. FedEx and United Parcel Service (UPS) maintain large cargo hubs at Oakland, and Southwest Airlines established one of their major hubs at Oakland in 1989. About 1980, construction began on an Executive Terminal at North Field. Terminal Two, the Lionel J. Wilson Terminal, was dedicated in 1985. In 2004, the 14.3-millionth passenger in a 12-month period passed through Oakland. In the same year, there were 339,163 aircraft movements, making Oakland the 30th busiest airport in the country. FedEx and UPS maintain large cargo hubs at Oakland, and Southwest Airlines established one of theirs at Oakland in 1989.

On March 17, 1964, Joan Merriam Smith made the first solo equatorial flight around the world, leaving from and returning to Oakland, in a twin-engine Piper Apache. On June 9, 1967, Ann Pellegreno took off from Oakland in a Lockheed 10A, similar to Earhart's plane, to duplicate her flight. She arrived back at Oakland on July 7 to be greeted by a group that included Vivian Maata (Earhart's secretary) and Glenn Plymate. On March 17, 1997, Linda Finch flew a Lockheed 10 in another commemorative flight, arriving back at Oakland on May 28 to be met by a large crowd and a dinner at the Western Aerospace Museum.

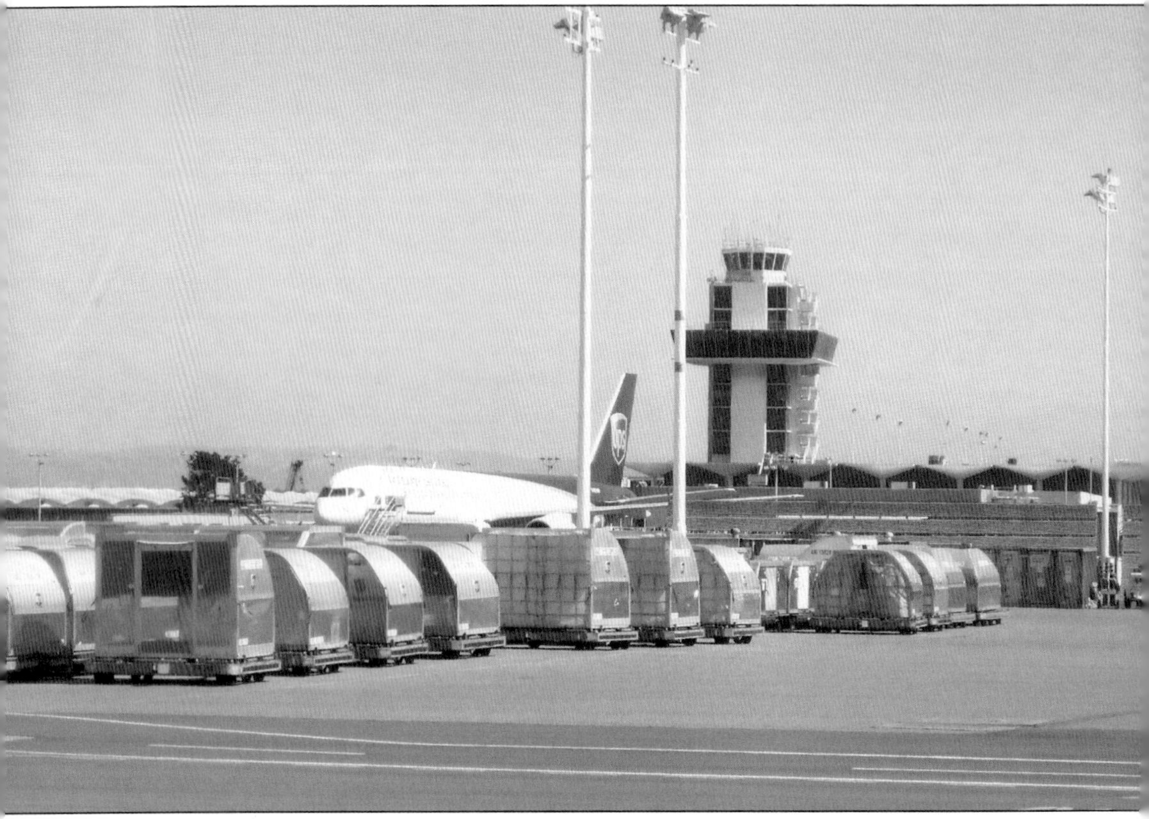

UPS opened a large cargo operation at Oakland in 1975, and it has grown larger since then. It is now second only to FedEx in size, larger than others such as Airborne Express, DHL, Emery Worldwide, and Kitty Hawk. This photograph shows some of the UPS cargo containers, a FedEx Boeing 767, and the Oakland Control Tower.

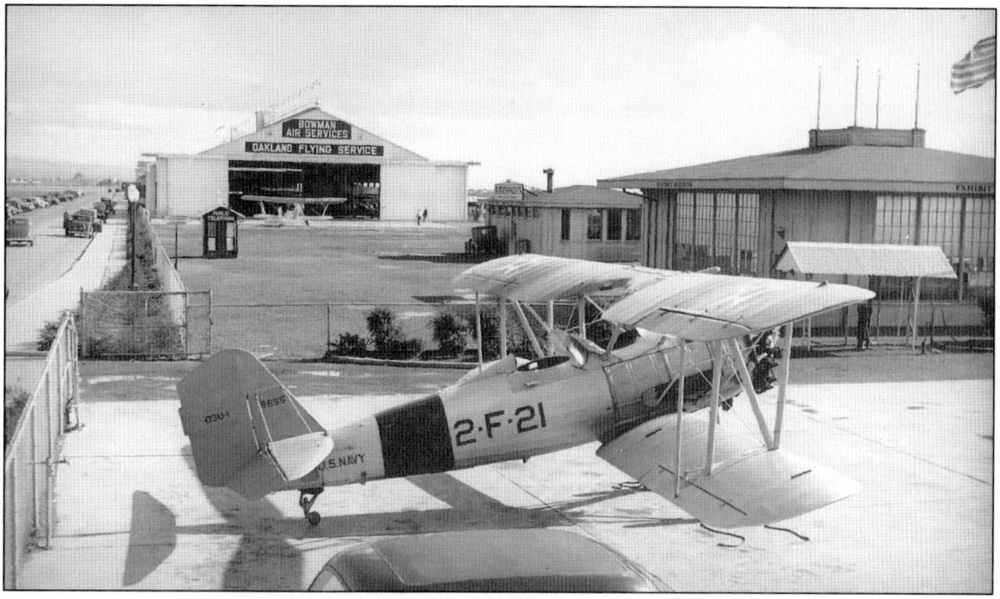

This 1937 photograph shows a visiting Vought O3U-1 (8855), a former U.S. Fleet observation plane now used as an instrument trainer for Fighting Squadron 2, San Diego, and a view looking south toward the exhibit building, coffee shop, and Hangar 2.

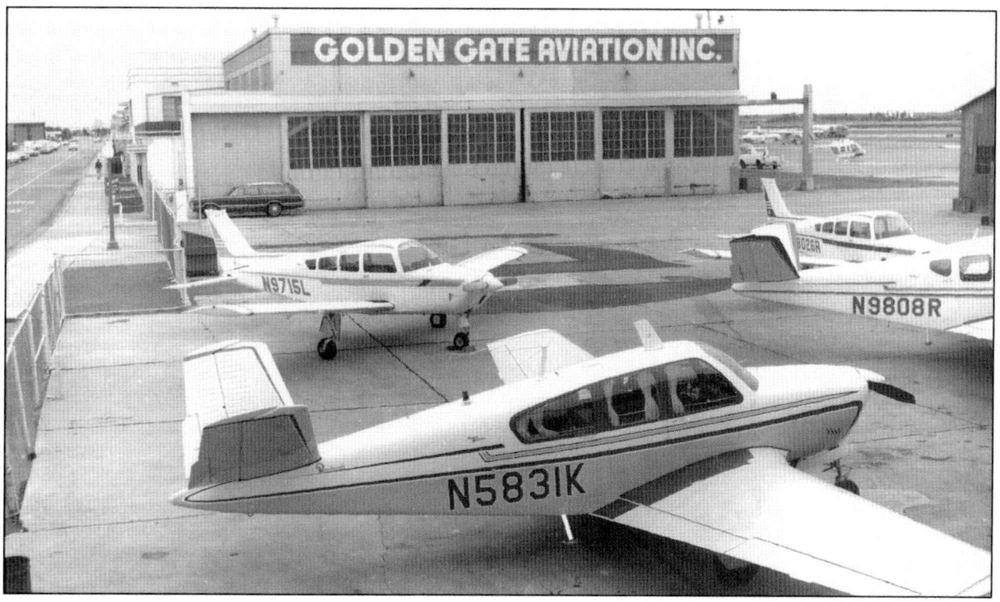

This shows a comparison view of the same area in November 1971. The exhibit building and coffee shop are gone, and a new hangar and repair facility originally built for Pacific Airmotive are in that space. Both photographs were taken from the same place: up on the ladder on the corner of Hangar 3 by coauthor Larkins.

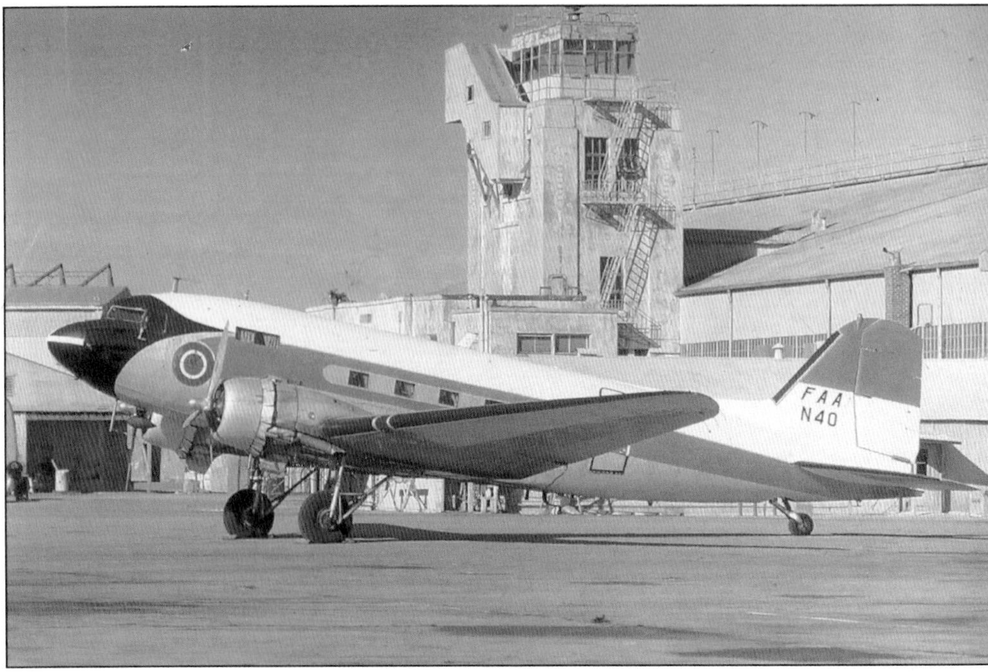

This Federal Aviation Administration (FAA) Douglas DC-3 (N40) was one of several DC-3s operated from Oakland by the FAA. The old postwar control tower on the field side of Hangar 5 is in the background.

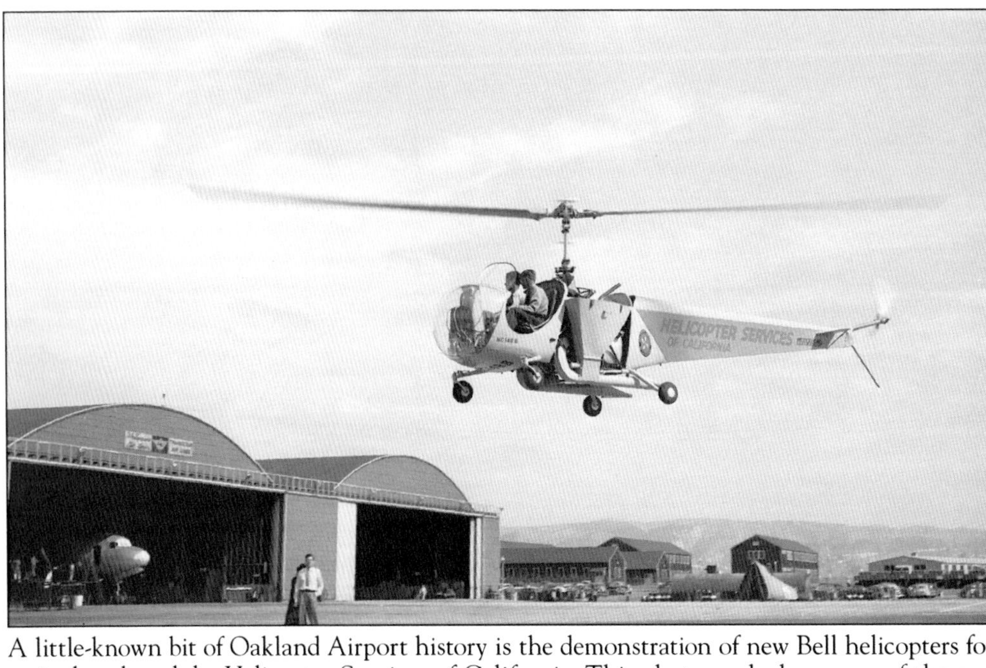

A little-known bit of Oakland Airport history is the demonstration of new Bell helicopters for agricultural work by Helicopter Services of California. This photograph shows one of them, a Bell 47-B3 (N148B) with side tanks for seeding.

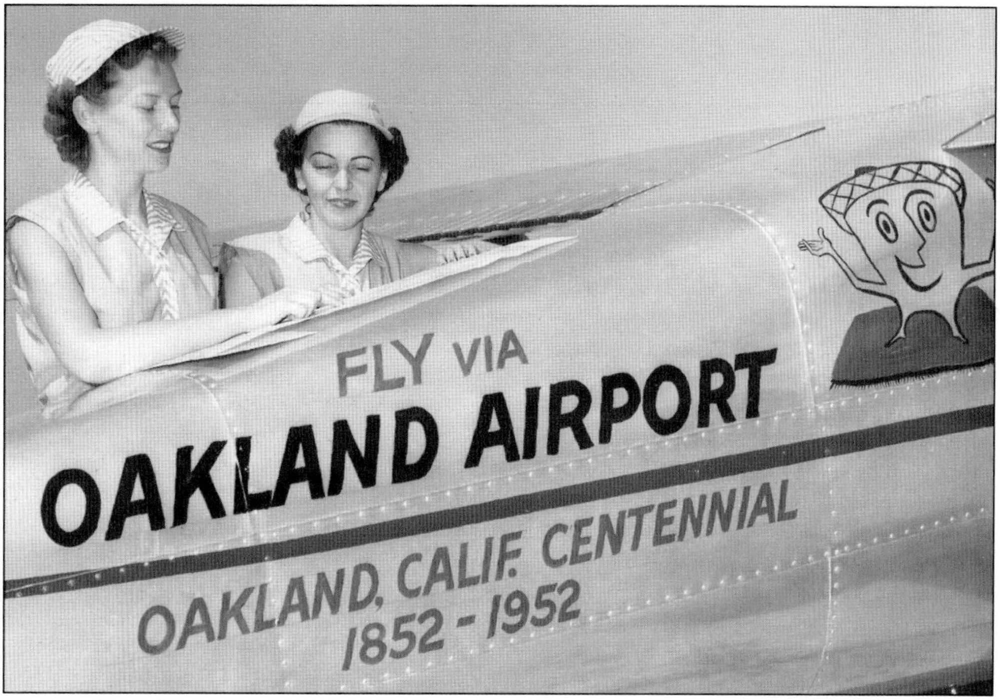

The Powder Puff Derby, an annual cross-country race later named the All Women Transcontinental Air Race (AWTAR), involved female pilots from Oakland. This photograph shows Lindy Boyes (left) and Margaret Callaway with their Cessna 120 about to fly in the July 1952 race from Santa Ana, California, to Teterboro, New Jersey. The 1962 race was from Oakland to Wilmington, Delaware.

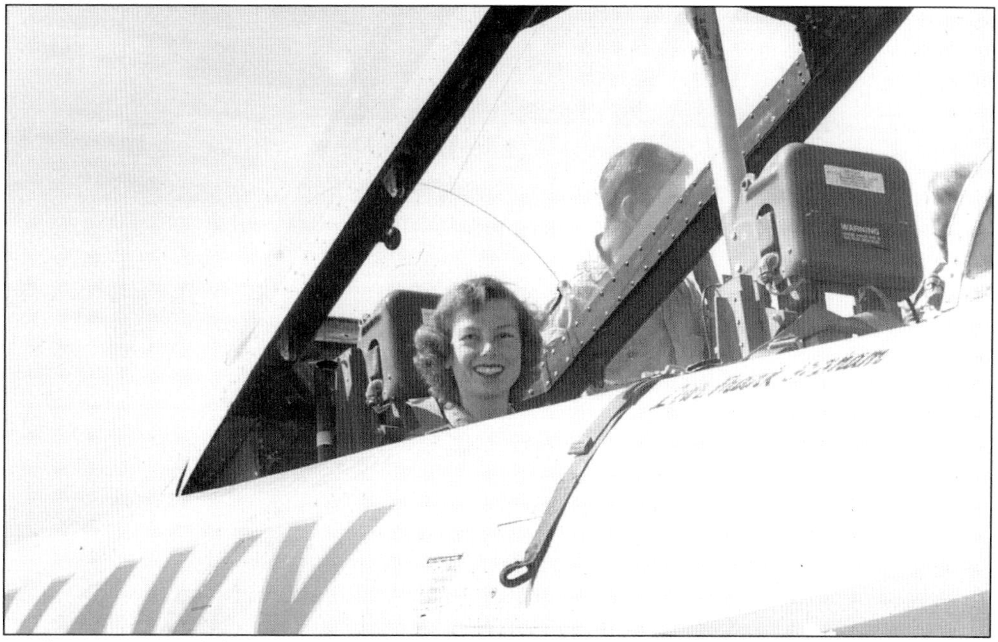

Lindy Boyes, one of the AWTAR pilots, was also an aviation writer for the *Oakland Tribune* and as such was able to get an orientation press flight in the Blue Angels Lockheed TV-2 when they were at Oakland for one of their several visits.

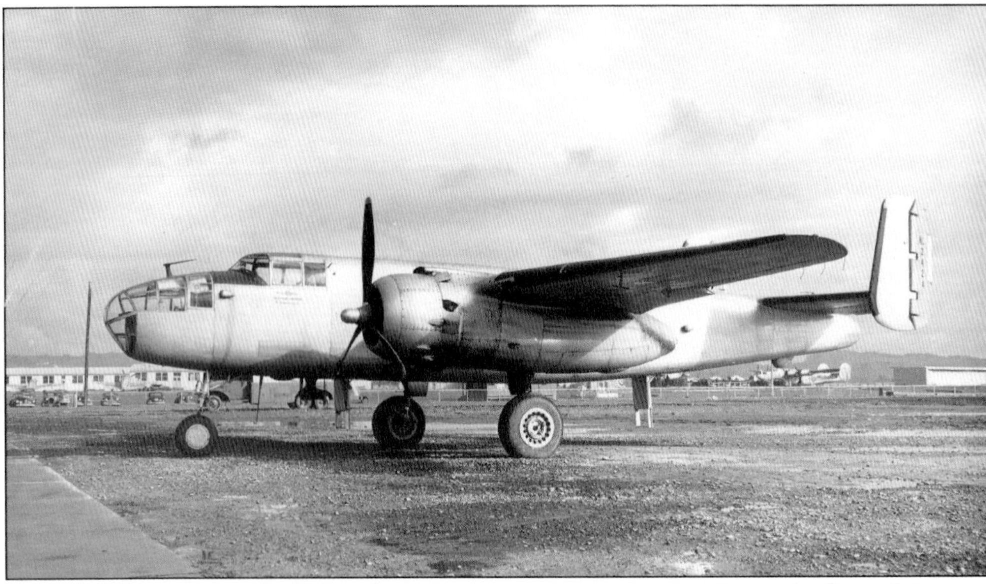

The Shell Oil Company had a long history of promoting aviation and owned a fleet of planes in the 1930s. This North American B-25J (N2424) was operated by Shell Oil at the end of the war. As Jimmy Doolittle was the head of their aviation division, it is believed that he flew this B-25 at some time. The legend on the nose reads, "SHELL FLYING LABORATORY For Aviation Research." This photograph was taken on December 20, 1947. Shell Oil also did fuel research with the USAF Douglas XB-26F operating out of Oakland Airport in 1949.

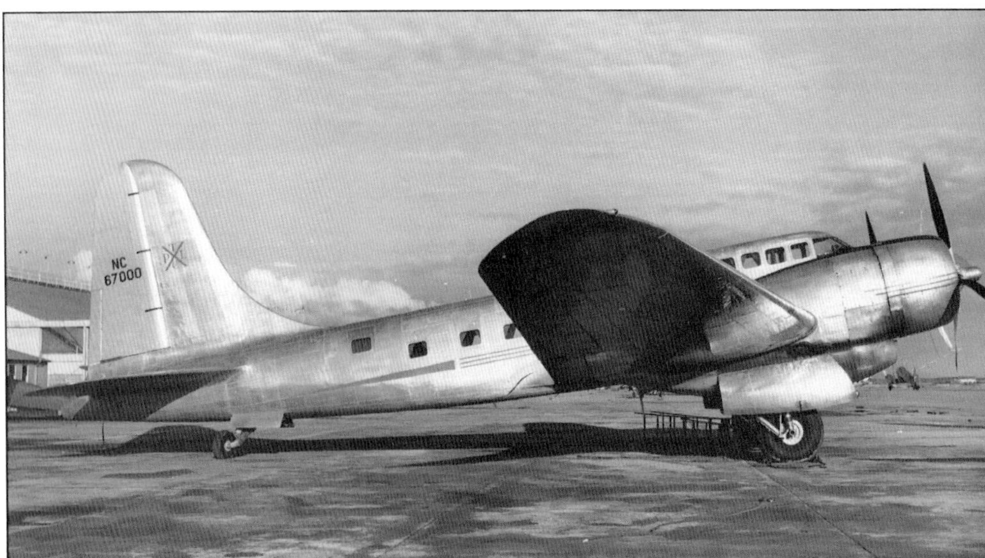

This Douglas B-23 (N 67000), owned by the Pacific Lumber Company in 1946, is representative of a number of surplus World War II planes that were converted into executive transports in the immediate postwar period. Standard Oil of California also flew a B-23 from Oakland.

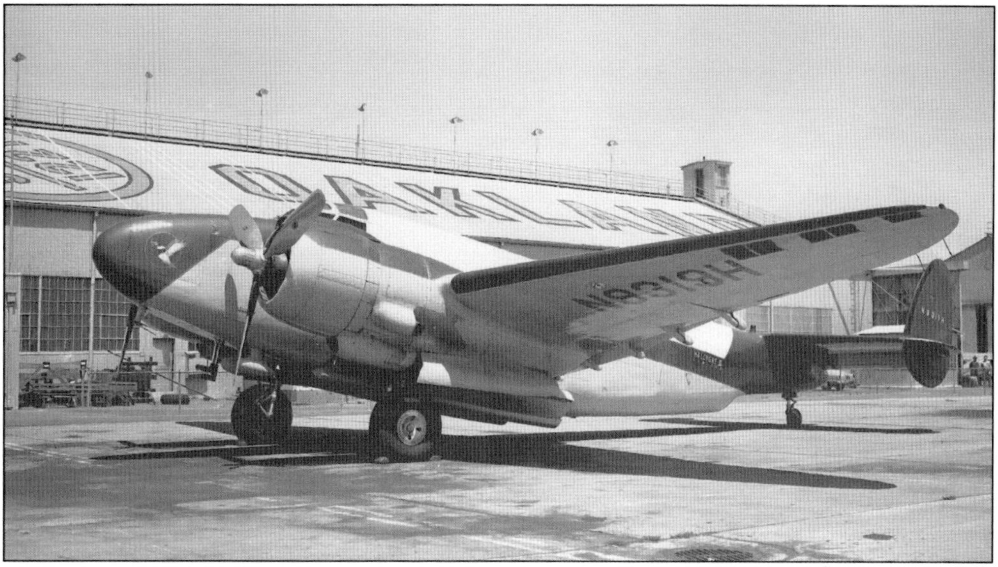

This war surplus navy Lockheed PV-1 Ventura bomber (N9319H) was modified as an executive transport and owned by the Henry J. Kaiser Company, who named it *Halcyone II.* The photograph was taken in October 1954, when Oakland was proud to have its name on Hangar 2. The Bechtel Construction Company operated two Lockheed 18s from Oakland for many years.

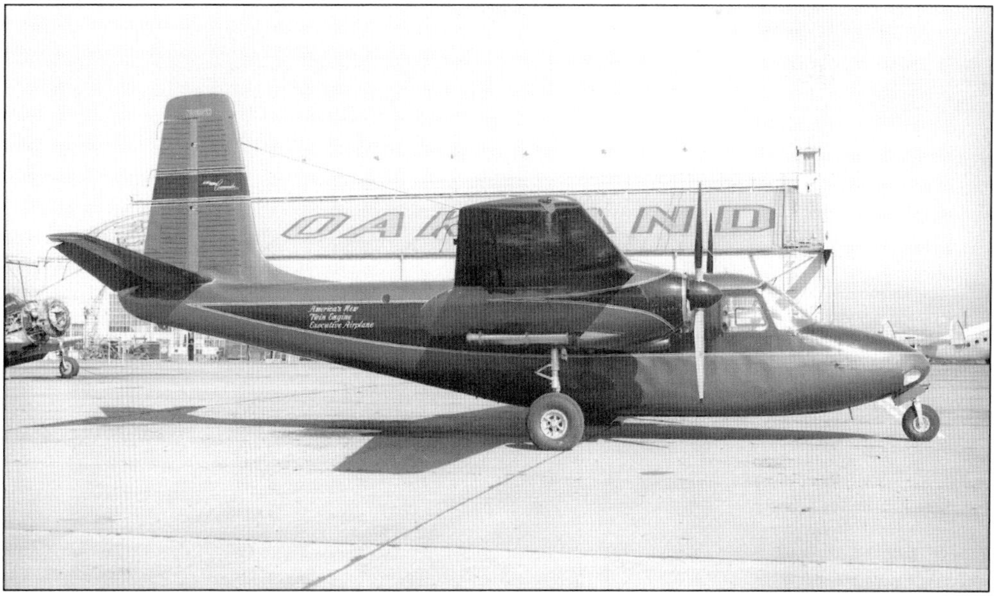

New aircraft to replace the small war surplus transports were slow to come, but by the 1950s, changes were under way. This new Aero Commander 520 (N2608B) is the example seen in February 1954. The logo on the side reads, "America's New Twin Engine Executive Airplane."

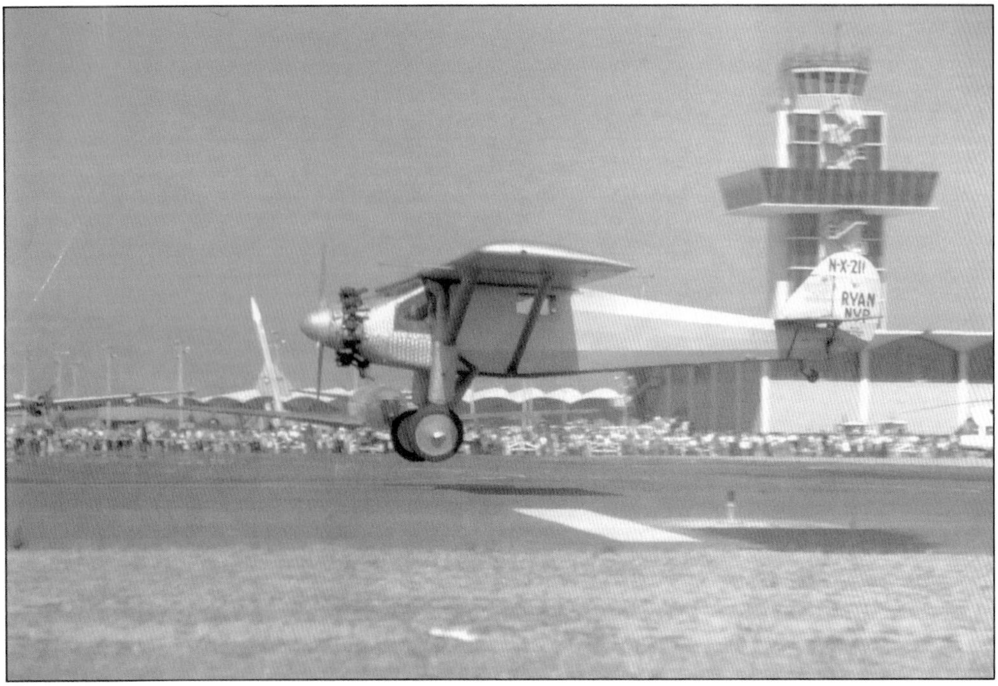

The opening of the new passenger terminal in September 1962 was celebrated by a two-day public show that included many of the Tallmantz planes from Santa Ana. Their Ryan NYP replica, shown flying by the crowd and new terminal, was a fitting tribute since Lindbergh had dedicated the airport in 1927.

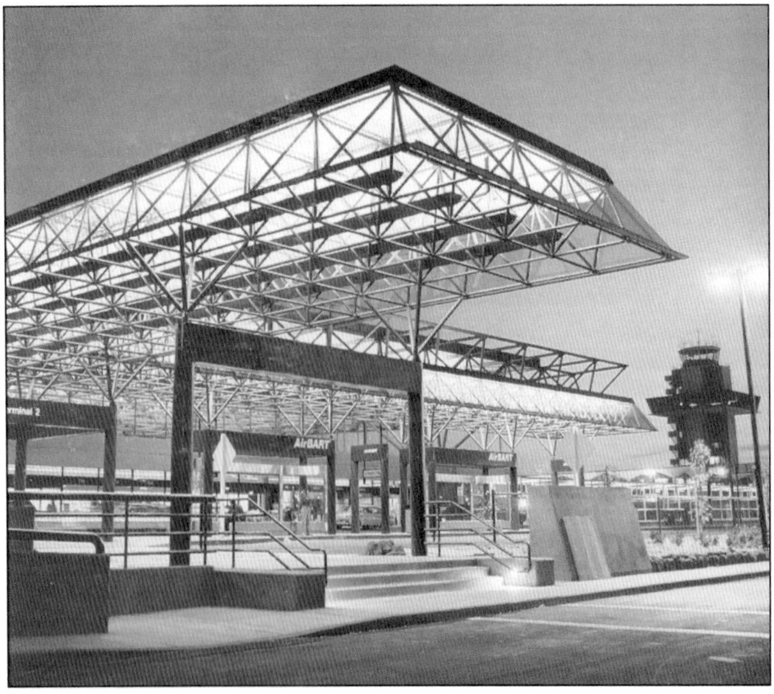

A further new addition to the terminal opened in 1985. Named the Lionel J. Wilson Terminal and designed by Ratcliff Architects, it was built to handle the high-volume traffic generated by Pacific Southwest Airlines and Air California.

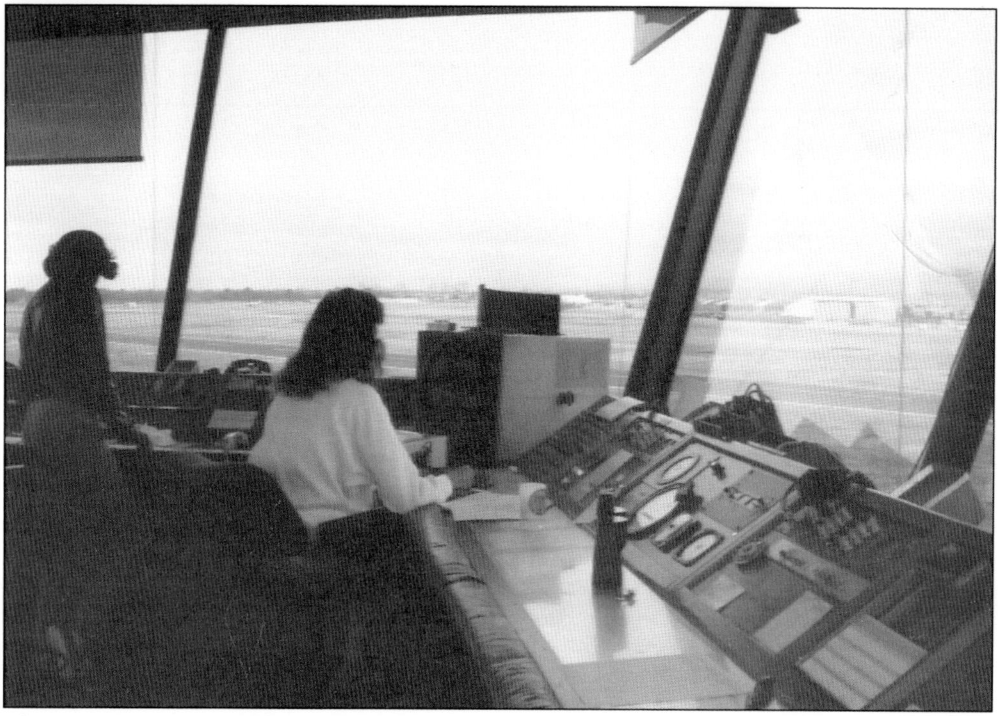

This is a view of controllers inside the current North Field Control Tower between North Field runways 27L and 27R and the new cargo area of the main Oakland International Airport area. It controls aircraft traffic taking off and landing on these two runways from 5:00 a.m. to 10:00 p.m.

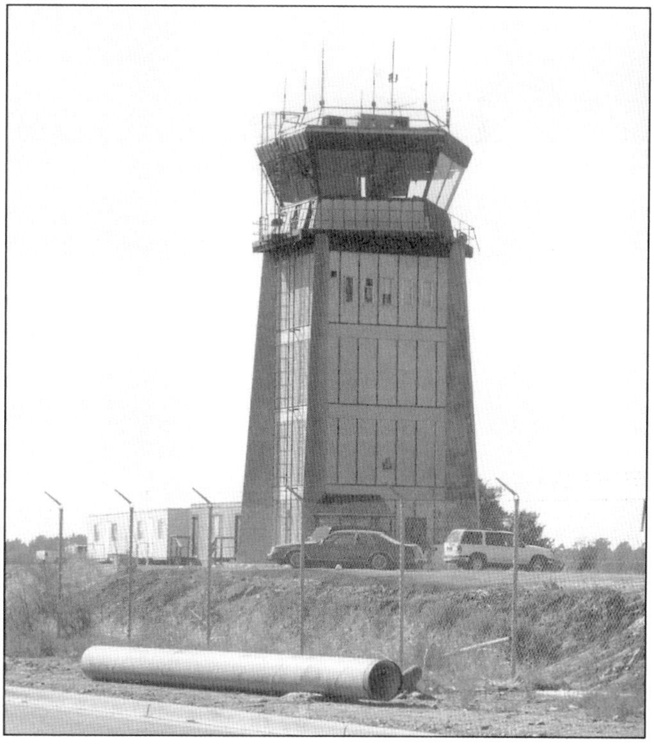

An exterior view shows the North Field Control Tower, built in 1973 as a result of the new large World Hangar obstructing the view of the first 1,200 feet of runways 27L and 27R from the main air traffic control tower on the airport terminal. A 20-story tower is planned for the future near the FedEx complex; when this is completed, the North Field tower will close.

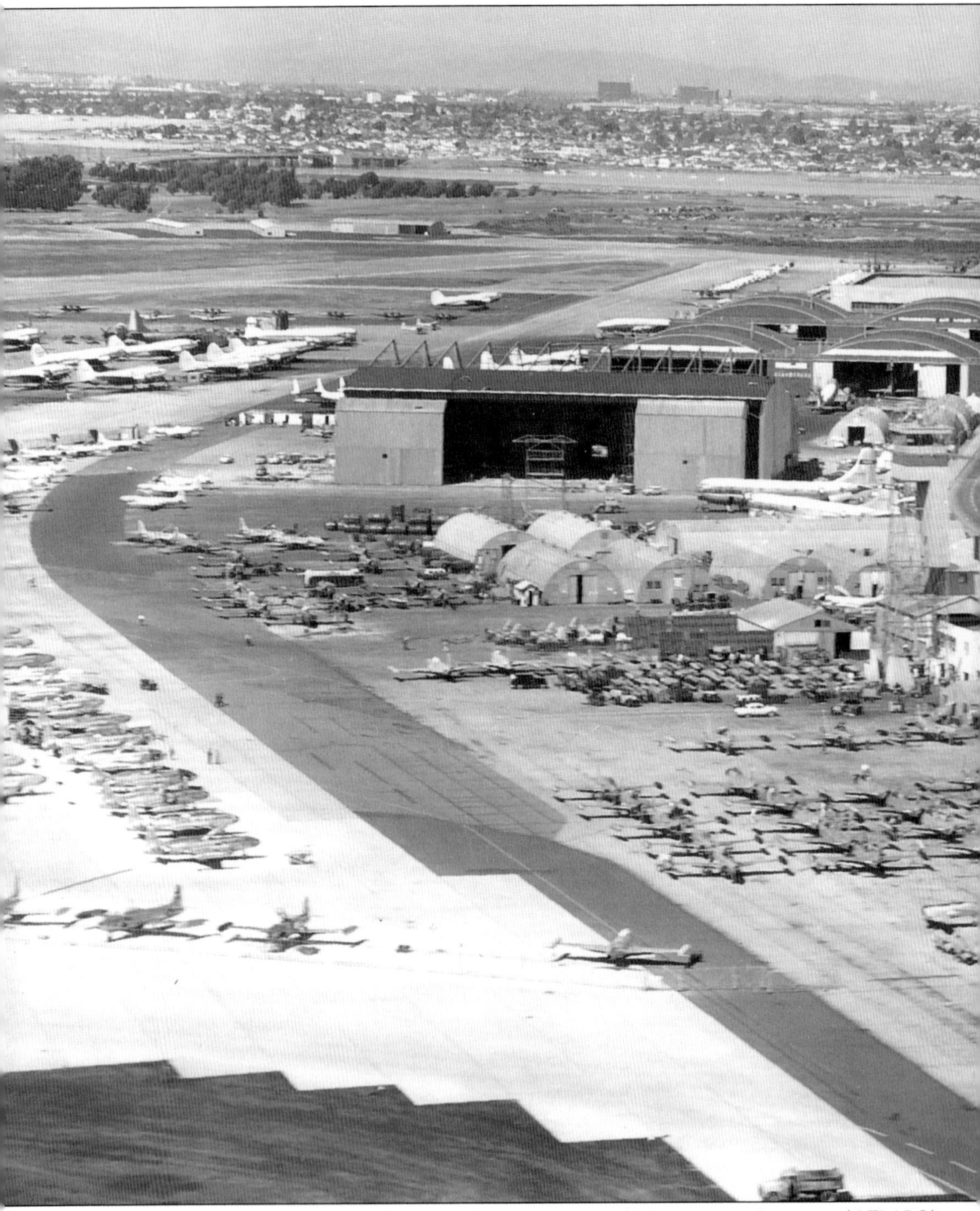

A fascinating aerial view includes the Aircraft Engineering and Maintenance Company (AEMCO) overhaul operation at its peak plus some of the surrounding area in August 1953. Hangar 5, with the control tower, is in the center of the photograph and was being used by AEMCO for an assembly line. The planes in the center and to the left are Lockheed T-33A two-place advanced jet trainers. There are two Boeing C-97s near the large AEMCO hangar, and the group at the top left shows

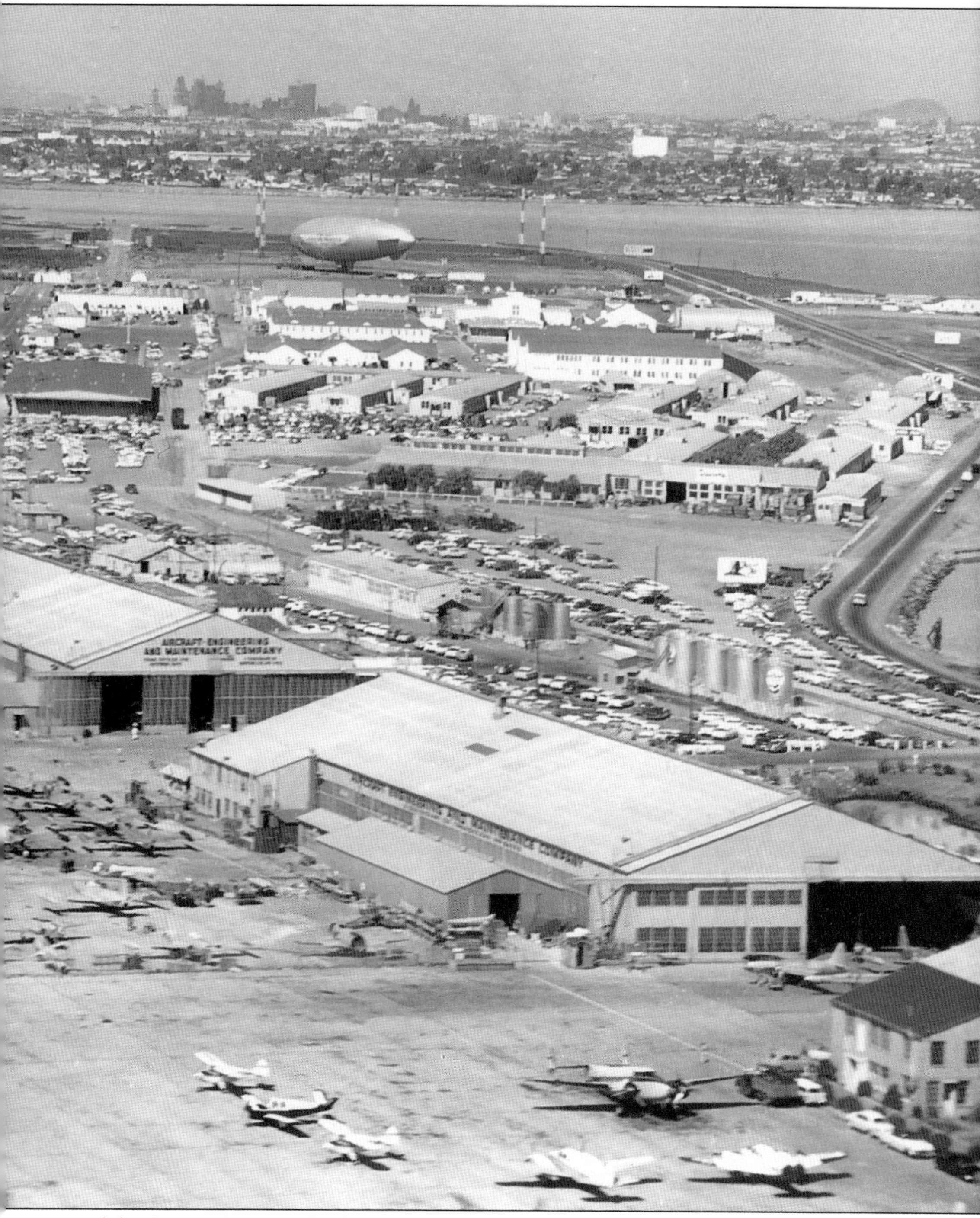

part of the Curtiss C-46 overhaul contract going on at the same time. The long building with the trees in the right center is the hangar being used by the Aero Industries Technical School, now housing the Oakland Aviation Museum. The Naval Reserve blimp is moored just above the buildings in the upper right.

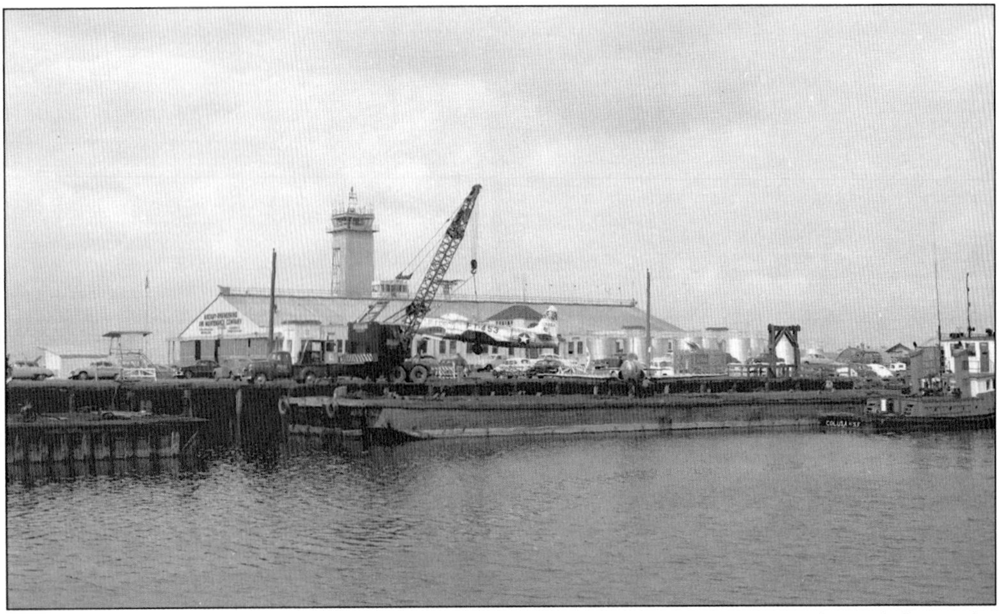

U.S. Air Force aircraft from McClellan Air Force Base in Sacramento were barged down the Sacramento River to the Airport Channel, where they were unloaded by a large crane and then towed to Hangar 5. This July 1955 photograph shows Lockheed F-80B (45-8453) being lifted off the barge.

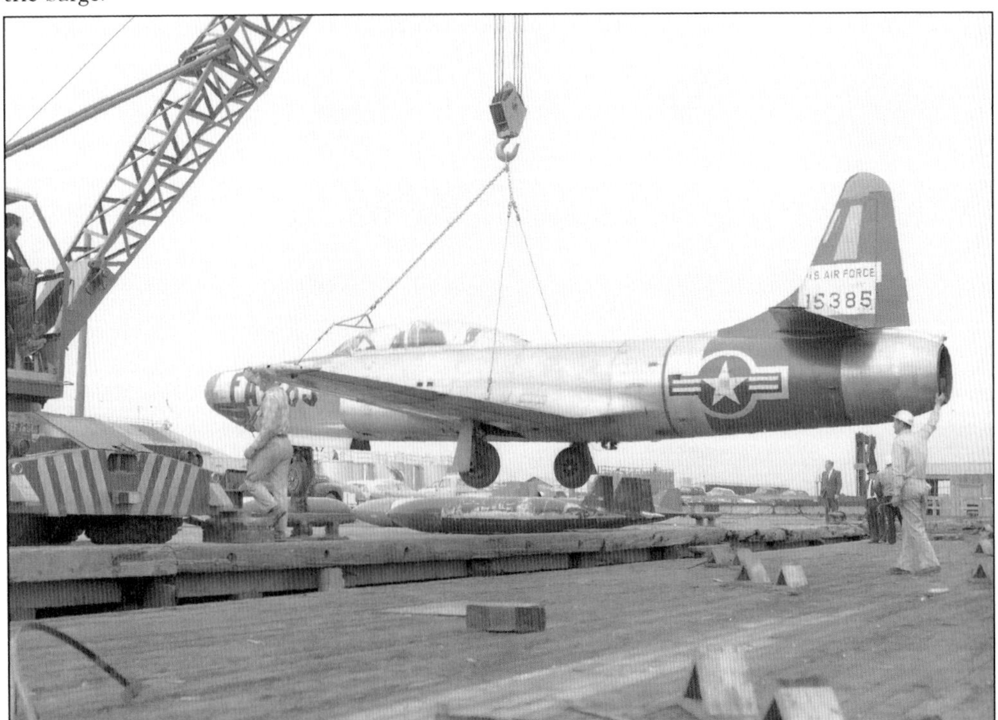

This is a close-up photograph of another type of plane being lifted off the barge in the Airport Channel in March 1955. This is a Lockheed F-94B fighter (51-5385) being brought to AEMCO for overhaul.

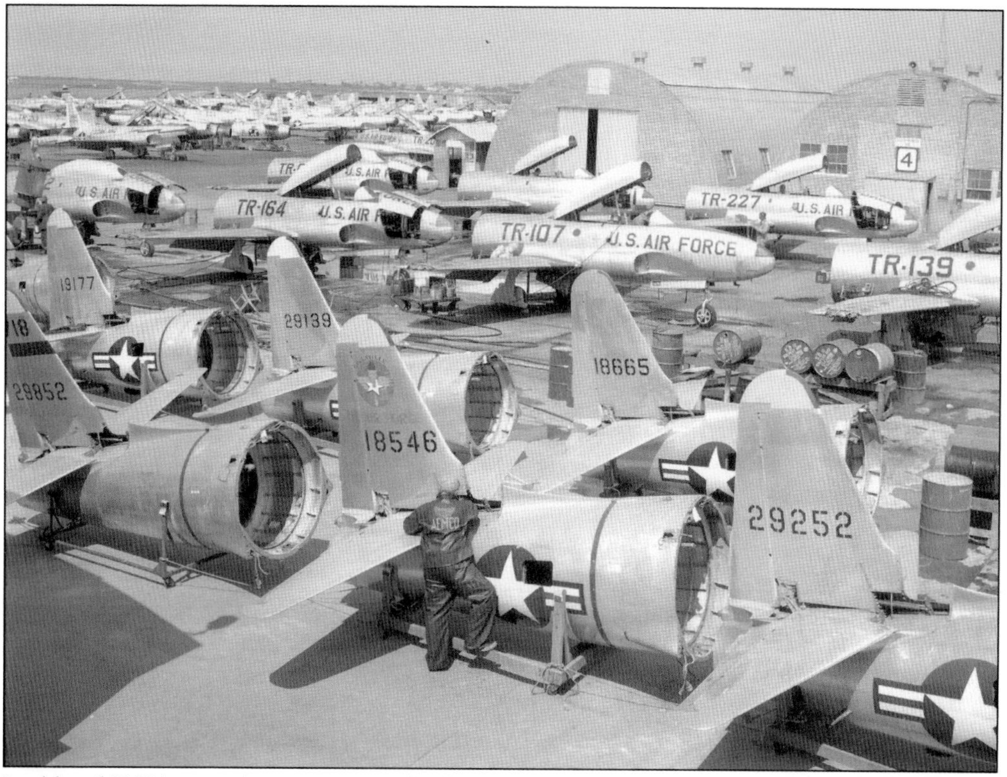

Lockheed T-33A two-place jet trainer fuselages were dissassembled during part of the overhaul and repair program done by AEMCO at North Field. They were reassembled in a production line inside Hangar 1.

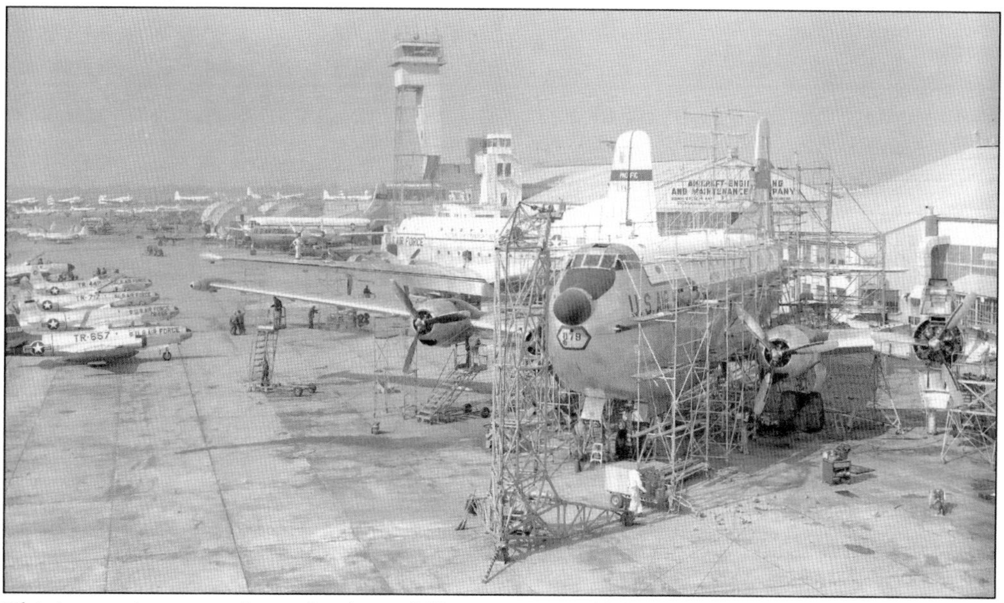

This interesting scene shows the Aircraft Engineering and Maintenance Company outdoor work stands that are necessary because of the size of the large Douglas C-124A transports. Hangar 5 and the Control Tower can be seen in the top center of the photograph.

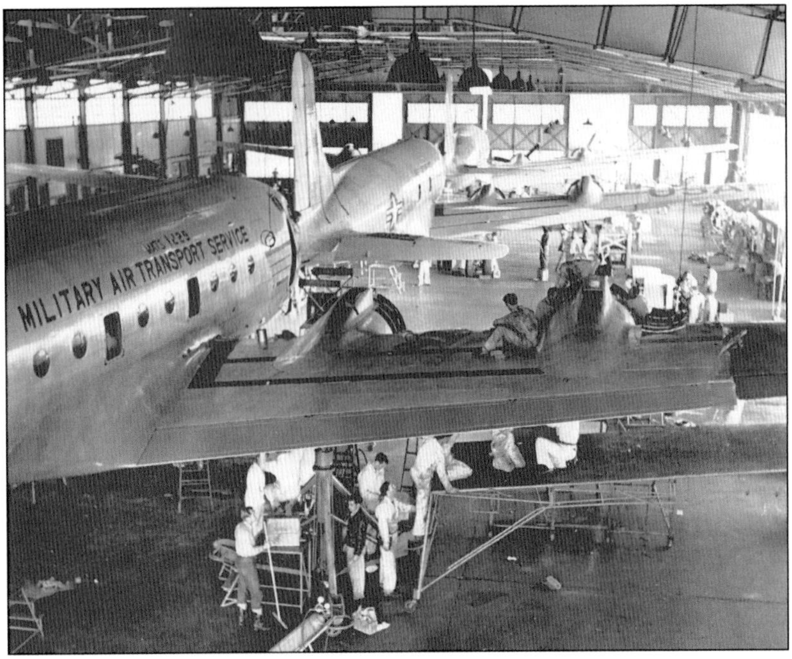

A view of the production line for the Douglas C-54 transports in Hangar 5 is shown here. This was the first large overhaul and repair contract for AEMCO after "Operation Vittles" in the Berlin Air Lift.

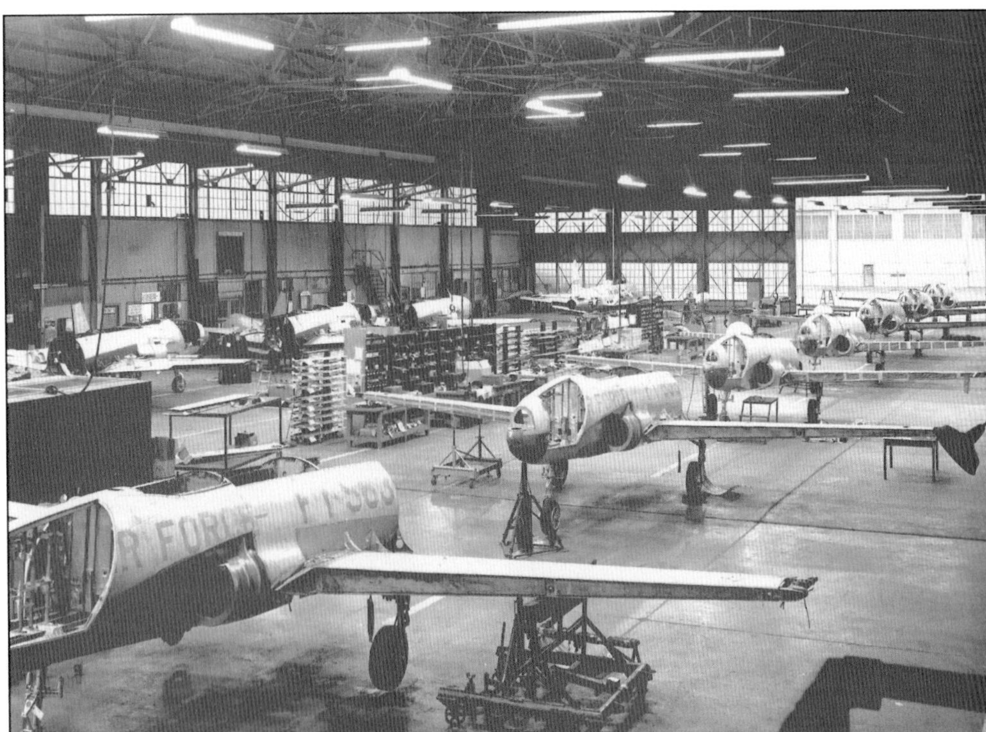

A similar production and assembly line for the Lockheed F-80Cs in Hangar 4 clearly shows the complete disassembly, cleaning and repair, and reassembly ready for flight testing.

Over 500 Douglas C-54 transports were overhauled by AEMCO under multiple contracts from the U.S. Air Force. Many of these were well-worn C-54s that had flown in the Berlin Airlift, and this special one was marked as indicated. One of the biggest problems in this program was cleaning coal dust from the inside of the fuselages because they flew coal as well as food into Berlin.

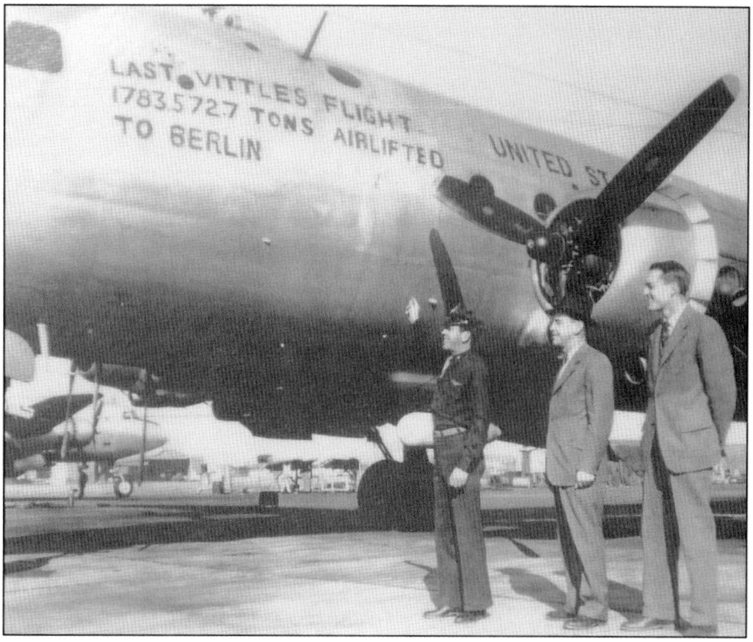

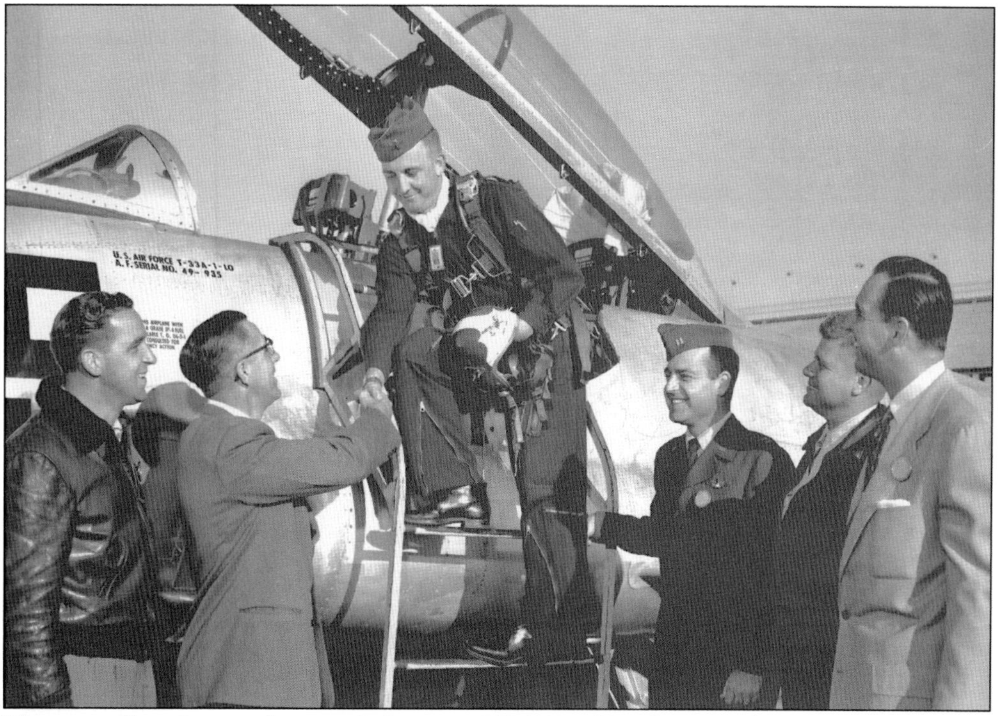

This is a public relations photograph showing a USAF Lockheed T-33A pilot accepting delivery of a newly overhauled plane from Aircraft Engine and Maintenance Company officials at Oakland Airport in 1954.

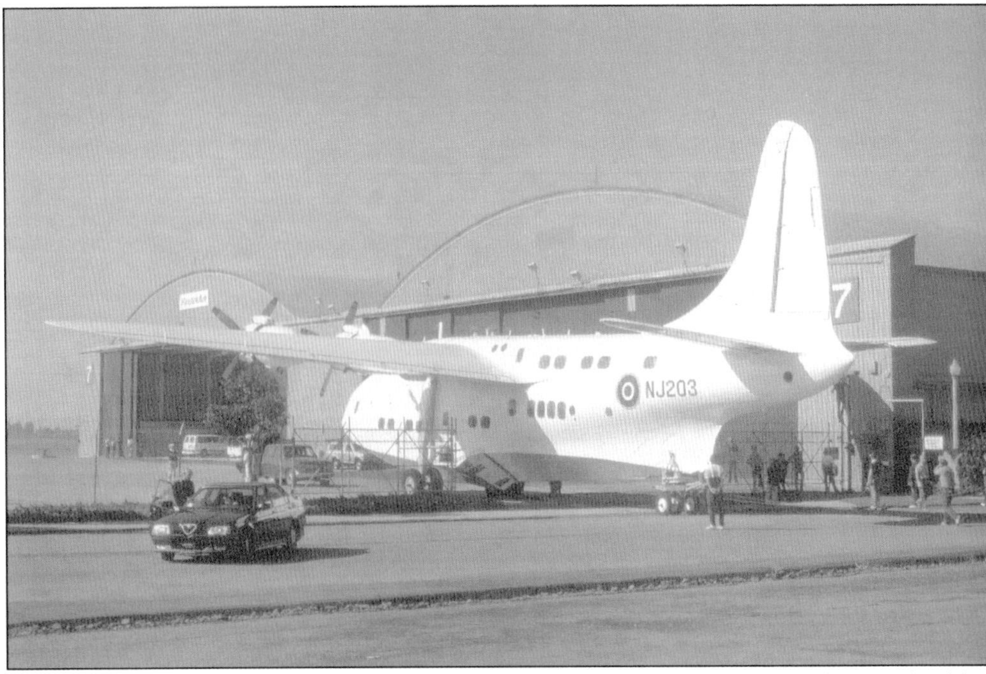

The Short Solent flying boat owned by Rick and Randy Grant is shown being slowly moved tail first through an open gate of the airport fence in November 1990 to bring it from the hangar area to the Western Aerospace Museum (now Oakland Aviation Museum), where it is currently on exhibit.

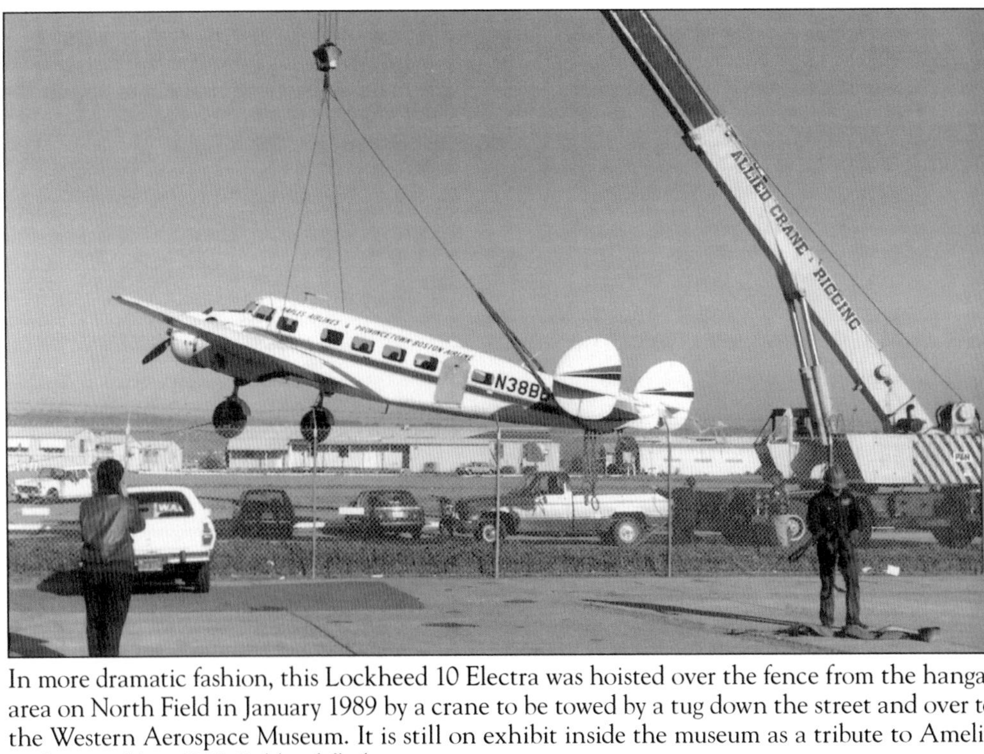

In more dramatic fashion, this Lockheed 10 Electra was hoisted over the fence from the hangar area on North Field in January 1989 by a crane to be towed by a tug down the street and over to the Western Aerospace Museum. It is still on exhibit inside the museum as a tribute to Amelia Earhart and her 1937 Oakland flight.

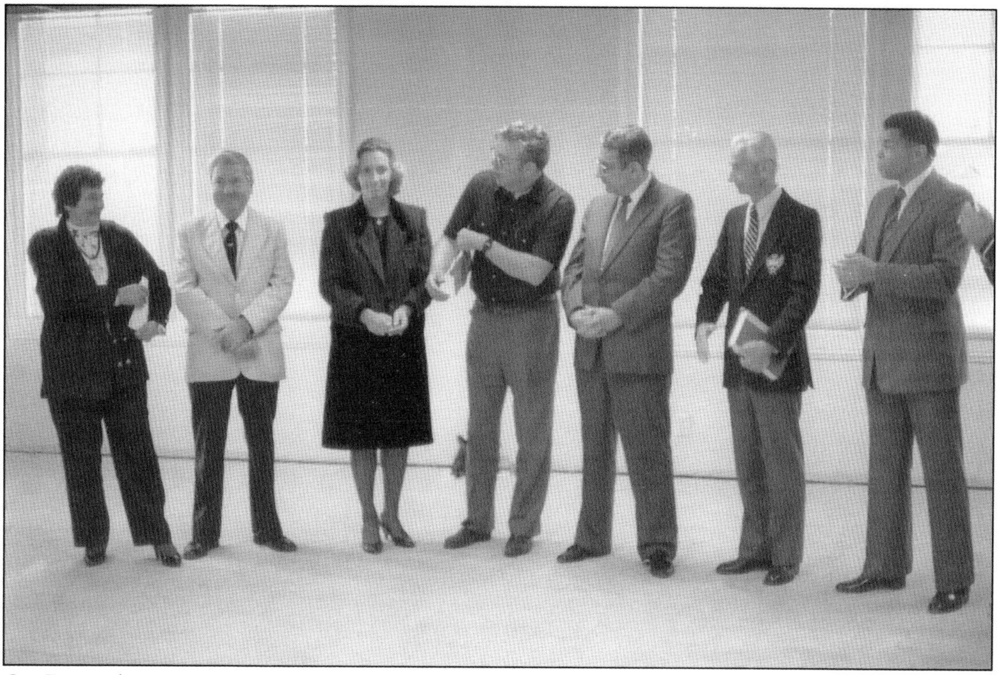

On December 7, 1986, the Western Aerospace Museum (WAM) held a commemoration of the founding of the museum in 1981 in conjunction with the opening of its first facility of one room in historic Hangar 5. From left to right are Marie Long, William Larkins, Louise Hammond, Ronald Reuther, Walter Boyne, Joseph Rebo, and Conway Jones Jr.

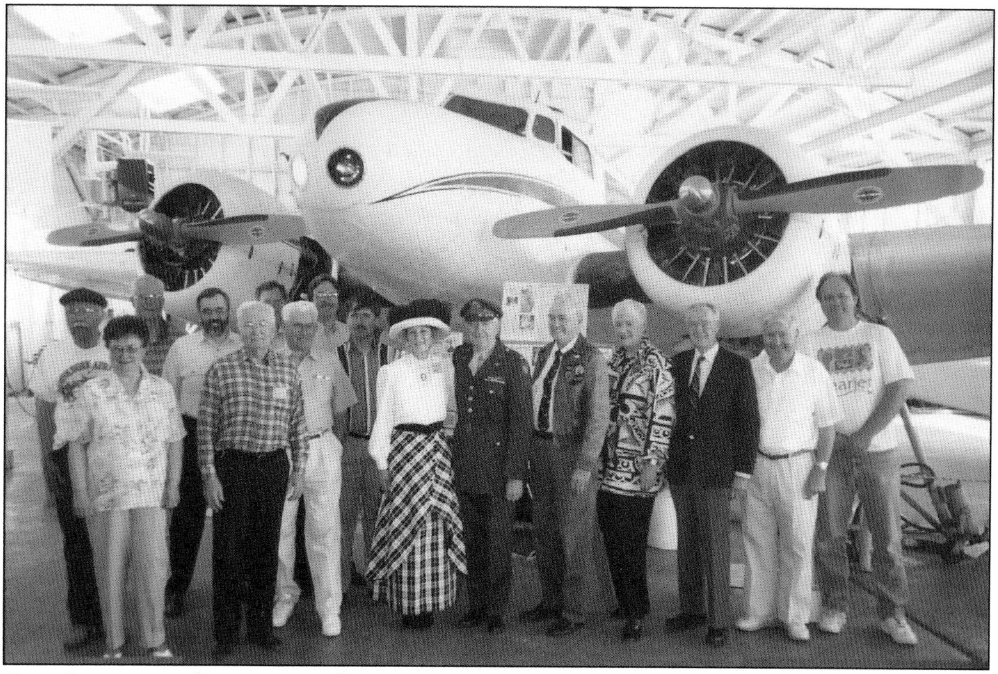

One of many special occasions at the Western Aerospace Museum was a gathering of aviation authors to meet the public in April 1995. This photograph shows the group appropriately posed in front of the historic Lockheed 10 Electra, exhibited by the museum as a tribute to Amelia Earhart.

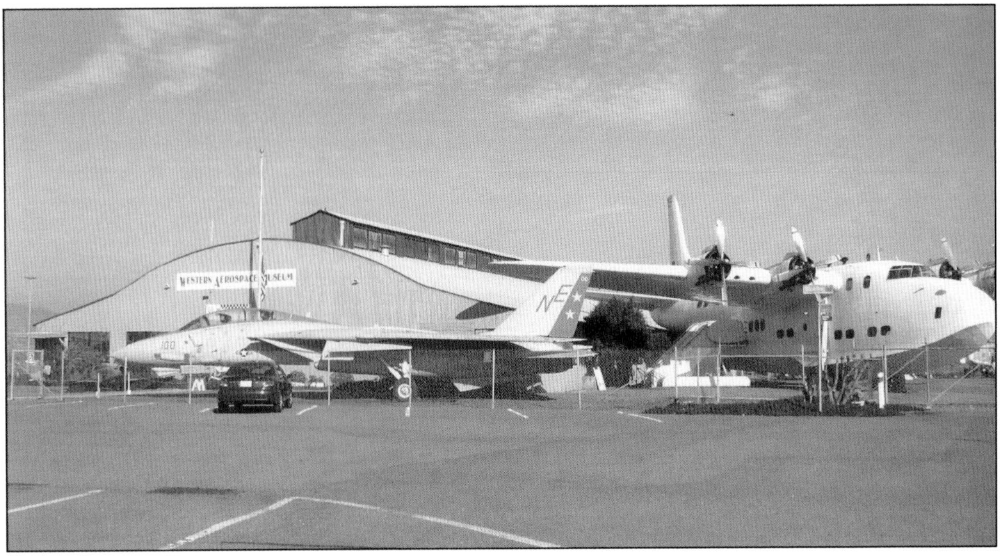

In November 1988, the Port of Oakland made the present home of the Oakland Aviation Museum (WAM at that time) possible by allowing the use of Building 621. This brought together the history of the field, exemplified by the 1940 hangar built for the Boeing School of Aeronautics to train Army Air Corps mechanics, with the space to exhibit aircraft indoors and outside, as shown in this more recent photograph.

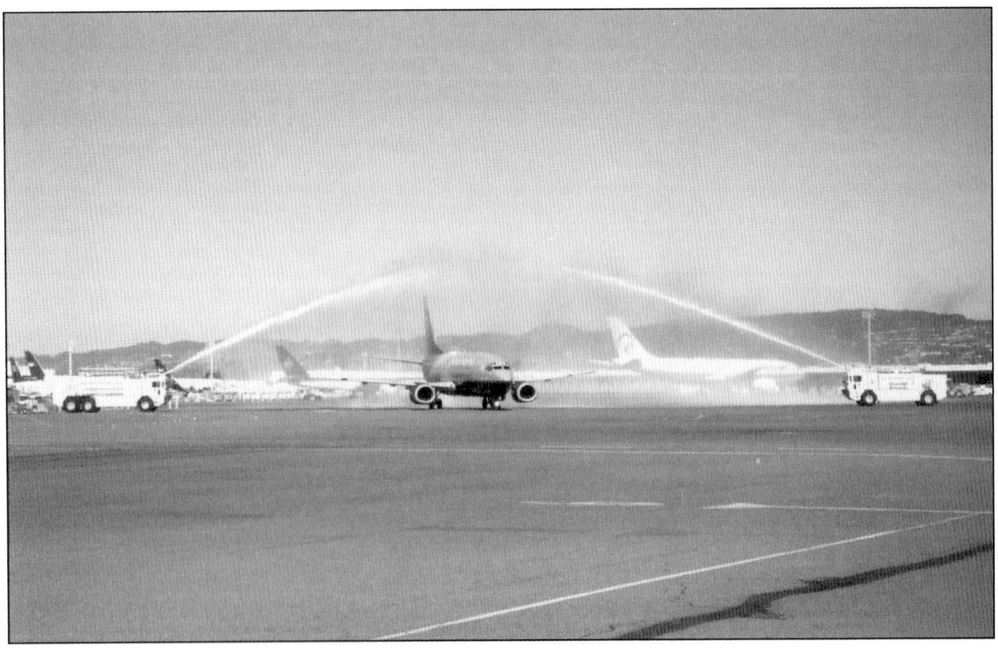

Airport Fire Station No. 22 performs a traditional "water bridge" for a United Air Lines captain's retirement in 2001. This is also done for inauguration of new service and other significant or important events at Oakland International Airport.

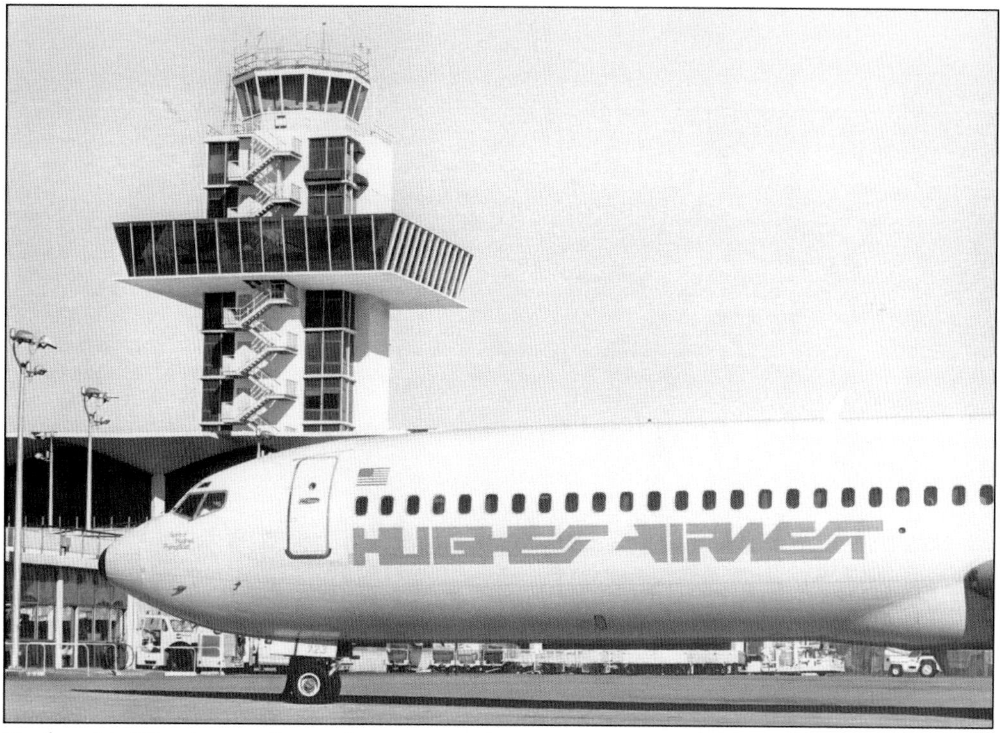

Hughes Air West is one of several airlines that have merged or gone out of business after having provided jet passenger service to Oakland Airport. This photograph shows good detail of the new control tower on the Lionel J. Wilson Terminal.

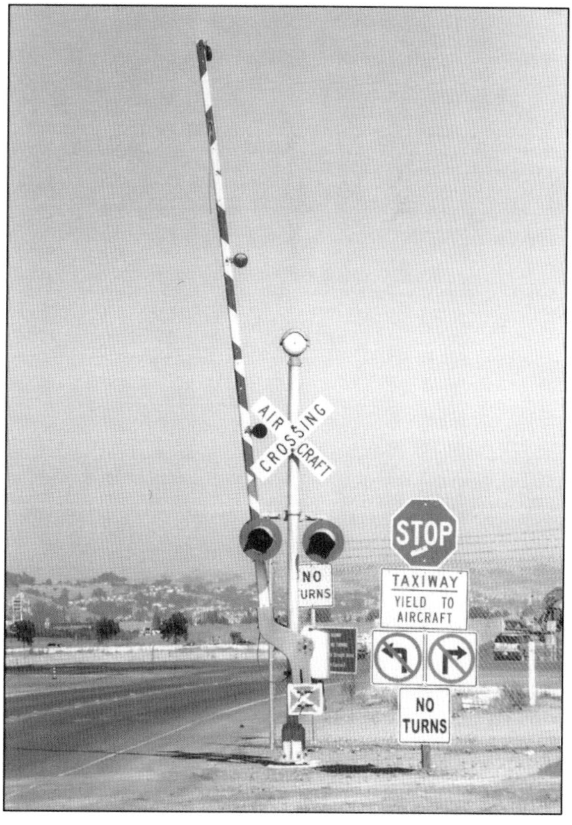

For a 10-year period, while construction was being done on the FedEx complex, a road crossed the active Taxiway Bravo. After an attempt to use traffic guards, this more efficient aircraft crossing was installed at Charlie Gate. The unmistakable appearance of a railroad crossing sign was successful, and at least one other has existed at the Anchorage International Airport.

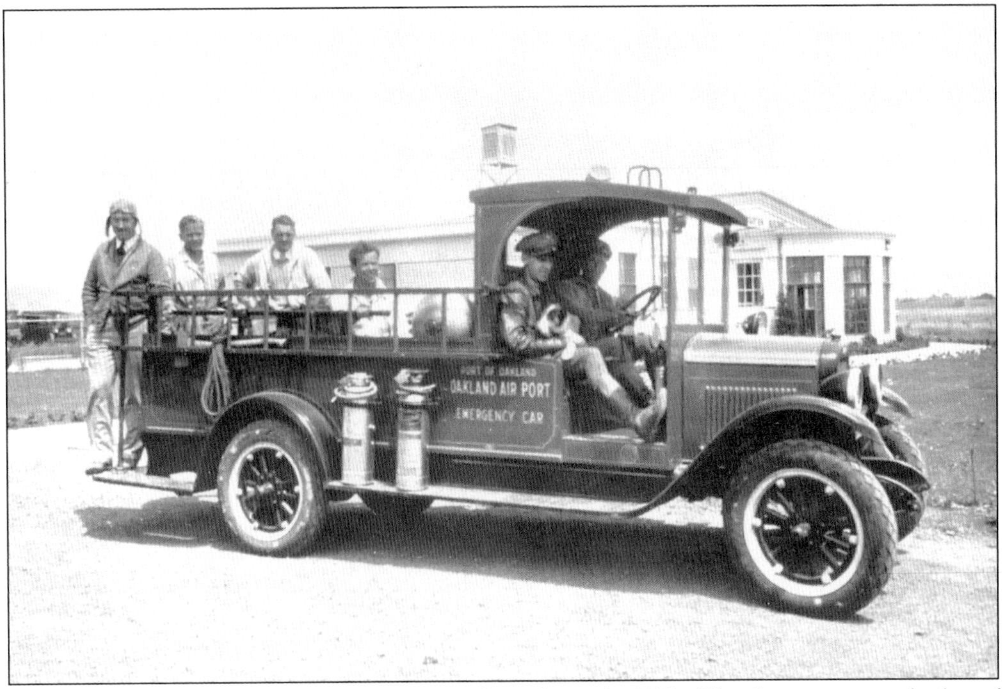

This is the Oakland Airport's emergency truck in the early 1930s. The dog sitting on the lap of the front seat passenger is Contact, owned by then–assistant airport manager Fred MacElwain. The dog is now buried beneath the Maitland-Hegenberger Monument in front of the old terminal building on what is today called North Field.

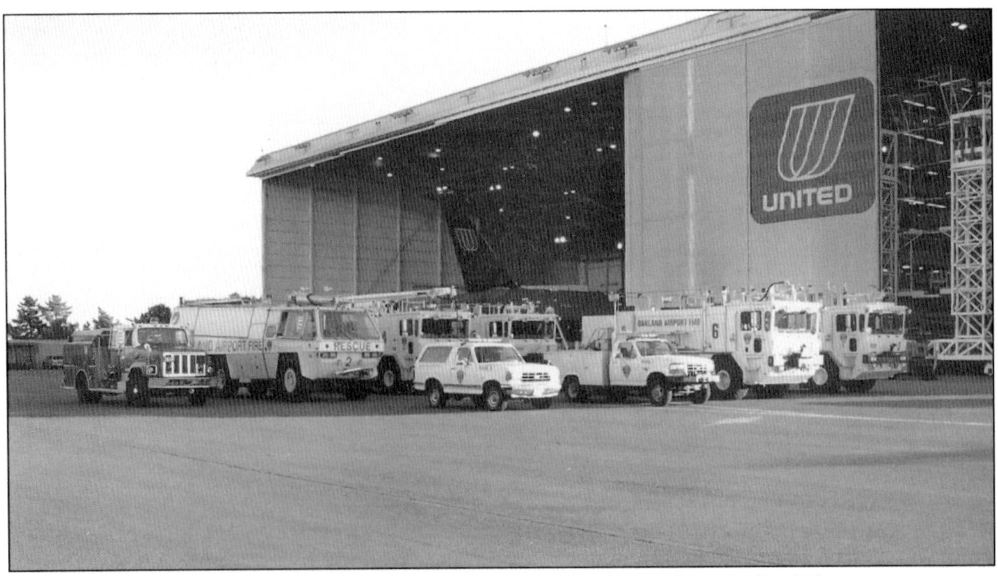

This October 1999 photograph of the emergency vehicles and crash firefighting equipment graphically shows the immense development and increase in service over the years between the original Oakland Airport and the current Oakland International Airport.

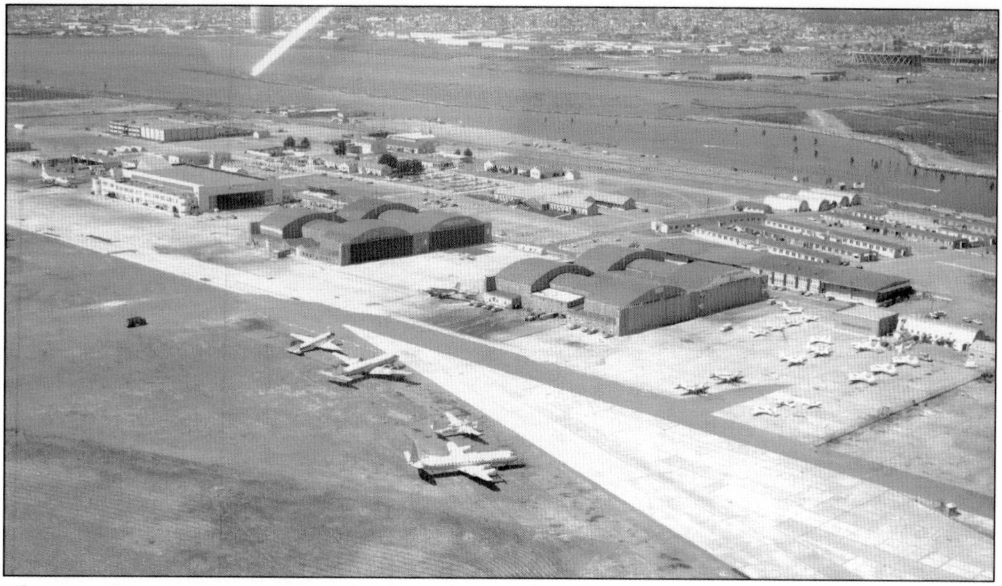

The two photographs on this page show the north end of North Field in July 1971. From left to right are Hangar 9 with SFO Helicopter Airlines Maintenance Base, Hangar 8 with Bayaire Avionics, and Hangar 7 with Kaiser Air and Western Airmotive. The planes in the foreground are, from left to right, a Douglas DC-3, DC-6A, B-26, and a Lockheed L-188 Electra.

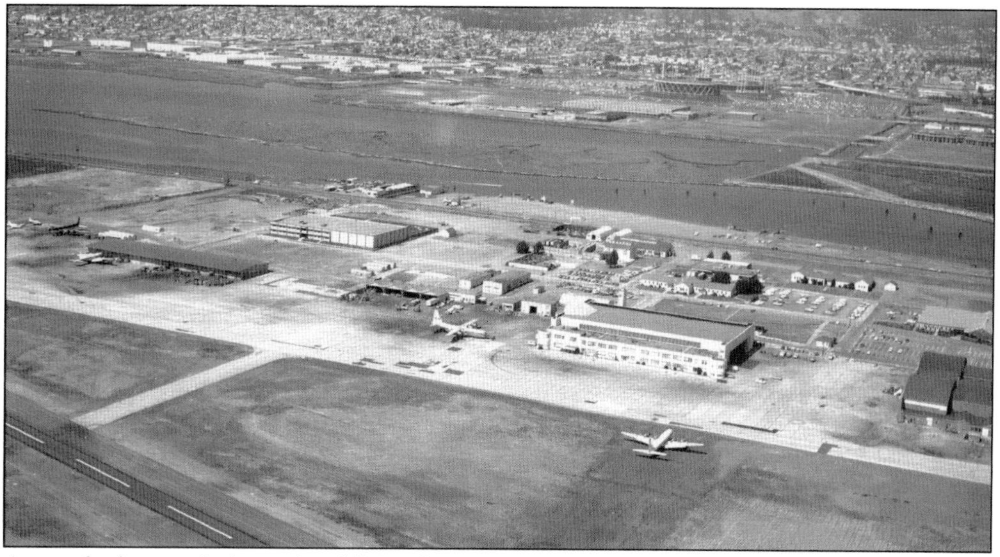

A view farther north shows the old Naval Air Transport Service shops, Hangar 9, administration building, and barracks. The Airport Channel can be seen just above that, and the Oakland Coliseum is at the top right of the photograph.

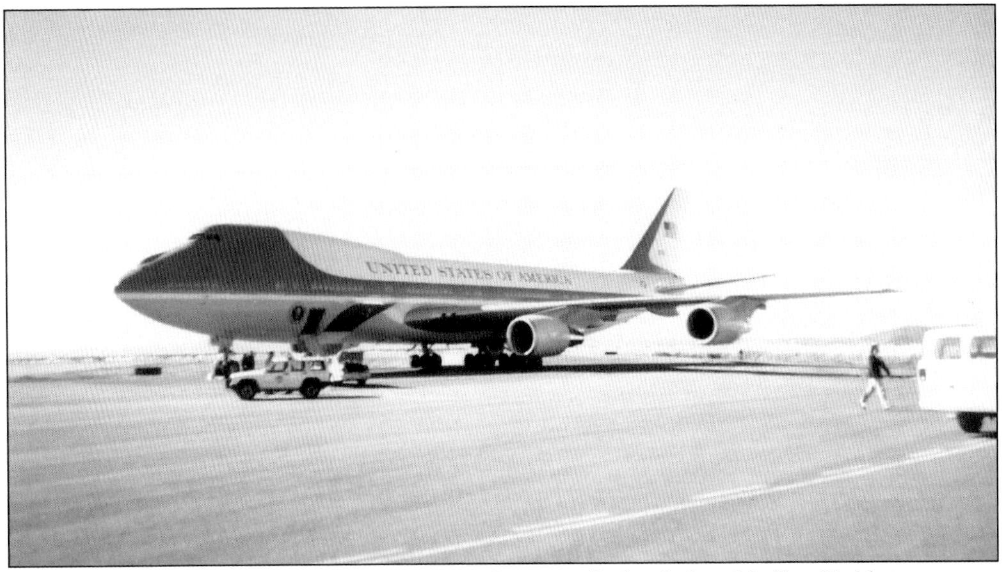

Although the special Boeing 747 Air Force One usually landed at Moffett Field, it came to Oakland Airport with Pres. Bill Clinton and his staff in November 2000. As usual, it was parked off in a secluded area away from the terminal and given special security by the airport police and fire departments.

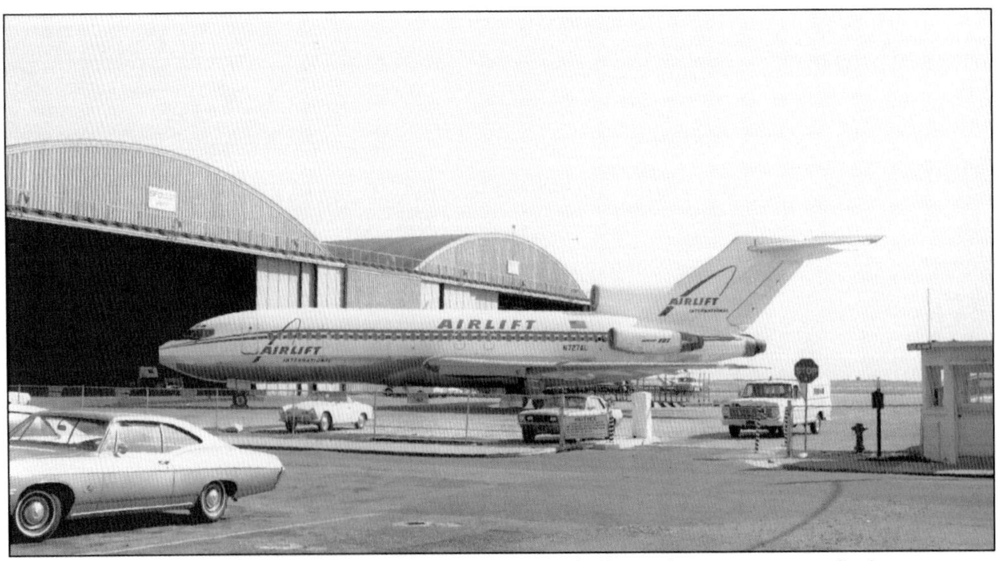

One of the many charter airlines, operating primarily for military contract flights to carry personnel and cargo for the U.S. government, was Airlift International based in Miami, Florida. It had a fleet of various jet aircraft types, including Boeing 727s like this one. The photograph shows N727AL headed into Hangar 9, with the guard gate and entrance on the right.

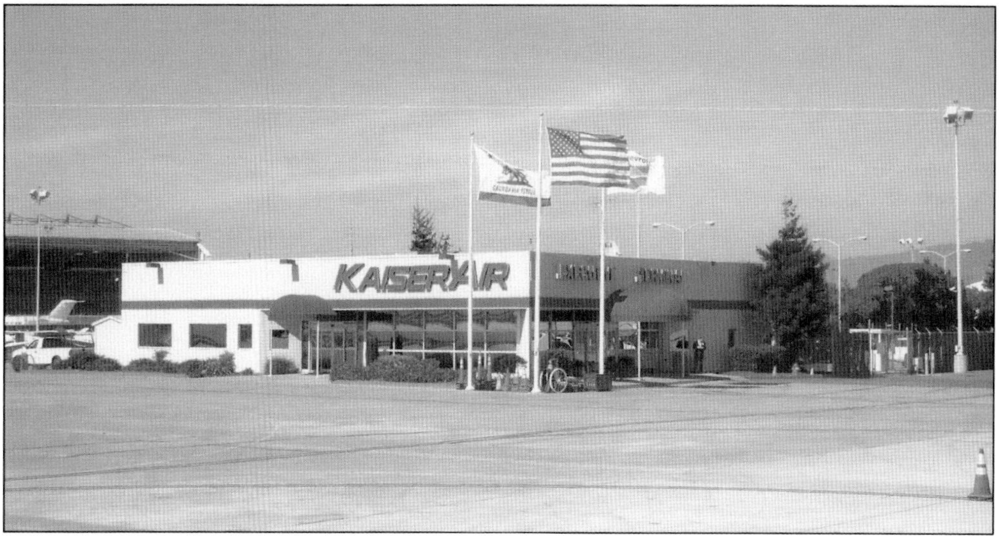

Kaiser Air, a division of Kaiser Industries, had its own small terminal built in the 1980s on North Field for arriving and departing executive aircraft. It has full facilities for passengers as well as the air crews. This view is from the field side as seen by arriving pilots.

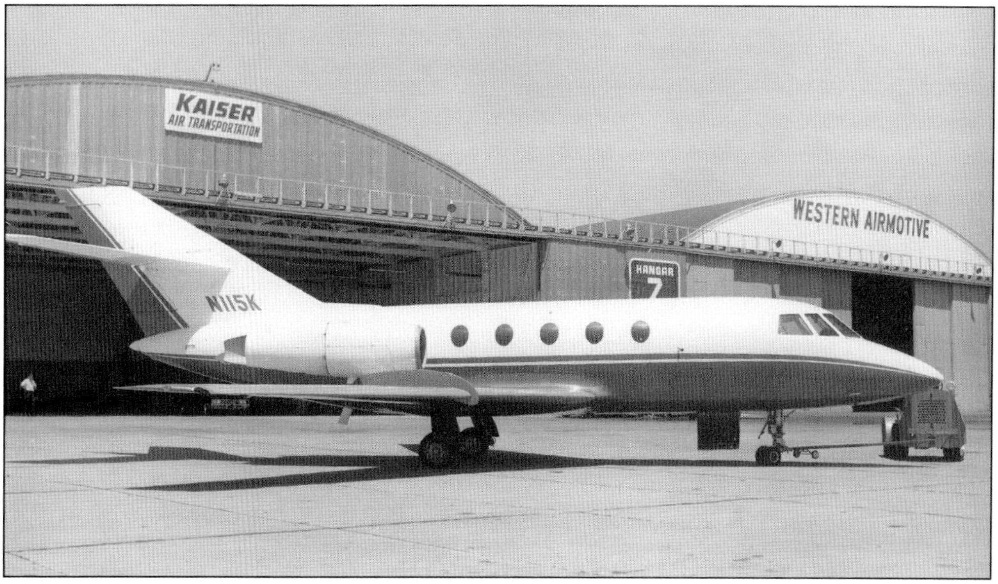

Kaiser Industries has owned a number of aircraft, such as this Dassault Fan Jet Falcon in front of its hangar in May 1968. The Kaiser Air hangar is one of those built during World War II for the Naval Air Transport Service airline operation, which flew Douglas R4D (DC-3) and R5D (DC-4) transports up and down the West Coast as well as to Hawaii and the Pacific.

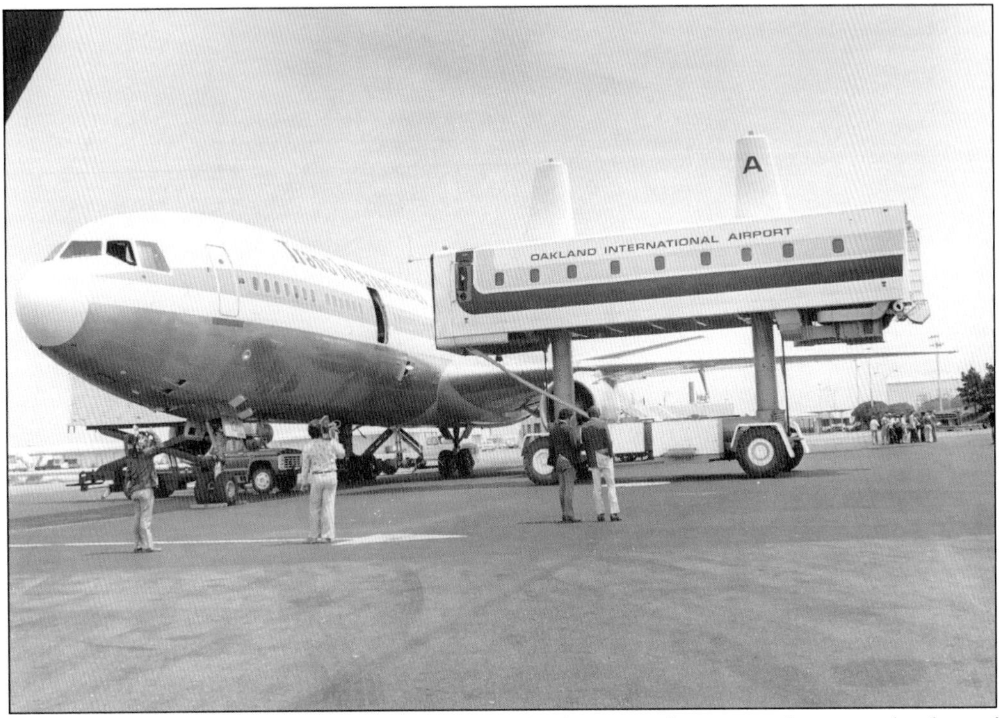

This photograph shows the new mobile passenger loading ramp being raised to meet the door of the Trans America jet transport.

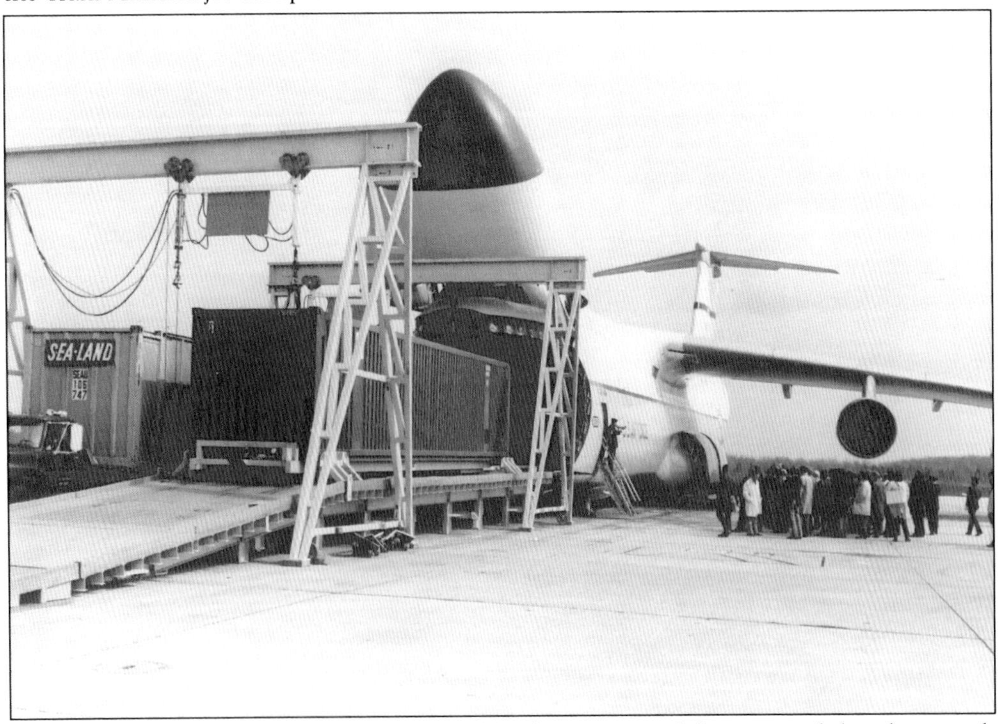

The giant Lockheed C-5A had flown into Oakland International Airport, and this photograph shows it unloading a large cargo container while a group of dignitaries watches the operation.

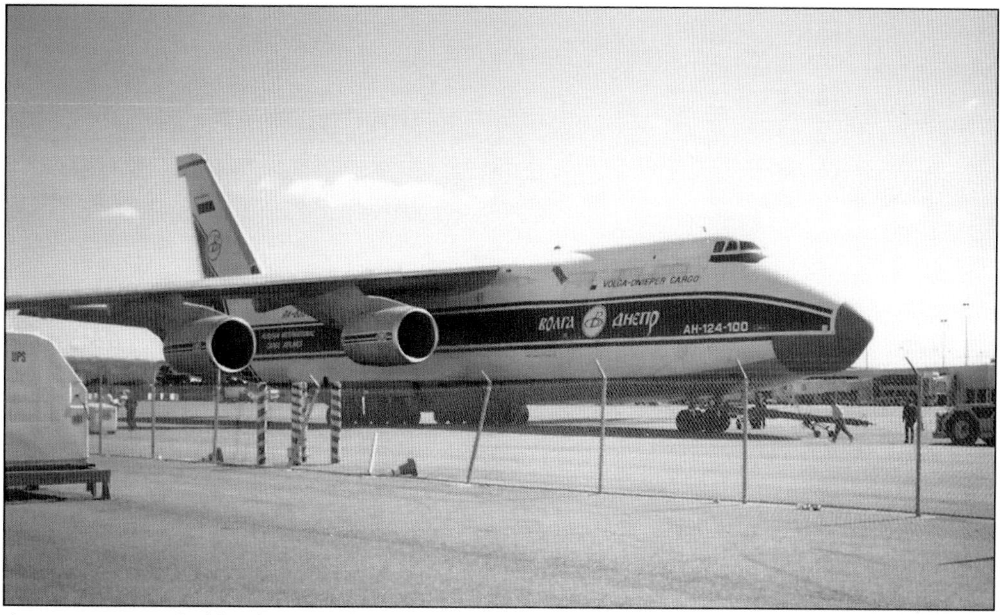

A rare visitor to Oakland in March 1995 was this Antonov AH-124-100 of Russian International Cargo Airlines. The world's largest plane at the time, with a wingspan of 240 feet, it could carry 330,600 pounds of cargo using 22 wheels for takeoff and landing.

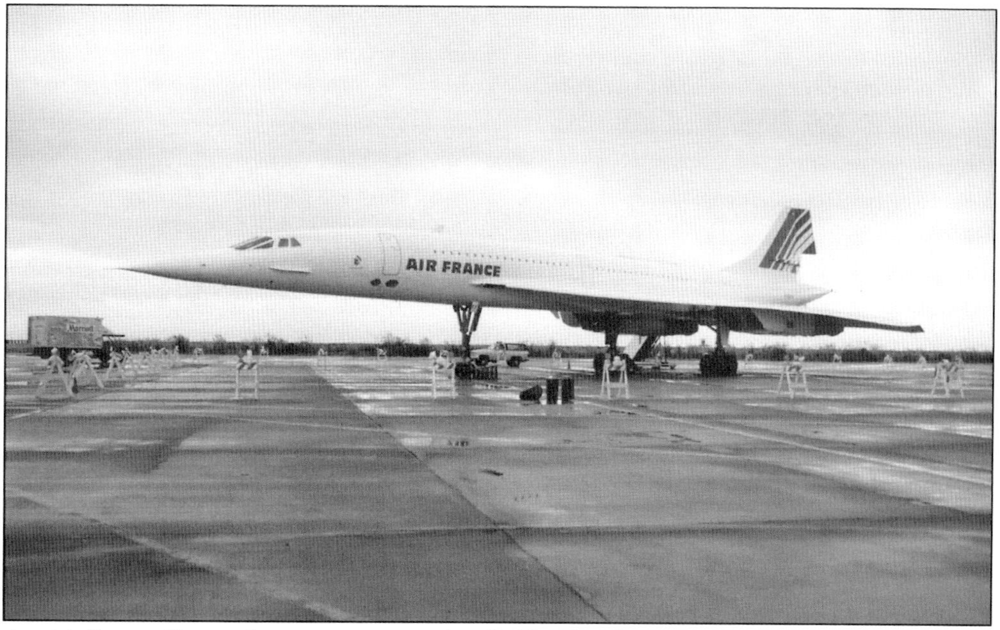

An Air France Concorde transport arrived at Oakland on January 8, 1987, to provide a chance for anyone to fly supersonic. Two-hour flights over the Pacific Ocean included breaking the sound barrier, Mach 2.3 at a 51,000-foot altitude, as the main purpose of the $895 per-person ticket cost.

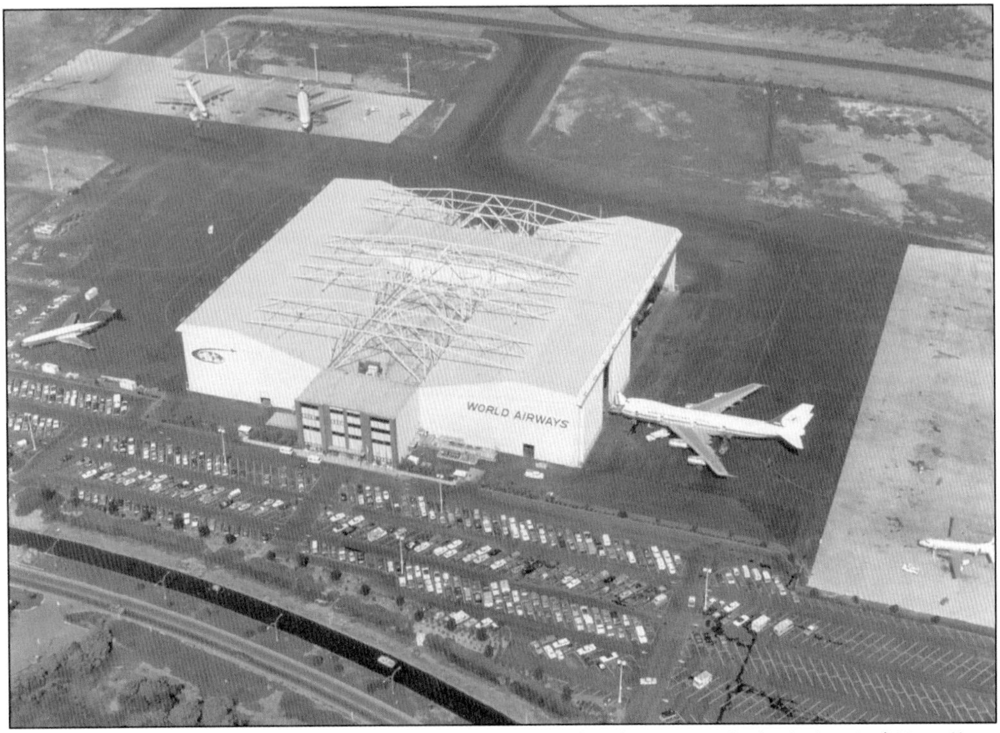

World Airways was able to build a giant 180,000-square-foot hangar with the help of a $10-million federal grant. It is so large that it could hold four Boeing 747s when it opened in May 1973 after several years of construction. World Airways moved their operation to the East Coast in 1987. United Air Lines took it over as a large maintenance base and continued there until 2003, when they moved to San Francisco. It has remained empty since then and is planned for removal to make way for a new international terminal.

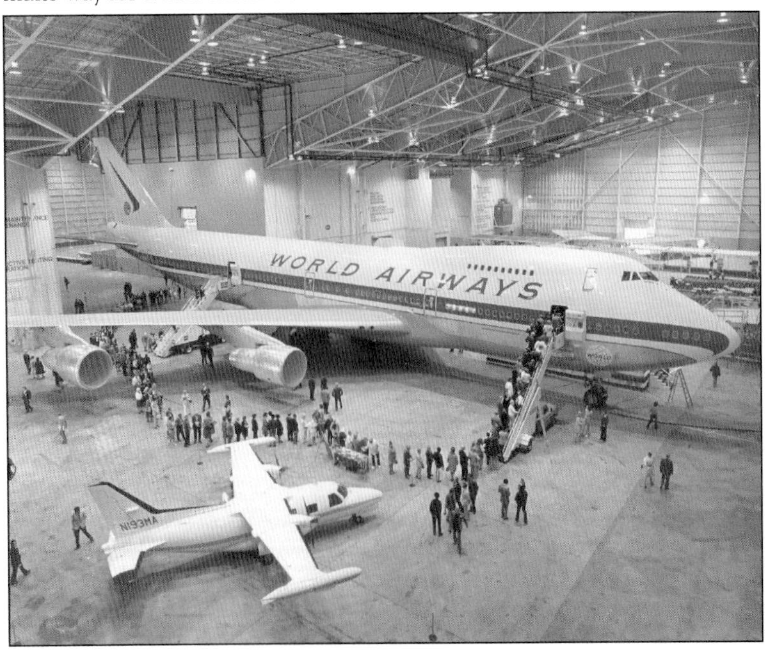

This photograph of the interior of the World Airways hangar was taken during the opening ceremonies, in which it was named for Congressman George Miller. The turboprop Mitsubishi MU-2 in the foreground is dwarfed by the new Boeing 747C about to go into passenger service in 1973.

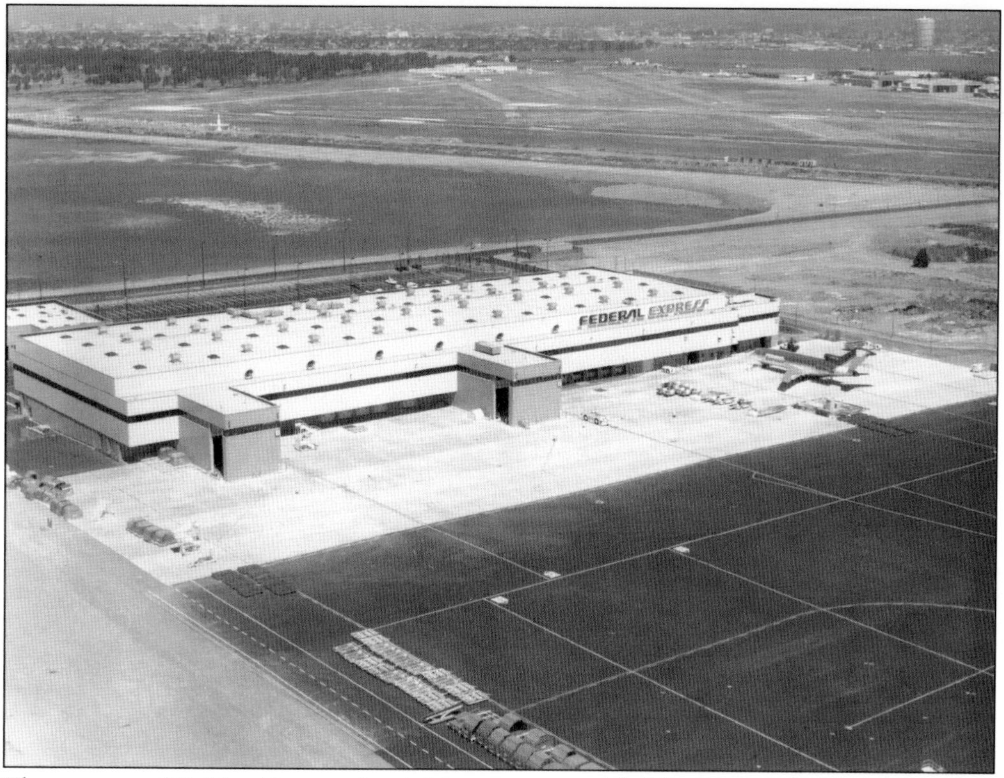

The new age of Oakland International Airport is exemplified by this aerial photograph of the large FedEx operations center north of the main terminal. The unique plan for central routing of air freight at specialized sorting and loading centers was developed by FedEx and has grown to a national airline fleet, which includes many McDonnell-Douglas MD-11 Freighters capable of carrying 20,800 cubic feet of cargo.

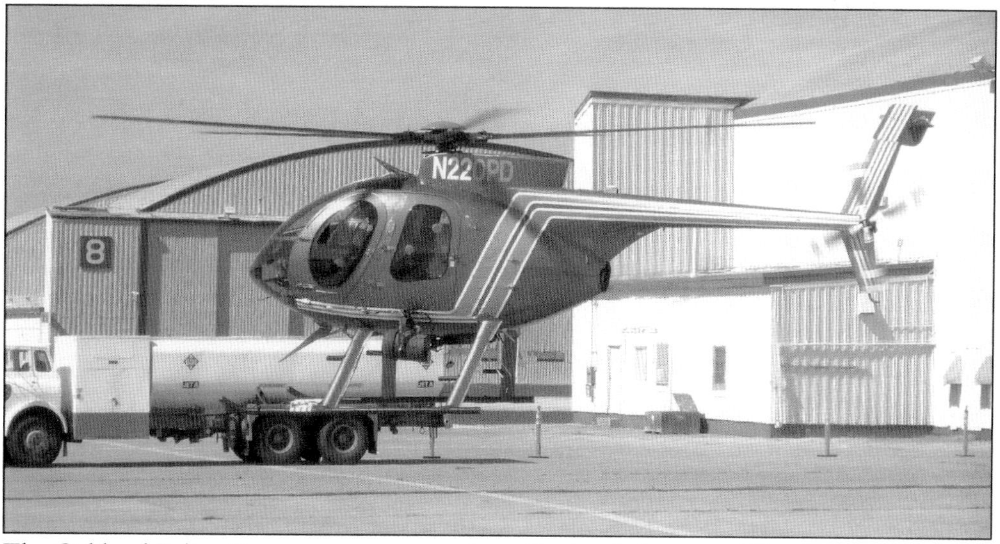

The Oakland Police Department operates three Hughes helicopters. This photograph shows N220PD, a Hughes 369E, taking off from its trailer platform. It uses a clever manipulation of the registration so that N220PD shows as N22*OPD* for Oakland Police Department.